RETURN OF THE THUNDERBEINGS

RETURN of the Thunderbeings

IRON THUNDERHORSE
DONN LE VIE, JR.

*A New Paradigm of
Ancient
Shamanism*

BEAR & COMPANY
PUBLISHING
SANTA FE, NEW MEXICO

LIBRARY OF CONGRESS CATALOGING-IN-PUBLICATION DATA

Le Vie, Donn, 1951-
    Return of the thunderbeings / Donn Le Vie, Jr., and Iron
Thunderhorse.

       p.   cm.
    Bibliography: p.
    Includes index.
    ISBN 0-939680-68-8

    1. Occultism.   2. Shamanism.   3. Indians of North America—
Religion and mythology.   I. Iron Thunderhorse, 1950-   .
II. Title.
BF1999.L3255   1990
299'.7—dc20   89-35848
                                            CIP

Bear & Company
Santa Fe, NM 87504-2860

Cover & interior illustrations: Iron Thunderhorse
Design: Angela C. Werneke
Editing: Brandt Morgan
Typography: Casa Sin Nombre, Ltd.
Thunderhorse portrait: Jack Stephens
Le Vie photo: Giddings Studios, Texas
Printed in the United States of America by R.R. Donnelley

9 8 7 6 5 4 3 2 1

CONTENTS

FOREWORD

In the course of our lives, every one of us is challenged to make an act of power that boldly acquits us in the face of destiny. There is a tradition among the pre-Inca peoples of the Altiplano of Peru that one must honor one's ancestors by being willing to stand on their shoulders in order to look to a more distant horizon. This is what we are challenged to do now, so that those who come after us will similarly be able to stand on our visions and deeds.

In *Return of the Thunderbeings*, Iron Thunderhorse and Donn Le Vie bring to life the essence of the ancient thunder teachings, bridging them into our modern world so that those teachings in turn can help us make our way sanely into the twenty-first century and beyond.

Never in the history of humanity have we been in greater need for healing and renewal of the Mother Earth and her peoples. I believe that we have all chosen to incarnate together at this critical time to send off the old millenium and bring in a new thousand-year period of human history. This is a time when all of the ancient teachings are being revealed to us: *The Tibetan Book of the Dead*, the ancient Hopi prophecies, and now *Return of the Thunderbeings*. I believe that these ancient teachings have been given to us as tools that we may forge a new vision of what it means to be human, a whole and holy vision that can take us sanely into the next millenium of life on Earth.

The knowledge and teachings in this volume are a gift of love to all of us, from all who have come before us. The authors have been faithful scribes, serving as a bridge of light from our past to our future.

But this knowledge also comes with a challenge. My teacher once said to me, "While everyone has a future, only very few men and women of power have a destiny." We live in an age when many are trying to escape the reality of our day by shaking rattles and waving feathers (which have their proper place in ceremony) and turning to the past, longing for a more simple time. *Return of the Thunderbeings* challenges us to put an end to ordinary history, to acquit ourselves of the past and settle for nothing less than our highest possible destiny.

Alberto Villoldo
Director of the Four Winds Society; author of Healing States *and* The Four Winds: A Shaman's Odyssey in the Amazon

PREFACE

In its deepest sense, this book is meant as an aid to spiritual unfoldment. It is intended to take you, the reader, on a guided tour of the ancient symbols and wisdom teachings that have aided shamans and medicine people in their journeys of self-realization for thousands of years.

Most people in modern society have all but forgotten such symbols and teachings, yet they are still as much a part of our psyches as they were in Paleolithic times—and they are just as powerful. It is our hope that this visual and intellectual review of the ancient shamanic pathways will spark the Sacred Fire within you and fan the flames of spiritual growth along your chosen path.

With this intent, the book is organized in an unusual way. It begins with a short autobiography of each of the two authors, in order to better acquaint you with your guides on this spiritual journey. Next comes a modern myth told sometime in the early twenty-first century. This is the story of how the manitous, or spirit beings, saved the world by re-establishing the ancient wisdom; how they provided for a dialogue between shaman and scientist that would reconcile and integrate the often-antagonistic forces of yin and yang, science and spirit, male and female. Not least of all, this special dialogue was meant to bridge the huge gap in modern humanity's psyche—the gap between left and right brains and between heart and mind that has caused such great chaos and destruction in the world.

This book, then, is meant as a tangible symbol. It is a part of the great dialogue that the spirit beings have arranged. With chapters alternating between the viewpoints of shaman and New Age scientist, it represents the melding of

ancient and modern wisdom that must take place before the New Age can come into full flower. As such, it represents not only the gift of ancient wisdom but also the path of spirit that leads back to wholeness.

Such dialogue, we believe, along with the psychic changes made possible through a deeper understanding of the ancient native ways, is an important part of the mental and spiritual bridge that modern humanity needs in order to pass safely over the shadowy chasm of disaster into the bright light of the dawning New Age.

May you read with insight and joy. May you gain from this dialogue the sparks of wisdom and understanding you most need to further your own spiritual flight to the nest of the Thunderbeings. And most important, may you always be steered by your own inner dialogue, your own heart, and by the milestones along your own path. For your own contribution to the healing of humanity and the Earth is unique, important, and as great as that of any other.

FLIGHT OF THE THUNDERBIRD
A Personal Journey
Iron Thunderhorse

I was born during the cycle the Algonquins call the "Wolf Moon," which is the first full moon of the new year. I was a breech-birth baby with a veil over my head. My birth was seen by everyone as an omen of some sort. I have often thought since that being born opposite the norm—feet first—descended me into the world upright and ready for action.

My father was Italian and my mother was of Algonquin lineage, of the Quinnipiac River band. My mother was raised by Irish foster parents, but she never denied me access to my native heritage. It was my *dudas*, and my Algonquin grandmother, who first began teaching me the medicine ways.

As a boy, I attended white schools, but when school was out I enrolled in an Indian-based summer camp. During these years, I learned much from my family. My paternal grandfather was a stone cutter and sculptor, while my maternal grandfather was an all-around woodlands craftsman. My maternal grandmother was a healer and midwife, and my paternal grandmother (who came from a small village near Naples, Italy) was a gardener and simple village farmer. My father was a carpenter, mason, and stone cutter, while Mother was an artist and a very hard worker.

I knew at a tender age that I was different from other children. I can remember events back to when I was hardly a year old, and my dreams were very vivid at times. I realized later in life that these were not really dreams, but heightened states of awareness.

Some of my early childhood dreams were very symbolic, such as flying like a bird, and falling into a huge spiral that was pulling me into a never-ending center. Many dreams repeated themselves over and over. They often gave me a euphoric feeling of otherworldliness which I took back with me into the waking world.

I also realized I could hear and see things that other children couldn't. For example, the mountain near my childhood home kept calling me to it. I began having visions and receiving psychic impressions from certain objects at about age six. I realize now that this was all part of an informal preparation for what was to come later.

Even as a boy, my life was filled with pain and tragedy. It followed me like a constant shadow. And though its meaning was beyond my grasp, something always seemed to guide me through it.

First my father was in a terrible car accident that crushed most of his body. He was a strong man; even so, he developed an aneurysm on a valve in his heart, and eventually he succumbed to a massive heart attack. I was miles away when he died, but somehow I knew.

When I was twelve, my mother moved to Quebec Province in Canada and married a French Canadian/Ojibwa man. I went to live with my grandparents in the New Haven, Connecticut area. I was in turmoil over my family falling apart.

At age thirteen I was expelled from school because I wore my hair long in the traditional Algonquin and Mohawk style. My Indian and Italian grandparents had taught me to be proud of my heritage, but school taught me to think I was white and to have a one-track mind.

I rebelled. I skipped school and became reclusive. Eventually, I was placed in a Connecticut reform school. While there, I was abused almost to the point of death.

In reform school, at the age of thirteen, I had my first out-of-body experience while spending 187 days in a small cubicle during an extended period of sensory deprivation. Again, an unseen guide kept me safe.

I was returned to my grandparents on my sixteenth birthday, and a year later I married my childhood sweetheart. Now I had a home and a good job as a carpenter, and soon my wife gave birth to a baby boy. Then tragedy hit once again. My wife and boy were both killed in a car accident.

I was devastated. At first I turned to alcohol to numb the pain. But something inside told me I must move on. I had to forget the past and find my future, my destiny. A giant, winged shadow pointed me westward toward the setting sun.

I really didn't choose my destiny or anything else; it chose me. In the late '60s, at age eighteen, I left Connecticut and traveled west. I just rode my motorcycle, searching and trying to find some meaning for my life. (To me, a motor-

cycle was an "iron horse" that represented freedom from the status quo.) Some biker friends rode with me, and eventually we wound up in Arizona, where I found work in a carnival.

Then one day, outside of Phoenix, I had my first peyote experience—an event that completely changed the course of my life.

A group of friends and I had taken a quantity of peyote buttons. It didn't start out as a spiritual ceremony, but it certainly ended up that way. We were sitting by a pool of water when suddenly an image appeared. It was a man—a Native American with long, flowing, brown hair. Lightning flashed from his eyes and all around him. He said he was my guide, Tashunké-Witko (Crazy Horse) and he showed me my future.

I saw phoenixes, Thunderbirds, and all kinds of giant wingflappers rising out of the hills behind him. He explained that I was to do his work for the Great Spirit and that the rest would be revealed in time. Next I was hit by a lightning bolt and experienced a sense of standing in two different worlds. Then it was over.

Amazingly, my vision was so powerful that my friends also saw, heard, and understood what I was experiencing. This led me to seek the peyote sacrament in a truly spiritual manner, and to find an experienced teacher.

I was in a state of otherworldliness for weeks after the peyote experience. I passed the word that I was looking for someone who knew about visions, peyote, and shamanism. I was led to a place in Mesa, Arizona, where I met Maynard White Eagle ("Mannie"), a Lakota brother. I smoked a pipe with him and told him about every detail of my experience.

Mannie explained that Crazy Horse was my guide and always had been. He said the peyote had simply given me the ability to communicate with him in the "real world." He also related that Crazy Horse has great power and can enter our world; that he is not earth-bound, but that he can communicate with anyone he wants.

Mannie also said that what I experienced was a Heyoka vision and that I must accept the call to become a Heyoka or I would risk being struck by lightning. I told Mannie what my mother had explained about my birth, and he said I was born a Heyoka and a seer and that I had been blessed to follow the path of a medicine man.

So Mannie began teaching me. I learned how to fast properly, and we had many sweats together. Then he showed me how to use peyote as it was meant to be used, in a sacred way. He taught me about the gifts of peyote; about its solar and lunar types; how to listen to its singing voice; and how to find it, pray to it, and ask it for guidance.

During my time with Mannie, I also began to learn more about the future, and Crazy Horse continued to instruct me. He gave me the secrets of the Wakinyan—the Thunderbirds, or Thunderbeings—and said one day I would be a chief like he once was. He said that I would build a new Thunderbird clan and bear his name as my own.

The name Crazy Horse was given to me in my vision. There were so many parallels between us that it seemed natural. But Crazy Horse is a holy name to the Lakota nation. And while some of the Lakotas felt there was no harm in my having his name, others believed it was not right.

I explained this later to a Lakota pipekeeper from whom I sought guidance. Then one evening after I was in prison I had a vivid dream. Crazy Horse appeared to me as a Thunderhorse along with his father, Worm. I discussed this dream with several people, and a new name was given to me: Iron Thunderhorse. This name is symbolic both of the dream and of the direction my life has taken since. Now Crazy Horse is still with me in the form of the Thunderhorse that came to me in the "iron house," and everyone is satisfied.

One day while I was still with Mannie, Crazy Horse told me I must go in search of other nations and learn all I could from the Old Ones—the elders and medicine people.

I left Arizona in mid-1971. My travels on my motorcycle took me through New Mexico, Oklahoma, the Dakotas, Nebraska, Nevada, Colorado, and California. I met Navajo, Hopi, Pima, Apache, Zuni, Cherokee, and many other people. I studied their legends, crafts, and medicine ways, and I was always accepted as a friend and brother. Everyone knew I was on a holy pilgrimage. It was a great time of learning and preparation.

During this time, I honed my skills as a craftsman and absorbed the legends, songs, chants, symbols, and healing powers of the elders from many nations. I also began to learn about the Civil Rights Movement and to participate in the American Indian Movement (the newly formed cultural and political organization called AIM) and Bikers' Rights protests. I experienced the true American Indian Movement renaissance and began to regain my "Indian-ness." In the middle of it, I recognized the fact that I was not the only mixed-blood or Native American to be abused or oppressed. I saw real suffering and real transformation.

During this pilgrimage, I participated in many ceremonies that were landmarks for my soul. Among these were healing and initiatory ceremonies which awakened the latent powers of the seven psychic centers. I learned that each of these centers, or chakras, is a kind of miniature brain capable of its own perceptions. I practiced releasing my consciousness to see and feel through each of these seven centers. In other ancient teachings, this is sometimes called "climbing the mystic ladder," or "listening to the inner worlds."

In 1973, after almost two years of traveling, I returned to Mannie again. We went deep into the Superstition Mountains east of Phoenix, and gradually I revealed to him all that I had learned. He said I was now ready for my first sun dance — ready to accept my path of sacrifice as a Heyoka. I fasted for several days and danced in the sun with buffalo skulls tied to my pierced skin. I danced until I collapsed, and then I visited other worlds, the nest of the Thunderbeings.

Later, Mannie gathered other shamans from five different cultures, and we conducted a ceremony called the Council of Five Fires. In this council were revealed the mysteries of five different types of power. Each power is associated with a different color and with the elements of earth, air, fire, and water, and spirit.

Mannie also put me through severe tests of endurance. I had to withstand extreme heat in the desert sun and periods of cold, bitter winds and rain. I learned how to reverse the effects of these elements on my body — how to cool myself in extreme heat and warm myself in the cold.

In subsequent travels, I learned mask-making, beadwork, leatherwork, woodcarving, jewelry, and how to make medicine shields. I also learned about the transformative powers of ancient symbols, as well as how to use medicine paint, masks, shields, and iconography to discover the latent abilities and qualities in people.

Later in 1973 I went to Southern California and began riding with a large motorcycle club. One year there was a big rally being organized by the Brown Berets (the Chicano activists), and it was rumored that police and undercover agents were going to cause trouble to break it up. Our motorcycle club was asked to help, and I was put in charge of security by organizing a mobile bodyguard patrol.

We had over 12,000 motorcycles from all over California at the rally. About 250 AIM members also showed up, and I met a lot of AIM contacts that I was close to for years to come. We had our parade and there was no trouble.

After the parade, I began to organize several concerted efforts with AIM, the Brown Berets, and the Bikers. These "occupations and blowouts," as they were called, occurred all over California and in other states. The U.S. Government and the California authorities soon had me pegged as a key organizer for these events, especially after I wrote a batch of articles for Biker magazines.

This was about a year after the government had begun a campaign to disrupt and disorganize motorcycle clubs. I was angry and aggressive in those days, and often under the influence of alcohol. Several days after a protest rally, I was arrested and charged with burglary. In 1974, I was sent to San Quentin, which by then had become a center for political dissidents.

I soon became active in the San Quentin chapter of AIM. I also attended all the Chicano celebrations, and I kept good rapport not only with all the racial minorities but with the whites as well. Whenever there was racial tension, I would be asked to act as a neutral party.

At San Quentin a group of Jailhouse Lawyers and I founded the Committee to Safeguard Prisoners' Rights (CSPR), which became the inside ad hoc branch of the National Lawyers Guild Jailhouse Lawyer membership. CSPR soon became a training ground for politically active convicts.

In 1975, I was also certified as a paralegal technician at San Quentin by the California Bar Association's Continuing Legal Education branch, and later CSPR was instrumental in setting up six pilot programs to train prisoners as paralegals. Needless to say, not everyone was happy about all this.

I was paroled in August of 1977 and was escorted home by a procession of over 300 motorcycles. There was a big celebration that lasted two weeks. The retired president of the motorcycle club gave me his patch, and there was little doubt who the club's new leader was.

I had a lot of security around me everywhere I went, and I soon began organizing events and runs for worthy causes (Toys for Tots, benefits for the Crippled Children's Hospital, etc). But drugs had become popular with young people, and they were fast being accepted by motorcyclists, too. I stayed away from hard drugs, but I still had problems with alcohol.

Besides this, the authorities didn't like the fact that I was back on the streets with so much influence among the Bikers—especially since I wrote articles for Biker magazines and because I had recently helped to expose a government plot to infiltrate motorcycle clubs. Along with many others, I became a target.

In September of 1977, I was tipped off that the California authorities planned to do something to set me up to go back to prison. I was advised to go underground, so I opened up a saloon in Oklahoma, just across the Texas border. I had every intention of staying out of trouble and living legitimately. But I had underestimated how much the authorities wanted me out of the way.

On November 11, 1977, I was arrested in Texas while returning from a routine trip to the store. I was charged with robbery and kidnapping, neither of which I had done or knew anything about—and which had not even occurred in the immediate area. All my witnesses mysteriously vanished, and the trial was a complete fiasco. Even one of the special agents used to testify against me later told me I had been set up. After three days of testimony about my "terrorist" leadership with the Bikers, I was given 99 years for kidnapping and 25 years for aggravated robbery.

After I filed for a new trial, one of the key witnesses broke down and admitted that all the key witnesses had lied; that they had made deals with the state to help put me away. I was acquitted of the kidnapping charge. But as of this writing, twelve years later, I am still serving a 25-year term for a robbery I never committed.

For years I felt angry about this. For years I felt bitter about being set up, and bitter about the brutality and persecution I underwent in prison. But there are deeper reasons for everything.

The first time I went to prison was for my stupidity and my alcohol addiction. The second time was an act of destiny. I went to prison because I neglected to honor my medicine visions and tried to be something else. I thought I was a Biker and a warrior. I lived like an outlaw and an activist with a chip on his shoulder. I was wrong. I really didn't know *who* I was.

But as prisons began allowing wider expressions of spirituality during the '70s, I slowly began to see a way out. I began to discover my true self and my true purpose. When I saw that my people were suffering more than I was, I decided to reclaim my heritage. My culture became not only my source of recovery from alcohol, but my new source of life and spirit. The path back to my ancestors became my personal journey to the nest of the Thunderbeings.

Looking back, I have always felt that what I was asked to believe in schools was not truth but conditioning to the established social system. I am not saying the system is all bad, but I have noticed that it often serves as a cloak to cover over the deeds of the "two-hearts" of this world: bigotry, greed, and abuses of power.

Often in my life I have chosen to buck the system. In my own quest for truth, I have frequently rocked the boat and sometimes even tipped it over. I am not saying I have always been right, but I have always learned, because I have trained myself to take everything as a challenge and an opportunity.

One of the things I have learned very profoundly is that prisons are metaphors. The concrete walls that surround me are not only my personal barriers; they are also the walls of fear, ignorance, corruption, greed, and violence that society has built around itself. The steel bars that keep me from personal freedom are also the self-created barriers that keep other people from fully experiencing peace, love, and joy in their own lives.

But inner freedom has not been the only benefit of my prison experience. Prison also gave me the opportunity to study the teachings I had wanted to learn more about, and to practice the methods used by other shamans and medicine people. I was guided to many literary works, and soon I began to use these to benefit myself and others.

As I write this, in the fall of 1989, I am still in prison. Yet now it is only a physical prison. In my own mind, I have long since come to terms with my past and walked through these walls. And as a shaman, I consciously leave this prison all the time. Yet even in here, I am actually better off than most people, for most people are in psychological prisons that they believe they cannot escape.

In prison, I have learned how to raise my own consciousness. Now I feel I have an obligation to raise the consciousness of prisoners everywhere, whether their bars are real or imagined—to teach them how to see the real world and how to transform the worst situations into something creative and positive.

Prison has also taught me more about the power of political involvement. Among other things, it gave me the opportunity to help organize the National Lawyers Guild Jailhouse Lawyer membership and the Committee to Safeguard Prisoners' Rights, Inc., and to start many Native American culture groups, including the Thunderbird Prison Alliance for Native American Rights and the Preservation of Traditional Sovereignty.

Also, had it not been for prison, I would most likely never have met my good friend, Donn Le Vie, with whom I wrote this book. Donn learned about me through the *Writer's Digest* Book Club, which did a feature on some of my work. We corresponded and visited. As we talked, I discovered that Donn's views of geology and other sciences were very much like the spiritual views taught to me by my elders. We decided to work together, and that is how this book on ancient teachings for a New Age came about—quite literally through prison walls.

None of this has been an accident. And as the years go by, I can see more clearly how my life fits into the greater scheme of things.

My Inca brother don Eduardo Calderon says that most people live in a "cultural trance." I agree with this—and the aim of shamanism is to awaken them. But as a shaman I had to awaken myself before I could really help anyone else. I had to transcend my own suffering and limitation. Strange as it may seem, prison helped me do that.

I do not enjoy digging up old bones, and I would not disrespect another person by digging up their personal skeletons, any more than I would the graves of their ancestors. But sometimes it is important to look squarely at the past in order to be done with it. I am not proud of some things in my past, but I make no excuses. All I have done has been part of my path. My past as an outlaw and my involvement with prisons has been part of my destiny: to help strengthen and prepare myself and those around me for the Great Purification and the Earth changes to come.

Today, we must all be strong enough to look at our skeletons and learn from them, in order to face the future with courage and clear sight. But if we become too attached to the past, then we will wake up some day to find that we have wasted precious time dwelling on our own ignorance—time that could be spent healing ourselves and the planet. The message of this book is to get people to let the past go, to look at now and the future and take responsibility for future generations. Crying about the past will not change tomorrow. Action now and preparations for the future are what we need. Who and what we were yesterday does not matter today. What matters today is who we are *now*. And if we don't know who we are, we had better find out soon, because time is running out.

Especially in these troubled times, my guides and allies in the real world of spirit make me aware of certain things. They have shown me how to read signs in nature and how to recognize certain cycles. Often I see far into the future, and my visions teach me how to flow with these cycles and how to prepare in advance to meet coming changes.

Many tribes have been studying these changes. The Hopis, for example, have repeatedly warned people in Congress of the coming Earth changes, and even many scientists have now become alarmed about what is occurring around the planet.

Humanity's wanton destruction of the environment has taken a huge toll. Holes in the protective ozone layer, the wiping out of entire rain forests, and the disappearance of thousands of precious species of plants and animals are just a few of the far-reaching consequences.

Today, pollution, acid rain, contaminated aquifers, and other environmental ills have become so widespread that a chain reaction has begun. Mother Earth is seriously ill, and she has begun to right the imbalance with toxic gases, volcanic eruptions, earthquakes, rising tides, and drastic weather changes. With time, this will get much worse.

Presently, we are beginning to enter another ice age. Glaciers purify the land, neutralizing everything in their path. Molten lava also purifies. Mother Earth knows how to heal herself, but her purging process will be hard on those who live on her skin.

Some researchers speculate that we may soon experience a shift of the Earth's magnetic poles, permitting the entry of ultraviolet radiation in dangerous doses. The Hopi speak of the "sacred twins" who guard the North and South poles, saying they will soon send vibrations to "shake and quake" the Earth.

These signs Mother Earth is releasing are omens with hidden messages. The outbreak of disease is one such warning. The mosquito breeds in the pit of the Earth Mother. Contaminated aquifers produce stagnant water, which affects the metabolism of the mosquito and other insects and brings on more disease. Toxic gases in Cameroon, Africa killed countless livestock and people. The cause was natural, but with it the Earth Mother was sending an urgent message:

"You are poisoning my skin! Please stop! Your radiation from nuclear waste is deadly, but I have far greater powers."

Many of the diseases today, including AIDS, are chain reactions — breakdowns in our immune systems caused by contaminants. These same effects are experienced by the Earth. The cause is humanity's greed and irresponsibility.

But all is not lost. Right now, there are many circles being re-established to deal with these Earth changes and to prepare for the Great Purification that the prophecies have foretold. I began to build mine long ago. Now that some of these circles are strong and stable, they have begun to interconnect. Eventually they will all be joined, linking the globe in one complete circle. I call this the Ancient Order of Shamanic Tribes. It is a collective ethos, a universal alternative society whose cycle has returned.

This should not be surprising. Hopi prophecies, among others, speak of a time when tribes will come together as one, when new clans will form and all will join hands in unity. A pictograph at Prophecy Rock in Hopiland relates that we are at the crossroads now. It says humanity will either be devoured by the beast of ignorance or transformed into an instrument for the balance of nature. Part of my job as a Heyoka is to do everything I can to help establish this new balance.

Heyokas are "contraries" with special powers of reversal. The Thunderbirds are the guardians of these powers and mysteries, and they are the ones who teach the Heyokas. The Thunderbirds have taught me how to use the thunderbolt as the voice of truth, and how to help channel its power to where it is most needed.

Negative power can never be destroyed, only neutralized by its reverse polarity. At the center, power is neither negative nor positive; it incorporates both into a state of reciprocal transmutation. The Thunderbeings come to test and transmute us. As a Heyoka, I help to channel these energies. The grandfathers do the judging. I am merely a tool they use, just as I might use a rattle or a mask in this dimension. But the power is all interconnected.

This transformative power has many different names: life force, kundalini, *wakanda*, chi, and *kupuri*, to name a few. Whatever one chooses to call it, this is what the Thunderbeings teach shamans to use correctly. Just as a t'ai chi master can raise a person's chi by simply touching the psychic centers, certain shamans use crystals to open up clogged centers, while others can awaken the same power in people at long distances through mental suggestion and prayer. Then when one person's psychic centers are open and unobstructed, that person can serve as a "booster cable" to jump start the worn-out centers in others.

As we evolve spiritually, our vibratory rates increase. The more awareness we gain, the higher the frequency of this vibration. People of like rates hear each other's inner voice like a spiritual timbre. They begin to resonate in harmony with each other. As this resonance spreads, more people begin to awaken spiritually. And as they awaken, they automatically feel more love and take more responsibility for themselves and everything around them. It is this spiritual resonance that will eventually heal the Earth.

The prophecies speak of this time as a cleansing period. It is a time when corruption, greed, ignorance, and disease will be purged by the healing forces. In mind, body, and spirit, every corner of our planet will become rejuvenated. Nations, tribes, and races will put previous differences behind them and join together for the good of everyone.

This is already happening. And healers of all kinds, both seen and unseen, are playing important roles right now, preparing people to come into balance so they can ride out the storm.

The knowledge I have collected in this book is part of my contribution to this process. Through it I hope that you will gain some insights and inspiration that will help to lift you up. And from your new vantage point, whatever it may be, I hope you will see more clearly that you, too, are being called to serve the Great Spirit—that you, too, have an important role in the Great Purification. What you do with that vision is up to you.

EMERGING FROM THE CHAOS
A Spiritual Sojourn
Donn Le Vie, Jr.

Visions have always played a significant role in my spiritual unfolding. They still do. (I call them visions rather than dreams because the symbology is easy to interpret and there is usually a direct message associated with them.) I place great value on these visions, as they have served as major guideposts along my path. Because of their importance, I have chosen several that have contributed significantly to my present awareness level. These visions and experiences illustrate my sojourn from initiation to apprenticeship as an explorer of my psyche.

My spiritual journey began on my mother's twenty-seventh birthday — the day I was born. As Geminis, my mother and I have always shared a special relationship, but, like my co-author, it was my grandmother with whom I would later learn my earliest spiritual lessons.

Ever since I can remember, this magnificent woman had a magical quality about her; Emma Mae was the embodiment of love, kindness, and compassion. And we never lost our closeness, even after her death from cancer in 1975. I was with her the day she died. I was twenty-four years old then. I remember being alone with her frail, emaciated body, reliving all the fabulous summer vacations I had spent at her home on the rocky coast of Massachusetts. It seemed so unfair for her to succumb to this dreaded disease that took her life piece by piece, day by day, when she had given so much of herself to family and friends.

My grandmother's death was particularly difficult for my mother, who had been taking care of her practically twenty-four hours a day. I knew the funeral would be difficult for all of us. But what I didn't know was that my first real spiritual lesson was about to begin.

The day of the funeral was cold, overcast, and rainy — certainly a somber picture as friends and family gathered at the graveside for the service. But as soon as the minister began speaking his comforting words, the rain stopped, the clouds broke away, and the sun bathed us in a glorious warmth.

At the conclusion of the fifteen-minute service, as we were returning to our cars, back came the clouds, the sun disappeared, and the rain and chill returned to accompany the procession leaving the cemetery. I *knew* that the break in the weather had not been a coincidence, it had been a message, a sign that my grandmother was nearby. I could actually hear her voice, I thought, telling me, "I will never leave you."

One week after the funeral, I had my first vision. In this vision, my family had just returned from the burial service, entered the house through the kitchen door (just as we had done one week earlier), and wandered into the living room. But seated at the dining room table with her back to the large picture window was my grandmother. I was the only one who could see her. Her head was illumined from behind by a powerful white light shining through the window. I could make out her silhouette and hear her voice as she told me, "Tell your mother to stop crying. I am very happy here, and it is so beautiful, but her grief is keeping me from enjoying this new place."

It was true, my mother had been releasing a tremendous amount of grief, especially when she was packing up my grandmother's belongings. When I relayed my "dream" to her, she thought that it was because my grandmother had been on my mind lately. She thought the dream was merely a subconscious replay of the previous week's events.

Not wanting to upset her further, I agreed. However, several nights later, I experienced another vision. This time, I found myself at my grandmother's house where I had spent my summer vacations. I was playing in the rear pantry, making dough "cookies" (just as I had as a child) while my grandmother was preparing dinner in the kitchen. And seated at the kitchen table was my great-grandmother, who had passed away in 1968 at the age of 92. My grandmother spoke to me once more: "Please tell your mother again to stop grieving for me." My great-grandmother interjected: "Yes, tell Shirley everything is wonderful over here. We are very happy."

The thing I remember most about this dream were the vivid sounds. My grandmother's house had a clothesline fashioned with a pulley outside the rear pantry. I always paid attention to the sounds in my surroundings, and I clearly recall those squeaky pulleys from my childhood. But the clarity and familiarity of the noise as the wind moved across them convinced me that I was indeed experiencing something other than a dream state.

When I told my mother of this second vision, she began to believe that there was some truth to the messages I had received from her mother. Soon, with her new awareness of her mother's ongoing spirit and her eldest son's unusual ability, her grieving all but stopped.

About a year after the first vision, when I was twenty-five, my grandmother's sister was hospitalized with a serious illness. One night, I had a vision of my grandmother and her sister dressed in long, flowing, white gowns. They walked hand-in-hand up a grassy knoll, only to disappear into the rapidly moving fog just on the other side of the hill. When I awoke, I immediately understood the significance of the vision: My grandmother had come to accompany her sister to the "other side." Later that morning, I received a phone call from my parents, informing me that, indeed, my great-aunt had passed away early that morning.

Not all of my visions have revealed events that have actually come to pass. For example, my grandmother's brother had been ill at his home in Massachusetts. This news saddened me, for my great uncle was one of the most colorful and memorable people from my childhood summers. He would always know just when to come around to take my brother and me fishing or riding around the North Shore so that my grandmother could get a reprieve from having us underfoot.

A vision appeared to me one night shortly after his illness took a more serious turn. In this vision, I was sitting on the porch of a cabin somewhere in the woods when my great uncle walked in. I was very surprised to see him and asked him why he was there. "I came to say goodbye, little buddy," he said. (He always referred to my brother and me as his "little buddies.") "But why did you come to see me? What about your kids?" I asked. "You know why," he responded, ". . . it's because you're the bridge."

I am happy to say that my great uncle is still around as of this writing. But being "the bridge" seemed like a very important responsibility, if I correctly understood its significance.

Since the vision involving my great uncle, I have had several more that have had a strong effect on my life. But my interest in metaphysics, the noetic sciences, and human development didn't emerge until several years ago during my career as an Earth scientist.

I was fortunate that my academic and professional training in left-brain disciplines didn't cause my right-brain hemisphere to atrophy from non-use. Quite often, the Earth and planetary sciences make room for the creative side of the mind to take control. Working with meteorites and lunar samples, for example, allowed my creative, scientifically disciplined imagination to attempt to solve the riddle of the solar system's age. Creative imagination is always necessary in order to formulate sound scientific theories—from how planet Earth evolved out of the cosmic maelstrom to what we must do to heal and protect the Earth.

My strong desire to become an active participant in the American space program came about in elementary school while living in south Florida. Living fairly close to Cape Canaveral and the Kennedy Space Center boosted my interest, especially whenever a Mercury, Gemini, or Apollo mission was scheduled for liftoff. I could either watch the launch on TV or step outside and see it for myself with the aid of a pair of good binoculars.

Shortly before my junior year in college, I literally came within a penstroke of signing up with the "Fly Navy" campus recruiter. I saw this as my ticket into the space program—first as a navy pilot, then as a test pilot for experimental aircraft. But this was during the early '70s, when bombing runs over North Vietnam had reached their peak. After considering this and several other factors, I decided to try to enter the space program as a civilian scientist.

Fourteen years later, I found myself a qualified candidate for NASA's Astronaut Training Program as a mission specialist for the space shuttle program. Even though I was not chosen as one of the fortunate fifty or so final candidates, I framed the letter I received from NASA, informing me of my non-selection. This served as a reminder of how close I was to my goal, and I resolved to try again.

Shortly afterwards, however, my career as an Earth and planetary scientist came to an abrupt halt. As the price of oil rapidly approached ten dollars a barrel, my position as a geologist/geophysicist was terminated.

Immediately I fell victim to the "Why me?" syndrome: How could someone with my technical and scientific background be out of work? It took some time for me to accept the fact that I would have to find a new career. I couldn't pull up stakes and move to another "oil town." The oil glut wasn't just affecting Houston; the entire planet was reeling from it.

The first thing I thought of after my termination was my qualified candidate status with NASA for the next group of potential astronauts. I had to keep NASA informed of any personal or professional changes. Trying to find a position as an Earth scientist in Houston or anywhere else in 1986 was next to impossible. There went my dream of exploring space, I thought. It appeared that my destiny was slipping from my grasp.

Then, through several more visions and related psychic events, my true direction was revealed. I had been correct about being called to space exploration; but it was *inner* space I was to pursue, not outer space as I had thought since the fourth grade. This "feeling" began on a rock climb several years earlier.

In 1982, my best friend and fellow geologist, Tony Vanacore, and I climbed Enchanted Rock, located in the scenic, central-Texas hill country. To a couple of geologists with a tremendous love for the Earth sciences (we had worked together as research oceanographers in Miami prior to moving to Texas), Enchanted Rock was a geological marvel: an exfoliated granitic batholith. However, neither of us had any idea of the local folklore surrounding Enchanted Rock. Neither of us knew it was an ancient power spot—that is, until we reached the summit. The view of the surrounding hill country was breathtaking in the crisp, clear, November morning air. I turned to Tony and told him that I had just felt a sudden surge of great power and great joy go through me. I thought this strange at first, because this was a very difficult and emotionally upsetting time for me, as I was going through many changes.

I couldn't find the right words to describe the feelings I was experiencing, but I told Tony that, "I feel like changing my birthday to today." That's how significant the moment was to me. I was a much different person on the descent from that magnificent rock.

Liver cancer claimed Tony's life in April, 1989. Doctors gave him a six-month prognosis, but he didn't make it past the first month. He spoke of us both scaling Enchanted Rock again, as soon as he was feeling better, but that day never came. My best friend, whom I have loved like a brother, is gone, and a part of me has made the journey with him.

Tony elevated the meaning of dying with dignity. In spite of his Roman Catholic upbringing, his Zen-like attitude toward his own death was amazing to behold. I visited Tony in Houston two weeks before he died, and I was totally unprepared for what I saw. His pain was almost unbearable, yet his spirit refused to acknowledge the ordeal his body was undergoing.

Somehow, we managed to laugh and even cry together. I spoke with Tony just before he slipped into a coma several days before his death. For some reason, we both could sense that this conversation would be our last. His last words to me were something each of us had felt for the other ever since we had met: "Souls as close as ours will always be able to recognize each other."

Like my grandmother, Tony died in a coma, his last few breaths drawn with great difficulty, his body ravaged by cancer. Several months after his passing, I scaled Enchanted Rock again—this time with my wife, Jeanette, and our good friends, Marc and Francie Schwartz. People who reach the summit can't help but sit still and quietly meditate with the feeling of *being* a part of nature. We did the same, and Jeanette and I both felt the presence of Tony's spirit. Tony's presence in my life not only enriched it through our intense friendship but, through these specific experiences, contributed toward a new understanding and awareness of my spiritual path.

In December of 1986 my life began to undergo major change. Nine months had passed since I'd lost my job as a geologist. In the meantime, I had been doing some consulting work and freelance writing, but it wasn't nearly enough to keep me from eventually losing my investment property and my life savings. I was on the verge of financial ruin, living on money my parents had loaned me to get through the Christmas season.

It was difficult for me to see all that I had worked for slip from my grasp. I believed even then that there was some lesson, some purpose in all that I was going through, though exactly what that purpose was I had no idea. I had mailed out over 200 resumes, knocked on doors until my knuckles were bloodied, and tried to call in favors due. But all I got for my efforts was a handful of interviews that led nowhere.

I literally lived each day for the mailman's arrival, hoping to find a request to come in for an interview, or at least a rejection letter so that a potential employer could be scratched off my list. The only things I read were personal mail and responses from employment inquiries. I had no interest in reading anything else.

Then one day I received my *Writer's Digest* Book Club newsletter. I had been getting this newsletter for nearly a year and never looked at it. But for some reason on that particular afternoon, I sat down with the December issue and began reading. It was there that I first encountered the name Iron Thunderhorse.

In an article about other members of the book club I remember being fascinated by this man's literary and artistic accomplishments—not to mention the hardships he had endured under the watchful eye of the Texas Department of Corrections.

Up until that day, I had never wanted to correspond with anyone in prison, nor had I known anyone who had spent more than a night in a county jail. But before the day's end, I had written a lengthy letter to Iron Thunderhorse, introducing myself and telling him about my literary and scientific background as well as suggesting that we might possibly collaborate on writing his biography.

I received an immediate and lengthy reply from Iron Thunderhorse. While the biographical collaboration didn't work, our views on the Earth sciences and humanity's interaction with the planet were remarkably similar. From there, other aspects of our lives—including our personal experiences and our academic and self-learning backgrounds—began to come together to form the two parallel perspectives that comprise *Return of the Thunderbeings*.

Ironically, about a week after my first communication with Iron Thunderhorse, I received an offer from a Texas software development company to come work as a writer, and I have been writing and lecturing full time ever since.

Looking back now, I can more clearly see the purpose of this experience. I remember how difficult it was for me to lose so much of a material nature. I also remember what a wonderful support Jeanette was for me at that time. We had only known each other about eight months but she repeatedly said she couldn't help but feel there was a much greater lesson to be learned from all this.

She was right. The loss of all those material things—all that I thought I depended on—was the loss of a way of being. Gradually I realized that even if I lost everything, I still had the skills and inner abilities to gain it all back.

Gradually I became more inwardly directed. And while there was great frustration in that inward journey, I also remembered the words of my Aikido master: "Take heart when you become frustrated, because you are about to discover something new."

I have often been told that I possess strong psychic abilities, but I never thought to further their development until recently. It was while researching this book with Iron Thunderhorse that I experienced one of the most profound visions of my life. At the time, I thought it was an unusual dream. Iron Thunderhorse and I had been corresponding for about six months, and I had visited him several times in Huntsville to discuss what direction our work should take.

One night, I dreamed of waking up and finding myself on a stone altar. Iron Thunderhorse was standing on my left and gently holding down my left arm while a medicine man on my right was holding down my right arm. I could clearly see that the medicine man wore a buffalo headdress, and under his eyes were two horizontal lines of white paint. I could barely make out silhouettes of other people forming an outer circle around us. I remember Iron Thunderhorse saying to me, "Don't worry. . . he will not harm you. . .you must trust him."

The medicine man then placed the end of a hollow wooden or bone tube about three feet long into my left nostril and blew into it from the other end. He then did the same for my right nostril.

As soon as he was finished, I remember watching the noon-day sun set into the western horizon—then move backwards, retracing its path across the sky to the noon-day position. From there I watched it set and return again—all in a matter of five or six seconds. I remember thinking, "This can't be real—the sun just doesn't move from west to east, or at that speed!"

I next felt myself being drawn up into the air and absorbed by the light of the noon-day sun. But just before total absorption, I recall looking at the medicine man as I floated up past him. He had an incredulous expression on his face as I became the light.

When I awoke the next morning, I remembered the exact details, colors, and conversation that had occurred in the "dream" and wondered if Iron Thunderhorse had sent it to me, as he has been known to do.

But the strange thing is that for months after that vision, I had trouble with my sinuses in the morning. My allergies to Texas pollen flare up in the spring and fall but never during the summer. I had been told that my problem was probably with mold spores, but I have never had an allergic reaction to them before.

I passed the "dream" off as an unusual journey into my subconscious and kept it to myself. But several weeks later, I had the exact same vision. The next morning, I immediately wrote to Iron Thunderhorse and asked him for an interpretation of my vision. Here is his reply:

"I had a good laugh because your dream is a typical shaman's call—especially a recurring dream. The stone platform is a typical altar where you sacrificed yourself. The man with the buffalo headdress is a medicine man, as you pointed out, and your guide to the upper worlds. The two white lines signify the second level of awareness. The color white is symbolic of spirit, wisdom, and purity. I was there to observe as your sponsor. Your spirit made this decision on its own—it was *not* projected by me. The tube you mention is one used in certain medicine rites—a hollow bone. It's used to suck out diseases. In this case, the blowing into your nostrils signifies giving life (breath is life) to your divine spirit. In esoteric language, the nostrils are metaphors for divine vitality and longevity.

"As you know, the brain hemispheres control opposite sides of the body. When your guide blew into your right nostril, he altered your left brain—the reasoning mind perspective; notice he enlivened the right hemisphere first, through the left nostril. And yes, he did send you a germ (your nasal problem). Read *Shamanism* by Shirley Nicholson and you'll understand this significance. It is a custom to act out a psychosymbolic disease. If you cure it, then you are a wounded healer—a shaman who has returned from the other world a new person. The disease is your left-brain reasoning. The balance of the new area of enlightenment is your cure.

"The element of watching the sun move in reverse is a Heyoka vision—the powers of reversal of the seemingly impossible. The dream shows itself as an out-of-body experience because you knew it couldn't be real. Also, you couldn't have known about the symbolism involved. Your own guide became incredulous because you still have some doubts. Since this occurred in a shamanic state of consciousness, it carried over into this world as a sinus infection."

After describing a shamanic technique to rid my body of the "infection" (the technique was more of a test of my ability to withstand pain), which Iron Thunderhorse referred to as my initiation, he continued by explaining:

". . .your initiation is a very mild one because you already possess a rapidly adaptive psyche. Some people go through hell, but once you endure the initial shock to the unknown, it will be euphoric from then on.

"By the way, I *knew* you would receive a call and I've been waiting for a sign."

I was, at first, somewhat surprised and amazed at Iron Thunderhorse's interpretation of my vision. And yet, deep down inside, I knew the significance of it.

So many experiences and visions in my life have seemed at the surface to be separate, disjointed occurrences. But now, having experienced the mystical state of consciousness and several other parapsychic events, they have all come into focus. The special people and events in my life take on even more significance as I continue my journey with a higher level of awareness.

Contrary to what we might believe, answering the mystic's call is not restricted to a specific cultural belief system or to preconceived notions about reality. I had to choose between ignoring the call and thereby questioning the decision for the rest of my life, or accepting the quest for which I had been chosen.

This personal revelation will surprise many who know me. Some may scoff at these experiences; others may come forward with experiences of their own that they have kept hidden within themselves. As philosopher-psychologist William James said, there is no certainty that a temperature of 98.6 degrees is the optimum temperature from which to experience reality. Through many investigations of meditative and other "altered" states of consciousness, Western science is now beginning to appreciate that alternate modes of cognition can yield truths and knowledge that are not accessible to us in the reality of day-to-day consciousness.

This has been a great discovery for me, and the exploration of these alternate realities of inner space is now one of my greatest joys. I hope this book will serve as a doorway to open your awareness to such realities, and to illumine important signposts on the landscape of your own psyche.

INTRODUCTION
Shamanism & the New Age
Donn Le Vie, Jr.

"The truth shall set you free." Largely because of this biblical passage, many traditional Western evangelical, charismatic, and fundamentalist groups view the New Age spiritual era as a threat that runs contrary to Christian doctrine. In their zeal to protect dogma, they overlook the simple truth that the New Age is really not new at all. Nor is it a religion by itself, any more than the "Age of Technology" or "Age of Reason" were religious movements.

On the surface, this New Age era appears to be a part of humanity's continued evolution toward some higher life form. It is not, as some believe because of its nonreligious nature, a paradigm shift of religious beliefs. Nor is it a "movement" as professed by others such as Ken Wilber. A movement, in my definition, is a cause that takes on momentum from a groundswell of public support (and sometimes from the overzealous attempts by its leaders to convince others to believe as they do). History records very well the social movements that began to destroy western Europe during the 1920s and 1930s: fascism and communism, for example.

The New Age does not seek converts or to "save" souls from eternal damnation; instead, it encourages each person to turn inward and to follow a self-chosen path. The goal of world peace lies not in convincing every person on the planet that global tranquility and harmony is a necessity; it lies with each person realizing tranquility and harmony *within themselves*. Then and only then will world peace become a reality without the conscious efforts of nations.

As an example of how "New Age" is a misnomer, consider the recent popularity and rapid growth in the fields of humanistic and transpersonal psychology that have been frequently but erroneously attributed to the New Age. Abraham Maslow, Rollo May, Carl Rogers, Viktor Frankl and others were pioneers in the field, but it was Maslow who coined the term "humanistic psychology" over 25 years ago. Shortly thereafter, Maslow advanced a new perspective he referred to as "transpersonal psychology," which concentrated on spirituality and "the farthest reaches of human nature." Maslow was one of the first to bring respectability to the scientific study of mysticism by explaining peak experience and other associated phenomena.

In our attempts to discover inner power, we sometimes leave our outer selves vulnerable to influences that distort our external sensitivity. These influences then distract our true being by *seducing* us (our female, passive nature) through vices. In the same fashion, in our search for uncovering inner sensitivity, we can become distracted by influences distorting our sense of outer power by *coercing* us (the active male nature) into vices.

This "spiritual chauvinism," as it is called by Buddhist teacher Ngakpa Chogyam, is one that hinders all religions and paths to enlightenment. It has done so since the institutionalization of mystical experience in the caves of the Paleolithic Period.

The people of the Paleolithic world lived close to the Earth as hunter-gatherer tribal families. Their existence, both biological and spiritual, was heavily dependent on the elements of earth, air, fire, and water. Food, shelter, clothing, birth, death, healing, magic, and mysticism were all tied together in a limitless field of experience. That which seemed impossible always remained just beyond the thin veil separating these people from their conscious perception of reality. "Possible" and "impossible" did not have the polarized relationship that they now occupy in Western culture and society.

Those who dared to gaze through the veil to heed the calling from beyond became the shamans. The shamanic experience transcends dimension. Through it, the world spontaneously reveals itself to those who remain open to *all* experience without prejudgment.

Shamans were revered by their contemporaries because of their vital connection with the elemental essence that allowed them to heal and guide others in the search for ultimate knowledge—truth. Where truth abounds, barriers, divisions, and hierarchies collapse because they only serve as points of distraction from the path. Whenever these impediments become lodged in the conscious mind, they immediately curtail any progress toward realization. The possession of ultimate truth is concomitant with making the truth available to all, so that every person can continue on the path of self-awareness and the attainment of higher knowledge.

Why is the Western church threatened by shamanism and associated mystical practices? The answer to this question relates to the discussion on outer power and sensitivity. As socio-political hierarchies arise, the shaman's sphere of influence contracts to almost nothingness—unless his or her activities conform to the behavior and laws set forth by the emerging hierarchy. But if shamans allow themselves to be bound by the very chains they are supposed to transcend, how can they still be called shamans?

Traditionally, because of their special powers and stature, shamans have always been non-conformists and anarchists. But they quickly became a necessary evil to the emerging order. Because of their power and influence, they were reluctantly absorbed into the socio-political structure.

When confronted with the alternative of practicing within the confines of the new order (to counterbalance its degenerative effect on humanity), many shamans undoubtedly opted to flee to more remote areas, away from the far-reaching grasp of the hierarchy. For those who chose to remain, the pressure on them to comply with the status quo was the beginning of the decline of true mysticism. In the course of time, true knowledge received only secondary mention to the prioritized, lifeless rhetoric of intellectually communicated dogma.

A significant characteristic of ultra-conservative religious doctrine is the view it holds of the individual as being intrinsically sinful, worthless in the eyes of God, and in need of punishment and correction. In contrast, the ethos of genuine mystical experience is that the individual is *always* in a state of enlightenment and merely in need of capturing a brief reflection of it as it passes through "the fabric of the self," which enables us to see ourselves for what and who we really are.

The path toward true knowledge is devoid of hierarchy, sexism, and prejudice; instead, it concentrates on the pursuit of liberation for everyone. True mystical experience is a real challenge to male-dominated religious hierarchies, overflowing as they are with weapons of pseudo-spirituality used to maintain their grip on elitism and socio-political order. But hope lies on the horizon, for shamanism and mysticism have enjoyed a rejuvenation with the global awareness generated by Harmonic Convergence of 1987.

Jesus taught that we are all divine beings; that the Christ and the spirit of God can be found within all people. Within *all* people, not just the few — not just the Protestants, not just the Catholics, not just the Hebrews, not just the Buddhists — but all people. The foundation for the New Age is the pantheistic philosophy that all is God. This philosophy is gaining wide appeal. So is shamanism, for shamanism is a cross-cultural form of pantheism with universal roots that is available to everyone.

A hundred years ago, in 1888, a theosophist by the name of H.P. Blavatsky predicted that if the churches did not divorce themselves from their "cherished

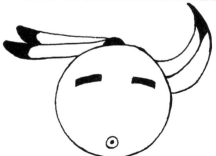

dogmas," the twentieth century would see the collapse and ruin of all Christianity. Madame Blavatsky further stated that centuries of blind faith would inevitably lead to crass materialism—*unless* archaic ideals built on the "shifting sands of human fancy" were replaced by universal ideals built on the foundation of eternal truth.

I personally know of evangelical organizations which sponsor "countercult" programs and target the New Age as a dangerous deviation. Leaders of these groups use hellfire and brimstone tactics to fill their coffers with money while filling their congregations with obsession and fear. Iron Thunderhorse refers to these ministers as "psychic vampires"—people who draw the spiritual life force from their hapless victims.

We see today the confrontations between the philosophies, beliefs, and teachings of many groups. This can be attributed not just to religion, but to the contemporary dross—the impurities—that we have all been exposed to and absorbed from society. What we need is a union—a cross-cultural collection of people who can inform and educate others, *by example rather than words*, that the journey toward inner awareness begins with seeking truth. The quality of the quest, as exemplified by how one lives one's life, speaks louder than any rhetoric. This is empowerment through *self*-communication, the language of *self*-direction and *self*-discovery that will cause others to take notice. After all, it took just one individual, Bodhidharma, to spread Buddhism from India to China. And it took just one Nazarene carpenter to capture the attention of the entire Roman empire.

Shamanism has always contained universal elements. For this reason, worldwide shamanic practices collectively form another framework for the New Age. This is the Golden Age which seeks to resurrect the ancient philosophies; therefore, none of the teachings and practices that have been labeled as "dangerous" by the conservative, fundamentalist, and charismatic groups is new. The underlying fear of these groups is that the re-emergence of shamanism and mysticism will inspire a more individualistic approach to salvation—an approach that is devoid of the religious pomp and circumstance established and perpetuated by the church since the Middle Ages.

The only thing new about the New Age is that we now have the freedom to join together, to associate and build a cross-cultural spiritual body. But before this can be accomplished, our own weaknesses and self-imposed obstacles need to be analyzed and removed.

The word "religion" has some ambiguity attached to it, partly because our minds perceive the lack of true substance associated with its implied meaning. Walter Houston Clark, in an article entitled "The Philosophy of Religious Experience," stated that even the definition of religion can find no agreement among scholars. Clark asked many experts in the field of religious studies to define the word "religion." Of the 68 replies he received, no two were exactly alike. Even when responses were grouped, the definitions were significantly different.

The reason for these many different definitions is easy to explain. Each one of us is endowed with a particular degree of perception, level of consciousness, and range of experience—in short, with a paradigm—a particular way of viewing the world and everything in it. All that we see, feel, hear, taste, smell, and think must pass through our unique perception, consciousness, and experience filters. What remains is censored and classified, often with clearly defined boundaries. One can be a Catholic, Protestant, Hindu or Shiite Moslem, but one's religious affiliation can never be a combination of traditions in the eyes of the respectful religious structure or church. How can one subscribe to both Moslem and Buddhist doctrine? In shamanism, these divisions and categories do not exist; one simply *is*. This "is-ness" is the knowledge of spirituality in harmony with the cosmos.

Anthropologist Michael Taussig notes that time, space, matter, cause, relation, human nature, and society itself are byproducts fabricated by humanity, just as are the different types of implements, clothing, housing, monuments, languages, and myths that humankind has made since the dawn of history.

Where do we stand today? South Africa, Afghanistan, the Middle East, Nicaragua: our once-heralded social conscience as global citizens has yielded to thought and processes that have left the world a stagnant place. Corruption ferments, from the hallowed halls of justice to the inner sanctums of religious institutions. How do we get out of this mire? Iron Thunderhorse provides one answer:

> . . .the shaman is a member of a special population of category-breakers. Ideally, the spiritual and cognitive combine in these men and women to render them powerful healers of their society. Shamans become epistemological mediators; that is, as they discover their art, they learn how to bridge different realms.

Therein lies a significant discovery: becoming bridges to each other. All too often, our society dwells on prejudices, on how different we are, instead of looking at the common threads that unite us in the family of humankind and universal consciousness. The greatest teaching a Native American possesses is the ancient truth: *mitakuye oyasin*—"We are all relations, all part of the whole."

The religious critics underestimate the transcendental powers of the shaman. This is why they fail to understand the New Age and fear its acceptance by an ever-increasing number of disenchanted people. Literal translations of

ancient doctrine blind these critics to the power of the symbology that represents the transformational process for shamans and others alike. Hence, the New Age is characterized as a cult and not "of God." The irony here is that the Bible is full of symbolism and metaphor. When read with this perspective, it is one of the greatest metaphysical pieces of literature ever written.

The shaman is not restricted to the ordinary readings, sermons, and pre-defined social patterns imposed on leaders of traditional religions. The shaman's role and power is to bring about necessary shifts in philosophical and cosmological direction, to re-establish balance and harmony for the people. This is described by Mary Schmidt in *Shamanism*, where she relates how the shaman begins by collapsing his or her own being, striving for controlled rebirth, then continuing to redirect the mental surety of others for the purpose of effecting cures for social ailments.

We can now see the importance of the shaman's role, both individually and collectively, in effecting a global shift in consciousness. Harmonic Convergence, for example, was celebrated with the complete involvement of a new shamanic underground. It is irrelevent whether others believe in the "literal" significance of this event. As stated before, the shaman is not out to win souls for anyone. His or her purpose is to light the way back to the self, away from institutionally imposed doctrine and dogma that imprisons the spirit.

The New Age shamanistic renaissance has received a good deal of attention from the media. At the same time, the fundamentalist empire shows signs of weakening in spirit, if not in finances. The scandals and controversy involving prominent TV evangelists and charismatic leaders in the late 1980s reeked of hypocrisy and deception. Was their exposure to the public at that time only coincidental with the rising interest in shamanism and mysticism? On a much larger scale, were the peace negotiations in Nicaragua and disarmament talks between the Soviet Union and the United States only coincidental with the beginning of the Aquarian Age?

Reintegration and reorganization of the collective unconscious is fraught with difficulties and pitfalls; nevertheless, it is happening. Today, the shaman represents a breaking away from official religious hierarchies to the individualized experience of direct association. The revival of interest in shamanism today, then, can be seen as a "democratization"—a journey back to the archetypal spiritual democracy enjoyed by primal tribal cultures and societies, where access to spiritual experience and direct revelation was available to most everyone.

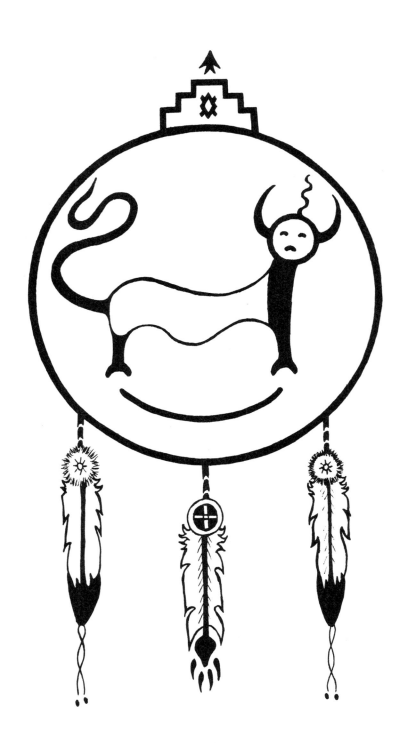

PROLOGUE
How the Great Council of Manitous
Saved the World
Iron Thunderhorse

Even though Mother Earth was still in a sad condition, everything seemed brighter now. The medicine circles were once again common, the elders were counseling the younger people, and the other invisible barriers seemed to be fading. Yes, there had been rough times when disagreement was rampant, but balance was slowly returning. The spirit beings had indeed saved the world, and now was the time of day to offer blessings and give thanks.

Thunderbird Sachem looked all around him. Hundreds of lodges were pitched in a great circle in the azure valley amidst rolling hills. In the background loomed the mighty forests, home of his Algonquin ancestors. Theirs had been a long journey, full of perils and heartaches, but today was a joyous affair, a new beginning. The Thunderbird nations had come together for a great celebration: the *Pauwau*.

Thunderbird Sachem reflected that this must have been how it was in days-gone-by when the medicine people, known as *pauwaus* in Algonquin, held sacred gatherings to share the wisdom of their ancient culture. This had not been done for hundreds of years. Finishing his offerings and prayers to the manitous at dawn, Thunderbird Sachem walked slowly toward the giant council lodge, savoring the sights, sounds, and fragrances. Life was good now, he mused, and it would get even better.

The people were gathering now to hear the *pauwau* shamans who were about to address the crowd. Thunderbird Sachem was scheduled to be the first speaker. All the relations were in attendance. While awaiting the preliminary stages of the *pauwau*, Thunderbird Sachem contemplated the vast history he had come to know from his own years of studies and his more recent acquaintance with his close friend, the New Age scientist whom he had named Double Sunset. The studies flashed into his mind like a kaleidoscope of images and colors.

First he recalled the prophecies of the Thunderbird nations—prophecies based on the sacred visions and dreams of the aboriginal clans whose history reached back more than 25,000 years. These dreams and visions, he knew, occurred in the dreamtime, a world which parallels this world, and were guided by the manitous and allies from the spirit world. The manitous were great and mysterious forces of nature that might take the shape of subtle creatures or terrible entities with great power. The most powerful were the Thunderbeings, whose wisdom comes with the terror of storm clouds, a dynamic metaphor for psychic disruption and reorganization.

The manitous and the *pauwaus* had taught Thunderbird Sachem that every individual is the sum total of all that has been experienced before, including the experiences of preceding generations; that through ancestry, every human being is but a single link in a chain that extends back through history to the beginning of time.

Thunderbird Sachem had also learned that past, present, and future are not interdependent markers on the scale of infinitude, that answers to questions from any time or place could be found within, if people would only take the time to stop and listen to themselves. The ancient ceremonies of the Thunderbird nations were designed to contemplate these profound questions in sacred space, called the dreamtime.

Then there was the Thunderbird totem itself, perhaps the oldest symbol known to all aboriginal peoples. The Thunderbird represented the rebirth of the soul, the rising of the spirit out of the ashes of ignorance, tyranny, greed, and oppression. Thunderbird was the aboriginal phoenix bird.

Thunderbird Sachem was well aware that much of the aboriginal history of the planet remained obscure in people's minds, and that much of it had been carved on rocks or painted on cave walls and cliff faces. Had humans lost the ability to recognize these symbols from their past? Had these ancient signposts become mere scribbles marking irrelevent events, or simply the link in modern minds that recalled unconscious images from the depths of our psyche? Thunderbird Sachem had been born with the gift of far sight. He recalled the meanings as well as psychic connections of symbols and hieroglyphics, so it was hard for him to understand why people could not see what he saw in the sacred images.

Yes, indeed, Thunderbird Sachem knew there was much more in these sacred symbols. But humans had become all too dependent on material things and had lost the ability to communicate with that part of themselves which is related to everything else in the universe. Science and technology had replaced the ancient hunter, builder, warrior, and even the ancient birthing rites. All people were connected in the great cycle of life—this he knew. The composite characters of the manitous illustrated these connections. Humans still had the power of creative intelligence; they had simply failed to use it wisely in modern times. (Modern conveniences did everything for them, so why bother, they thought.)

For centuries, science had been reluctant to accept the ancient teachings that tell of the spirits found in trees and animals alike. Now science was learning that there may be some truth to the ancient wisdom.

In the midst of his musings, Thunderbird Sachem suddenly remembered the modern discovery that certain trees release a poisonous sap which serves as a defense mechanism against damaging insects. This was nature — a living nature that aboriginal peoples cherish and are committed to preserving and protecting because they are the caretakers of natural law.

Yes, thought Thunderbird Sachem, all things had intelligence. Brother Eagle knew just how to soar high above the Earth. Brother Fox also knew how to use the natural geography of the land for cover while swiftly stalking prey. The Salmon Mother always knew just where and when to migrate in order to find her special spawning place, just as Goose knew when it was time to fly south to her ancestral mating grounds. Grandfather Moose knew just where to go when it was his time to cross over the spirit trail and leave his physical body behind. Younger Sister Doe knew how to stand and walk, even at birth. These, he thought, were all acts of intelligent spirit — the same spirit that animates all human beings.

Thunderbird Sachem then reflected on the intelligence of Mother Earth. He considered how wonderful it was when a portion of the environment became imbalanced, that nature automatically took corrective measures. This was the basis for teachings that had been passed down from generation to generation. Such teachings concerned the connections between all living things.

Thunderbird Sachem had often heard it said in ceremonies that we are all relations. He had been taught that the first Earth cultures were based on the metaphysical rhythms associated with fertility and procreation of all life. Because of this, he was convinced that the first shamans must have been females. Today, for example, the rites of womanhood and the celebration of the nurturing Earth Mother could still be observed in the *inipi*, or sweat lodge ceremonies. In recent years, even scientists had begun to study the concept of the living Earth Mother. This study was called the Gaia concept, after the Greek goddess of the Earth. However, much of this research seemed unnecessary to Thunderbird Sachem. Aboriginal peoples did not need satellites and microscopes to know these things.

Thunderbird Sachem also remembered the Hopi and other tribal nations who still conduct ceremonies of great antiquity to celebrate the mysteries and cycles of life. He remembered how these practices were outlawed as westward-expanding Christians had oppressed aboriginal spirituality because it was different and therefore considered "heathen." Ethnocentricity was usually the result of ignorance or tyranny, he imagined. But now, finally, the contest had been narrowed down to a final match between natural law and the artificial law imposed by man.

Thunderbird Sachem smiled. He had also learned much about the spiritual prophecies and legends of the aboriginal people. Years ago, those people had spoken of a day when the teachings would be lost. But those same people also said there would come another day when the teachings would be re-established for all to share. Thunderbird Sachem knew in his heart that day had arrived.

The Hopi and many other nations had a prophecy about Pahana—their lost brother—and it spoke of a time when this lost brother would return to them with the missing portion of a sacred stone tablet originally given to the Hopis by the Creator. The brother's return would be a sign that the ancient prophecies would be fulfilled.

And what did this tablet represent? None other than the teachings of the Thunderbird totem from the ancient confederacies; none other than the return of natural law that would once again be understood—and hopefully, respected.

The legends also said that the aboriginal people of this land had arrived here through different routes. Thunderbird Sachem had learned that approximately half of the oral and pictographic histories left by aboriginal nations revealed that their people were indigenous. But the other half spoke of migrations—not just one mass migration over an ice bridge, but many migrations by boat and over island "stepping stones" leading to this world. All of this, he knew, had taken place thousands of years prior to the so-called "discovery" of North America.

The aboriginal legends also said that all humankind can trace its roots to one tree. Those roots, he recalled, were the aboriginal people themselves, growing beneath the Thunderbird totem and the Great Tree of Life.

Thunderbird Sachem remembered that these teachings had once been shared with all nations. But the rise of civilization had created divisions, the illusion of material wealth and an unhealthy imbalance on Mother Earth. Now the prophecies told him that the time for this negative imbalance had expired. The signs were right.

All these things ran through Thunderbird Sachem's mind as he considered what questions the people would ask of him. Whose questions should he answer first? The questions of the little ones, of course. Their observations were always fresh, honest, and free from any bad feelings.

Ghost Horse, the Spiritual Firekeeper, delivered thanksgiving prayers, taking care to recall the blessings bestowed upon the people. Next, Buffalo Medicine Sachem held the sacred wampum in one hand while speaking briefly to the assembly. He concluded by announcing: "Thunderbird Sachem will now speak to the people."

Thunderbird Sachem approached the front of the assembly. He seated himself on the robes before the people in the great council lodge and began.

"It is good to be home," he said. "This is a joyous day for us all. Let us celebrate our blessings together as we did in the long ago. Much work lies ahead in healing ourselves and our Earth Mother. The clan mothers have done very well keeping our sacred teachings alive, from mother to mother and daughter to daughter. We owe them our love and respect for this. We are here to remember how to share our insights and special knowledge with the people. Let us do so in the ancient way of telling stories.

"Is there a special request for a medicine story?" asked Thunderbird Sachem. "Let the little ones speak first. Their new eyes are eager and inquisitive. Ahh—I recognize Morning Star. Speak up, my niece, and tell us what story you would like to hear."

"Thank you, Uncle Thunderbird Sachem, for recognizing my request," came the melodious voice. "Would you be kind enough to tell us all the story of how the Great Council of Manitous saved the world?"

Thunderbird Sachem smiled broadly. "You have made an excellent choice, as I suspected. One day you will carry on as your own mother before you. Then you will carry the sacred crystal that has been passed on from generation to generation. One day you, too, will be known as a *pauwau*, or medicine woman. The story you chose also happens to be the most important one known to me because it explains how we acquired our great knowledge as caretakers of the sacred laws of Mother Earth and Father Sky."

Thunderbird Sachem spoke to the medicine woman who stood by his side. The woman handed him a sacred medicine shield. Thunderbird Sachem held up the shield and everyone saw the pictographic symbols of the manitous painted on it. Cedar and sage offerings filled the enormous lodge with a pungent odor as the story began to unfold:

"At the center of the universe," began Thunderbird Sachem, "there is a place called Skyworld in the Star Nations galaxy. This is where all our nations originated.

"This is the place of the alter ego of Earth, the *nagual*, or shadow. It is where the manitous live as human beings on our Earth Mother. The manitous are either medicine animals or composite entities representing the forces of nature. They are part human and communicate telepathically. Once, in ancient times, the manitous were able to speak directly to us in dreams and visions. But very few humans in the recent past remembered how to use their powers of communication with them.

"Because of this fact, one of the manitous decided that something drastic needed to be done. He spoke to the other nations and discovered that all of them felt the same way. They all became worried as each of them spoke of the terrible things on Earth Mother—the pollution, corruption, war, greed, and hate—which they saw in these dreams and visions. They decided to summon Gitche Manitou, the Great Master of All Life and Spirit, to hold a council.

"As was the custom there, Gitche Manitou summoned all the other manitous to assemble in the grove where stood the Great Tree of Peace, a majestic, towering pine.

" 'The Great Council of the Manitous will now commence,' declared Keca Manitowa, the gentle manitou maiden whose voice was as sweet as the scent of fresh pine needles.

" 'The Great Council has been assembled to hear a specific complaint that the human beings on Mother Earth no longer have the powers or abilities to communicate with us in our special way,' thundered the looming voice of Gitche Manitou. 'Let the Keeper of the Sacred Shell, Otter Manitou, begin these discussions.'

"The air immediately became electrified with the sounds of rolling thunder as traces of sheet lightning danced behind the wispy treetops.

"Next, Mana-Bozho, Manitou of the Dawn, Fire, and Air spoke to all those assembled in the sacred grove of the Tree of Peace. 'We have tried to reach our human relations in their dreams and visions, but they are no longer able to see us or hear us,' he explained. 'Their dreams are full of strange things. These are not natural things, but new and artificial things and thus merely illusions. They are not real like us.'

"The grove erupted with a resounding clamor from the manitous, who voiced their collective agreement.

" 'It must be this thing called science,' cried Yo-He-Wah, Manitou of the Grass.

" 'What is this thing called science?' petitioned Wisa-ka, Manitou of all Culture.

"Gitche Manitou responded to the queries of the Council with a low rumble of all-knowing assurance.

" 'This thing called science is an artificial way of looking at what is natural,' he noted. 'It is a sign that the Keepers of Natural Law, the manitous, have not been diligent in their duties of maintaining spiritual equilibrium in the world. The Great Cycle of Life has run its course and it must be rejuvenated as is the natural order of things. It is time for a new world cycle to begin. The Age of Flowers is upon us.'

" 'I attest to this law,' responded Kukulcan, the Feathered Serpent, Manitou of the Laws of Astromancy.

" 'And I, too, attest to the other half of that law of cycles,' seconded Kolowisi, the Horned Serpent, Manitou of the Laws of Geomancy.

" 'Well, then, what about the Medicine Rocks with the talking pictures carved on them? Didn't we give these to the humans in the last world so that they wouldn't forget the sacred laws of nature?' inquired Ketanto-wit, Manitou of the Great Power of Mysteries.

" 'That may have been so in the last world cycle,' countered Unkatahe, Manitou Mother of Fertility and Good Health. 'But this science seems to have many new distractions and devices that have destroyed or covered up the rocks—such as cities and roads.'

" 'And don't forget the little ones who have lost their original instructions and guidance from parents,' added Manitowa Mimiwa, Manitou Mother of the Song Birds who appears in the form of a giant turtle dove. 'Why, they are so mischievous without the sacred laws that they deface the talking rocks with toy weapons or they paint a new type of artificial symbol on them, called graffiti.'

" 'Well, then,' interjected Gitche Manitou, to let the Council know that a possible solution was at hand, 'I truly believe that what is needed is a spiritual renaissance of natural law on the Earth Mother. To accomplish this great task in the new time cycle will require a special liaison who knows how to communicate with us so we can once again teach these relations the meaning of the symbols carved on the sacred rocks. Do I hear any suggestions?'

"Peteikunau Naiota, the Manitou with the Sacred Bundle on His Back (who is also known as the Flute Player and guards the rocky ledges and cliffs) was next to speak. 'Only the *pauwaus*—the shamans, as they are called in this new world cycle—are capable now of ever understanding the sacred laws carved on the Medicine Rocks which I have so painstakingly struggled to preserve.'

" 'Yes, I agree with our elder brother,' snarled Gitch-a-nah-mi-e-be-zhew—the Manitou of the Underworld Powers who has the body of a panther and the antlers of a deer. 'There are very few left who are truly *pauwaus* and who see and hear us in their dreams and visions. Let us give to these shamans the powers of clairvoyance and clairaudience so that they will clearly understand and see the natural law on the sacred Medicine Rocks.'

"Baho-li-kong-ya, the Crested Mammae Manitou who watches all young people and animals, raised an objection. 'The Council has spoken wisely, as always,' she said. 'Yet, I foresee an obstacle that is as ancient as we manitous. We know that the law is based on duality. So how will we show the human beings that are the scientists what is true yet unexplainable in their terms?'

"Gitche Manitou sensed the magnitude of this problem and once more responded to the deference of the council. 'I have heard there are a few new-comers on the Earth Mother world who know this science and who are also cognizant of the ancient laws of metaphysics,' explained the grandfather manitou. 'We must see to it that the Shaman and the New Age Scientist come together in their own ways of council and devise a middle ground. Once this is done, let us reveal to the Shaman a special method of initiation to insure that all humans will understand our laws. The Shaman and New Age Scientist are the Sacred Twins in human form; the Lost Pahana will meet the counterpart spoken of in Earth prophecy. The initiation will be a three-part test to coincide with the three phases of life, yet with a built-in duality that remains reciprocal. The Shaman will be given the Medicine. Then the Medicine will be revealed to the Scientist, who will analyze it and report on it in the language of this New Age science. In this way, the human beings will have the natural law so that the world might be saved from destruction.'

" 'Yes, this is all very good,' agreed Athenesic, the Manitou of all Beautiful Things. 'The *pauwau* Shamans are the only ones capable of restoring balance. With the help of the New Age Scientist, humans can verify our laws as interpreted by the Shaman. Otherwise, there will always be disagreement. This is a very wise plan, my brothers, sisters, and elders.'

" 'Then it is settled,' bellowed Gitche Manitou, with an urgency that gave notice to the others that the council was about to end. 'Advise the Shaman that it is time to reveal to the Scientist the laws written on the Medicine Rocks. Let a spokesperson from each side be selected to assemble these Medicine Laws in a way that the entire world will see and understand. Then, when you are assured from their dreams and visions that all is understood and the tests have been developed, I shall send a summons directly to the human beings. If this summons is heard by all the humans from the four sacred directions of the Earth Mother, then we will know our plan has worked and the world may proceed through the test of purification and renewal.'

"And that, my brothers, sisters, elders, and little ones, is how the Great Council of Manitous saved the world. The Medicine Laws are now available for everyone to behold. The Shaman and the New Age Scientist will now come forward to give their revelations directly to the people. The old and the new, the right and the left, will merge. All polarity is but the half of a true whole. Let the Great Tree of Peace bear fruit at the center of the world. Let the Thunderbirds arise from the ashes and return to the nest. Let nature flourish and peace prevail on our Earth Mother."

Chapter One

ART & THE
SHAMANIC AWAKENING

PART I
Iron Thunderhorse

Archaic shamanism spanned a wide spectrum of roles that went beyond the more popularized role of healer. The shaman as artist, crafter, poet, storyteller, keeper of legends and genealogies, songster, entertainer, and teacher are vital areas of the shamanic repository too often neglected in most contemporary studies. These areas are highly significant as aids to cultural reintegration and transformation. For this reason, it is necessary to recognize their role in contemporary shamanic practices. Hidden beneath the surface of the story, craft, legend, dance, or song lies the true spirit of the shamanic quest: the wisdom of thousands of years of intimate relationships to nature.

The contemporary renaissance of shamanism began several decades ago and continues to build momentum. Today there are many isolated examples of shamanic entertainers and artists who demonstrate the proper uses of metaphysical lore. Vast amounts of shamanic lore, however, have been lost to the prevailing winds of acquiescence and technological dependency. Establishing a shamanic lifeway, which entails developing a modern paradigm for the future, also includes the wisdom of thousands of years of intimate relationships with the environment. Such is the wide scope of the shaman's roles described herein.

The Storyteller

Whether told by a traveling monk, a Druid bard, or at a winter campfire on Turtle Island (Native America), the drama of storytelling was and still is a vital means of passing on the acquired lessons of shamanic self-introspection. In many contemporary circles, such storytelling is categorized as "folklore."

Folklore is the substance of a people's culture perpetuated in the beliefs, practices, customs, observances, myths, and legends of mutual acceptance. Arts and crafts express the genius and creativity of a tribe or group rather than that of an individual. The people are guided by their repository of folklore.

A good example of a modern-day shamanic storyteller who strives to revive this ancient craft is Joe Bruchac. Bruchac was born in 1942 during the Moon of Falling Leaves (October) in Saratoga Springs, New York, and is of Abenaki-Slovak/English ancestry. He published the *Greenfield Review*, operates the *Greenfield Review Press*, and facilitates the Native American Authors Distribution Project. He has written over 25 books of poetry and fiction, as well as hundreds of articles.

Joe often conducts storytelling workshops. He is also one of this country's foremost authorities on Native American writing, along with Maurice Kenny (Mohawk) and Diane Burns (Chippewa-Chemehuevi). Joe has been strongly influenced by the Mohawk elder, Ray Fadden (Tehanetorens), who operates the Six Nations Museum at Onchiota, New York. Tehanetorens is a Mohawk educator, historian, and master storyteller. Bruchac's insight into the need for storytelling and its underlying foundation as metaphysical education is indeed a valuable reference for a future shamanic paradigm.

In an article entitled, "Thanking the Birds: Native American Upbringing and the Natural World," he notes: "The teachings that have been given to generations of Native American children in stories are ones that need to be understood by all of us."

One story Bruchac uses to demonstrate the principles of ecological well-being and respect for the environment deals with the Abenaki transformer hero figure, Gluskabe.

One day, Gluskabe goes off hunting and returns unsuccessful. Disappointed, he angrily consults with his grandmother and talks her into making a magical game bag. This bag stretches to allow anything to be put into it.

Gluskabe returns to the woods with his game bag and discovers a large clearing. He begins to cry and moan, and the animals come out to see what the noise is all about. At first, Gluskabe claims that the problem is too terrible to reveal. But after persistent inquiries from the animals, he announces that the world is going to be destroyed. The animals become alarmed, but Gluskabe saves the day when he tells them of his magical game bag. "You can hide in my game bag," he tells them, and all the animals in the world climb inside.

Gluskabe takes the game bag home, and his grandmother notices its fullness. She asks why it is so full. At first, Gluskabe pretends it is nothing, but finally he tells her it holds all the animals of the world.

"Now we will never go hungry," he says.

But his grandmother reminds him, "Animals cannot live in a game bag. And what about our children and our children's children? If we take all the animals now, what will they have to eat?"

Gluskabe then understands his error and returns the animals to the forest.

This particular story is very clear in its meaning. It teaches a person the foolishness of hoarding, greed, gluttony, and waste.

Another story Bruchac uses to demonstrate the uniqueness of Native American storytelling is one that applies to contemporary issues. This is the story of Swift Eagle, an Apache who is visiting the Onondaga Indian Reservation in New York. Swift Eagle is walking in the woods one day when he hears some boys playing in the bushes. The boys have killed a few birds for sport with a BB-gun. Swift Eagle decides to teach them a lesson, but in a unique manner.

Swift Eagle walks up to the boys. "Oh, I see you have been hunting," he says. "Pick up your game and come with me."

He then takes the boys to a spot where they can cook the birds. He instructs them in the proper way to give thanks to the spirits of the birds before they begin to eat. As they eat, he tells them stories of the importance of birds—their gifts of song, feathers, talons, and their flesh as food. Swift Eagle's last comment especially makes a lasting impression.

"You know," he says, "our Creator gave the gift of life to everything that is alive. Life is a very sacred thing. But our Creator knows that we have to eat to stay alive. That is why it is permitted to hunt to feed ourselves and our people. So I understand you boys must have been very, very hungry to kill those little birds."

It is known to all shamanic peoples that a healthy environment is the primary source of survival. To disturb the environmental balance is to invite disaster to our own well-being. At a time when our entire world is threatened with environmental destruction, the shamanic modes of folklore storytelling are desperately in need of resurrection.

Storytelling is somewhat different from most other literary disciplines. Storytelling involves an aura of drama, usually with pantomime and other forms of visual playacting. Storytelling, then, is experiential and holistic rather than merely literate. It touches the entire being—emotionally, spiritually, physically, and mentally.

The Performer

The shaman as songster, dancer, actor, orator, and poet is another vital area of study. As a performer, the shaman enacts the ancient wisdom for the people to observe and absorb. The observer experiences this wisdom both consciously and subconsciously, and it becomes stored in the memory.

Song played an integral role in Native American folklore. Every experience, from birth to death and all things in between, had a celebratory song.

The death song was sung when a person knew the time for transition was near. In 1882, for example, 37 Sioux warriors shared the same death song when they were executed at Mankato, Minnesota, for defending their land:

I, _____ , do sing:
I care not where my body lies,
My soul goes marching on.
I care not where my body lies,
My soul goes marching on.

The Eskimo culture had a unique use for song in settling personal disputes. Whenever one Eskimo accused another of some misdeed or misbehavior, a "song-duel" was held in a ceremonial community dwelling. Each of the adversaries used their creative talents to win the approval of the audience, and the winner of the dispute was the one who gave the best performance. No punishments were meted out; nevertheless, the adversaries were able to vent their frustrations and hostilities in a creative manner which averted violence.

It is interesting to note that the Italian opera had its roots in similar shamanic song-duels that ended in dispute resolutions. Also, some songs, such as the Abenaki Snake Dance song recorded by anthropologist J. Walter Fewkes in 1890 (Figure 1-1), have words that are apparently all vocables—nontranslatable syllables that carry the melody. Finally, songs and art often overlap, such as when a dream song is recorded as a talisman. In the subarctic regions of the world, an apprentice Mide (a member of the Midewiwin Medicine Society) often inscribed sacred songs on a piece of birch bark to help in memorizing the key elements.

Ho ho ya no ne— ya— hoya he ne we-hoya— ne-we ya— ho ya ne

Wo ho Yo ne he yo ne-ho yo ne ho— yo ne— ho yo ne yo yo ne ho

Figure 1-1. *Algonquin song from "New England Music," by David McAllester, a chapter in* Rooted Like the Ash Trees, *edited by Richard G. Carlson. Naugatuck, CT: Eagle Wing Press, 1987.*

Divination

In most shamanic cultures, poetry and divination seem to go hand-in-hand. Elder Druids in Irish shamanism, called *fili*, were classified as "poet-seers," a caste authorized to practice divination. These *fili* memorized magical alphabets, which took an average of twelve years to master.

These Druid shamans constructed an alphabet known as the Tree Ogam. Each letter of this alphabet was represented by a lunar month and a particular tree. For example, the lunar month of Duir was associated with the oak and lasted from June 10 to July 7. It is said that the Native American moons of the lunar calendar were acquired from the markings on a turtle's back.

In Native North America, reciting of long poetic myths was a ubiquitous, time-consuming tradition. The Lakota Sioux creation myth, for example, takes several days to recite in verse.

In Mesoamerica, the sacred myth of the Quiché Maya is the *Popol Vuh*. This is an esoteric allegory of the creation of the Mayan ancestry. A leading scholar on Native American lore, Dennis Tedlock, recently authored a definitive edition of this sacred book.

Tedlock was taught the secret of the *Popol Vuh* by a Mayan shaman or "day keeper," as they are properly distinguished. The verses are actually mnemonic devices for positive and negative augurs (predictors of omens) and deities associated with the Mayan sacred Tzolkin or ceremonial calendar. Thus, the poetic teachings were used as a form of astrological forecast to divine the future and the past.

One of the fundamental roles of oral poetry in traditional learning is to create a bridge between the past and present. The shaman, again, is a symbolic mediator. The new renaissance in shamanism can thus be understood as a contemporary transformation in folklore. Contemporary shamans have assumed new roles in the cultural reintegration of tribal traditions.

The Dance of the Shaman

As with song, shamanic cultures also use dance to symbolize all experience. Through dance, the shaman enters sacred space through the shamanic state of consciousness.

Shamanic dancers do not merely imitate an animal; they *become* the animal. Indeed, such transformation is central to all shamanic ceremonies. In other sections of this book, we will discuss the association of Earth and sky mysteries and how certain archaeoastronomical sites were used to celebrate the connections between Mother Earth and Father Sky.

Even today, Taoist shamans practice a meditative trance that projects their spirits to the stars. And the Taoist "star treader" enacts a journey of celestial

ascent which is celebrated in dance form (Figure 1-2). Some of the instructions
are amazingly vivid. The novice is told to first hold the breath, then turn left
after reaching the seven stars. Next, he or she is told to travel the length of three
circuits above the clouds of the Big Dipper. These detailed expressions are
actual recollections of the soul's travels released in flight.

Native American dances associated with certain celestial observances have

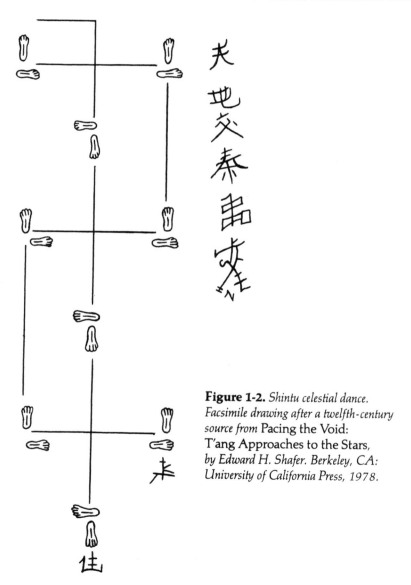

Figure 1-2. *Shintu celestial dance.*
Facsimile drawing after a twelfth-century
source from Pacing the Void:
T'ang Approaches to the Stars,
by Edward H. Shafer. Berkeley, CA:
University of California Press, 1978.

definite connections to the merging of Earth and sky via the ecstatic shamanic state of consciousness described by Dr. Michael Harner.

The Hopi observe an annual new fire ceremony called Wuwuchim which also utilizes song and dance that are coordinated by the position of the constellations. The Hopi singers wait for the stellar positions to align with certain markers as viewed through the kiva skylights. The songs then continue until dawn, ending in a public dance.

All roads to the village are closed off at the end of Wuwuchim by using sacred corn meal. One path, however, is left open as a small spirit trail. Sealing off road access to the village keeps contaminating influences outside the area. Thus, at the peak of Wuwuchim, the sacred Kachina spirits are allowed to dance merrily into the Hopi village. During this time, the two worlds of heaven and Earth emerge as one.

The Arts of Shamanism

Daily life, as well as the ever-present ceremonial life of shamanic peoples, necessitated the crafting of artifacts. Shamanic crafts included an endless array of ceremonial aids, such as rattles, feather fans, staffs, masks, headdresses, necklaces, medicine bags, and so on. Every piece of art produced by shamanic tribes was created with a purpose—from a stray piece of driftwood to an entire tree transformed into a totem pole. Nothing was wasted.

Masks played an especially important role in shamanism. They were used to enhance a multifaceted personality and bring out latent psychological emotions, or to confront repressed emotions, thus serving to guide troubled individuals out of crisis.

The places where sacred art can be found indicate a great deal about how such art was utilized in ritual. For example, caves were used as a natural form of sacred place long before the community ceremonial lodges were constructed. In Wyoming, at the Wind River Reservation, cave paintings can still be observed, many with anthropomorphic figures. For centuries, shamans underwent initiatory transformations in these caves and recorded what they experienced. During such initiations, totemic spirit allies were imbued with power and served as focal points for the novice.

Rock art situated near rivers, lakes, ponds, and marshes heralded the *genii loci*, or sacred spaces protected by the spirits. Entire villages of people are thought to have once inhabited these locations. Rock ledges and certain rock formations endowed with unique features also became spiritual objects (Figure 1-3). The sacred pictographs of the Chumash Indians at the cave known as Painted Rock in the San Joaquin Valley, California, are well known to most rock art enthusiasts (Figure 1-4).

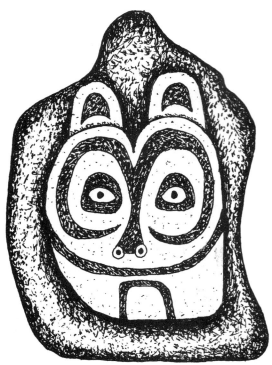

Figure 1-3. *Legend tells that this figure represents a mythic chieftess called "She Who Watches." The chieftess, who was turned to stone for breaking taboos, must now watch over her people forever. Facsimile drawing from photograph of a rock painting on a cliff over the Columbia River, Washington State.*

Sacred art also served as a mnemonic device to record metaphysical principles associated wih geomancy, astronomy, cosmology, and the pantheon of spirits.

Conclusion

All over Turtle Island, there are many signs that a contemporary renaissance is taking place in these more specialized and intimate aspects of shamanism. As one example, Michael J. Caduto, Joe Bruchac, Carol Wood, and John Fadden have blended their talents and creativity to produce a wonderful teaching gift entitled, *Keepers of the Earth: Native American Stories and Activities for Children.* This book is a collection that promotes understanding, empathy, and responsibility toward people and the environment. Similarly, Moses Nelson Big Crow's children's book, *Legends from the Crazy Horse Clan* (published by Tipi Press) relates legends learned from his grandfather. The book is illustrated by the renowned artist, Daniel Long Soldier.

Nadema Agard, spokesperson for the Little Rabbit Dancers, reveals that a group of Native American children is taught many aspects of culture through dance. She explains: "Sometimes these dances tell stories which often emphasize American Indian social and moral values."

Singers such as Floyd Westerman and Buffy St. Marie, and performers like Kevin Locke, are also solid indications that dance, song, and drama are alive and well beyond the popular pow-wow circuits.

New literature, such as *Yaqui Deer Songs* by Larry Evers and Felipe Molina, and *Song of the Sky* by Brian Swann, are signs that Native American shamanic songster collections will be passed on to other generations.

Poetic anthologies by Joe Bruchac (*Songs from This Earth on Turtle's Back* and *Wounds Beneath the Flesh*, edited by Maurice Kenny), as well as a host of other titles in the Native American genre, are additional examples of the stability and rise of the Native American shamanic voice in literature and poetry.

Crafters such as Richard Dobson (feather fans and ceremonial rattles), Susan

Figure 1-4. *Sky Coyote. Facsimile drawing of Chumash cave rock art, from Painted Rock, San Joaquin Valley, California.*

Valadez (Huichol beadwork), Adam Fortunate Eagle (pipes and sculptures), and Art Thompson, Ellen Neel, and Nancy Dawson (wood carving) also demonstrate a wide range of folk art from a shamanic perspective. And more and more unique forms of expression are emerging as the shamanic renaissance unfolds.

PART II
Donn Le Vie, Jr.

As we have seen from the discussion in Part I of this chapter, shamanic art forms are not just art for art's sake; rather, they create a sacred awareness of the universe. Shamanic art also becomes a survival mechanism because of its ability to give structure to the mystical and abstract. The shamanic awakening is recreated in artistic form which then becomes a vehicle for transformation.

As artist, dancer, songster, poet, crafter, and medicine person, the shaman is able to "exert" some influence over ethereal powers by entering worlds of extraordinary reality at will. He or she then returns with power, knowledge, and wisdom to be used for those who are suffering physical or psychological ailments. In such an elevated social position, the shaman also becomes counselor, judge, psychologist, and interceder because of his or her unique relationship with spirit and the forces of nature. The shaman is also endowed with wisdom that frequently serves to quell social and environmental difficulties that might otherwise threaten tribal survival.

Shamans represent only one of several types of religious practitioners and healers; however, they are probably the archetype of all healers and practitioners, since their presence predates recorded history. Modern psychic healers, clairvoyants, and mediums are only shadowy remnants of these once-powerful mystics. As religious institutions gained a stronger grasp on evolving society, the emerging priesthood assumed the religious role of the shaman, and mediums and seers took over such tasks as contacting the spirits and communicating with the dead. Almost immediately, the shaman's task was reduced to the primary function of healing.

Emergence into industrialized society has forced many cultures into leaving behind traditional teachings, not the least of which are those of the shaman. There are far fewer practicing shamans today than in centuries past, and fewer still who retain revered and active stature in a tribal society.

The transformative process of the shaman, from the profane to the sacred, is often revealed in dreams or visions and released through creative expression. Through shamanic art forms, the human condition achieves elevated status, becomes incorporated into myth, and is finally comprehended collectively. Thus, shamanic art forms function as a transpersonal communication bridge, portraying in detail the shaman's innermost psychic experiences.

But perhaps they are even more than this. Much of shamanic art is a mythical portrayal of some sort of human suffering, designed to give meaning to a particular human experience or event. Clifford Geertz and Claude Levi-Strauss emphasize how the language of myth can be highly integrative—a collection of the "real" with the "imagined" that knits together very different states of consciousness.

According to Dr. Joan Halifax, in her book, *Shaman: The Wounded Healer*, the emotionally overwhelmed psyche of the shaman coordinates itself by means of mythological concepts. The result is a rational accounting which gives human suffering importance and direction. The extraordinary perils the shaman encounters in his or her psychophysiological journeys become at first tolerable, then later receive celebration.

Shamanic cultures in all times and places have had a special reverence for the sun, and this reverence is very often reflected in their art forms. The sun represents the culmination of the shaman's journey, for it is the sun's fire of transformation that sears away all that is impermanent. First, the emancipated, everlasting spirit of the shaman is absorbed by the sun. Then the self-sacrificed shaman, stripped of all that is temporal, is made pure—is transformed. With great illumination, the Sacred Fire within is released, allowing the true inner self to shine forth and replace the false outer shell.

Because of his or her association—indeed, unification—with fire, the shaman is the embodiment of an intense and blinding heat—a heat of spiritual brilliance that represents purity and knowledge. In *Shaman: The Wounded Healer*, an Eskimo shaman explains that the true shaman must feel an illumination inside the body or brain that glows like fire and provides the power to see with closed eyes in the darkness.

One of the tragedies of Western scientific dogma is its need to equate the physical state—the state perceived by the senses—with reality. In other words, if something has measureable properties, such as length, width, height, or mass, it must exist in the physical sense. If something cannot be quantified or scientifically categorized, then its validity falls into question. This is why the world's religions and mythological traditions have, through the centuries, resorted to physical, artistic manifestations of spirit through ritual, ceremony, sacrament, and meditative imaging. Representations of the numinous evoke strong emotions as the mystical spirit stirs within. Whether it is cave art in southern France, cliff drawings in the American Southwest, or desert rock art in the Sahara, the function of this art proclaims the mystical awakening.

Mythology and art contain revelations about reality. These many facets of reality are all continuous and contained within our physical bodies. For example, Christianity speaks of the resurrection of the body. That is, our bodies accompany us into the Kingdom, for the Kingdom lies within. This Kingdom is not somewhere else, nor does it exist in some other time frame. Resurrection is how we perceive our world, our reality, our existence, and how we respond to it by transforming our senses.

Several years ago, I attended a Fourth of July memorial service at a cemetery in the small East Texas town of Groesbeck. While we were all gathered under a large tent for the religious portion of the service, a local minister pointed to the granite markers in the cemetery and spoke of how the dead in Christ would rise from the grave during the Second Coming as their bodies joined their souls in heaven.

The image conjured up by this description puzzled many of the children in attendance, including my daughter. When I explained to her the metaphorical significance of the minister's message, she wondered why he hadn't said that in the first place. "Because," I said, "the truth is sometimes hidden in things we hear or see. When we understand the true meaning of what we see or hear, it has the effect of changing how we think of ourselves, the world, and each other." So much for wandering skeletons.

Meditative practices from around the world often incorporate the multidimensional universe into the microcosm of the individual body. Shamanic meditative practices plunge the initiate into a trance-like state where he or she experiences dismemberment, evisceration, and reconstruction of the body. This is symbolic of the death and rebirth of the spirit.

The mythologies of India and Tibet teach us that the physical body is but the densest of five sheaths, crystallized from our consciousness. Interpenetrating these sheaths are four even more subtle sheaths, consisting of the vital body, the personality body, the consciousness body, and the universal consciousness (bliss) body. The physical body represents the link between heaven and Earth, the "sacrament" by which personality, depth consciousness and universal bliss are manifested in the world of experience and represented in shamanic and mystical art forms.

In kundalini and tantra yoga, there is variation on this mythology. Both describe power centers located within the body, known as chakras. Chakra meditation focuses on these power centers to open the flow of energy throughout the entire mind-body system. The seven chakras are: survival, located in the spinal base; sex and sensuality, located in the genital area; power and ego mastery, located in the solar plexus; love and compassion, located in the heart; devotion, located in the throat; wisdom, located within the center of the mind;

and enlightenment, located at or slightly above the crown of the head.

The seventh chakra, also referred to as the "thousand-petalled lotus," represents the connection with the universal consciousness that lives in all and that observes through the individual's perspective. When the seventh chakra is fully open, the enlightened being, as a separate entity, is gone; perspective vanishes as the enlightened discorporates and turns into light. It is consummated by the Sacred Fire within.

The objective of meditating on this kundalini energy is to "sacramentalize" the experience of embodiment, to allow the physical to manifest the spirit, and for the spirit to perceive and act through the physical.

Fire, sun, light, purity, knowledge: What is the connection between these that causes them to be celebrated in art forms throughout different cultures across time? Are they primitive representations of gods that received special attention by Paleolithic peoples because of their celestial uniqueness? We cannot be sure. However, we do know that Amenhotep IV, ruler of Egypt from 1367-1350 B.C., respected the sun as the visible source of creation, life, growth, and activity. He declared that God was a vital intelligence existing as a single entity upon which all things in the universe depended. The creative forces of God, he said, radiated through the sun.

Perhaps we can come closer to an answer through the Mayan mysteries recently unraveled by José Argüelles in his book, *The Mayan Factor* (Bear & Company, 1987). After 33 years of investigating the Maya, Argüelles raises an unsettling but interesting proposition. "Solar cults," such as the Egyptians, Incas, and Mayas, held that the sun is literally the source and sustainer of life. But Argüelles takes the concept one step further. Could the sun also be the mediator of information focused to and through it from other star systems? Here is what he has to say:

> So-called sun worship as is imputed to the ancient Maya is in actuality the recognition and acknowledgment that higher knowledge and wisdom is literally being transmitted through the sun, or more precisely, through the cycles of binary sunspot movements. The Tzolkin, or Sacred Calendar, is a means of tracking the information through knowledge of the sunspot cycles.

Interestingly enough, sunspot activity occurs in periods of cycles—eleven years of active polarity and eleven years of negative polarity—each with its own series of peaks and valleys.

Impossible? Unbelievable? The point here is not whether Argüelles is speaking from fact or fancy, but that he has opened up another doorway to what lies beyond the obvious—to the numinous. Himself an artist, Argüelles has provided a new paradigm with which to view art—in this case, the functional art of the

Tzolkin. During the painting of his famous "Doors of Perception," Argüelles was guided by the vision of the ancient Mexican and Mayan painters that laid the transformational foundation for his work in *The Mayan Factor*.

An ancient Nahua saying gives special reverence to the artist:

> The good painter is wise, god is in his heart.
> He converses with his own heart.
> He puts divinity into things.

Joseph Campbell once stated that the artist's true function is the mythologization of the environment and the world. Mythologization keeps ritual concurrent with the status of cultural knowledge. Ritual, he says, throws us out of our sphere of domesticity. The problem with our society today is that we no longer have rituals of deep personal significance to pass along to children as rites of transformation. Ritual must be kept alive for society's survival. We must, therefore, turn to times and cultures where ritual and art forms provide the connection between heaven and Earth—the shamanic awakening.

In order to fully appreciate (though not necessarily accept) perspectives such as those offered by Argüelles, one must shed the skin of prejudgment and temporarily suspend the objective Western attitude that "not physical means not real."

As an exercise in doing so, consider the example of visible light. Visible light occupies but a minor interval along the electromagnetic spectrum. Yet X-ray, microwave, ultraviolet, and infrared radiation also exist; in fact, they dominate the spectrum. These other types of radiation are not detectable by the human eye or any other sensory organ. But do we question their presence? And what of other phenomena that still remain undetected? Must we also await the invention of instrumentation that will detect them before we can accept their existence? Absence of evidence is not evidence of absence. In order to understand from a different perspective, one must step outside the self and search without prejudice.

I close this discussion with a quote from the *Apothegm of Narada*: "Never utter these words: 'I do not know this, therefore it is false.' One must study to know; know to understand; understand to judge." Denying the mystical from a position of ignorance robs the spirit of bliss. Denying the richness of symbology in all shamanic art forms prevents the awakening of the mystical. For in shamanic art forms, the artist is a storyteller—bringing mind into a harmonious relationship with questions of immortality, and bringing the physical body to its appointed destiny with death.

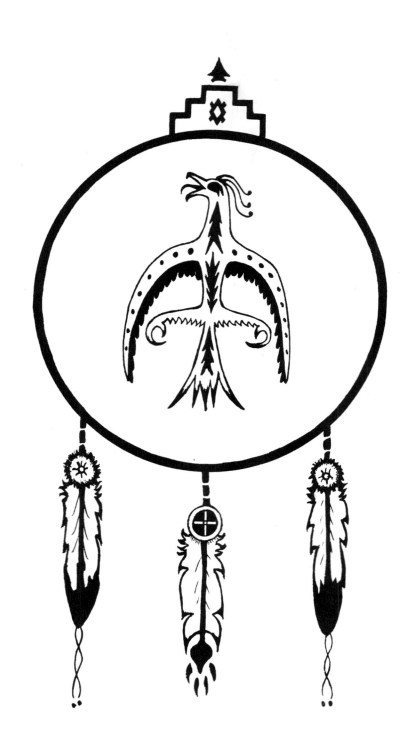

Chapter Two

THE THUNDERBIRD ANCESTRY

PART I
Iron Thunderhorse

One of the oldest, most widespread, and important motifs of Native America's aboriginal folklore is that of the Thunderbird. The Thunderbird is the messenger of the Great Spirit and has always been characterized as an awesomely powerful creature.

The Algonquin tribes refer to Thunderbirds as "our grandfathers." These birds of the supernatural realm play a major role in the folklore of the Eastern Woodlands tribes, the Northwest Pacific Coast tribes, the Southwest and Plains tribes, and even the tribes of Mesoamerica.

The Crow Indians and other tribes depicted the Thunderbirds as wearing eagle cloaks. The eagle, as a supernatural messenger, flew the highest and therefore closest to the heavens. In much of Native American shamanic art, the eagle is identified with the Thunderbird. On the Northwest Coast, the eagle moiety (Na'as) of the Tlingit tribe was at one time one of the most powerful clans. The eagle and Thunderbird clans were related and were very widespread as a result of pre-American aboriginal migrations. The eagle clan cult of aboriginal Australia and the mythic eagle of the Hindu Rig Veda, the guardian of the all-healing tree, are just two examples found in other world religions.

The eagle dance as recognized throughout North America is a celebration of the powers of the Thunderbird. The Thunderbird is the elder brother of the eagle and represents the physical and metaphysical aspects of nature. The eagle flies high above the physical world, to the edge of the spirit world. When it disappears beyond the clouds, it becomes transformed into the Thunderbird. Thunder, rain, lightning, and hail are the powers of the storm god, and the Thunderbird is its divine messenger.

Eagle dances, such as the Iroquois *ganegwa'e* and the Comanche *kanani kiyake*, are usually performed in the spring. There is a definite purpose for these spring-time performances. A study performed by anthropologist A. Irving Hallowell

Figure 2-1. *Animiki, deity of thunder and storms. Facsimile drawing of pictograph from Algonquin territory, northeastern United States.*

offers several important observations. Hallowell discovered what Native Americans have known for centuries: namely, that the Thunderbird follows a behavior pattern which is phenomenally coincidental with certain meteorological events. This is especially true of the frequency of thunder in the months from April to October, which coincides with the nesting and migration of most species of hawks and eagles.

Thunderbird Legends

In legend, Thunderbirds are the giant birds responsible for creating thunder and lightning. In North America, they are the heralds of the storm god, Animiki (Figure 2-1). Among the Native North American tribes, thunder and lightning are considered inseparable because the Thunderbirds produce thunder by flapping their giant wings, and lightning by opening and closing their eyes.

In Mesoamerica, thunder was also perceived as a powerful deity. In Peru, white llamas were sacrificed in its honor. In fact, any site struck by lightning in the Americas was considered sacred ground. In some instances, thunder and lightning were (and are) believed to be weapons of moral retribution from the spirit world. This concept is similar to Old World beliefs in the thunderbolt.

In North America, the spotted eagle is the totem of the Thunderbird. In Mesoamerica, the giant condor preceded it as totem for the Thunderbird far back into history. In one South American legend passed down through the centuries, it is believed that after the passing of a storm, the giant condor was seen, the "Thunderbird who lives with the lightning."

Thunderbird Shamans of North America

During the period when Tiahuanaco, Peru flourished as a major Incan cultural center at Lake Titicaca, the Incas built a classic piece of monolithic architecture known as the "Gateway to the Sun." This gateway, which has survived the effects of the elements for centuries, stands ten feet high, is more than twelve feet wide, and weighs approximately ten tons (Figure 2-2). On its face are peculiar images carved in sculptured relief: A central anthropomorphic figure holding two bird-like staffs, one in each hand, is flanked by alternating rows of bird-like figures and shamans.

Figure 2-2. *Drawing of iconography above entrance to Gateway to the Sun, Tiahuanaco, Bolivia.*

The symbols that make up this ideographic sculpture are very significant to Thunderbird lore. I believe this sculpture marks the gateway as an important stronghold of the Incan Thunderbird shaman.

CENTRAL FIGURE: The central figure is strongly anthropomorphic. Around the face is a plumed headdress ending in a puma head containing discs. The eyes of this figure are centered within the pattern of a stylized bird tail and wing. This deity wears a necklace and fringed tunic bearing trophy heads. In its hands are two staffs, each decorated with stylized condor heads.

It appears that this central figure is the Mesoamerican storm god. The condor, as mentioned previously, represents the Mesoamerican Thunderbird. Hence, this deity holds Thunderbird staffs — a unique method of illustrating thunderbolts. As the storm god shakes its staffs, the Thunderbirds create thunder. As the deity opens and closes its eyes, the Thunderbirds inscribed around the eyes cause lightning to flash.

The headdress with puma and disc motifs also has an interesting interpretation. Much like its cousin, the jaguar, the puma was associated with darkness, eclipses, shamanism, and the mysteries of the jungle. In this part of the world, legends prevail that a great feline covers and devours the sun, subsequently causing eclipses. When the sun leaves the sky, it enters the underworld guarded by jaguars. The disc represents the hole in the sky — the portal through which the shaman passes back and forth to participate in the affairs of the spirit world. The trophy heads marked the awesome power of the deity and indicated that it was a malevolent, potentially volatile figure.

The deity stands atop a double-headed puma. This represents Mother Earth and the guardian pumas of the underworld that devour the sun at night (the west) and give birth to it at dawn (the east). The deity stands at the center of the Earth on a very high plateau. In Peruvian culture, Tiahuanaco is the center of the world and the highest elevation in Mesoamerica. Thus, it was ideal as the location for major cultural and religious center to worship the storm god.

FLANKING FIGURES: The rows of figures flanking the storm god are very similar in nature. They all have wings, carry thunderbolts, and wear headdresses and necklaces. The top row of figures bear human-like faces. These represent the Thunderbird shamans who personify the powers of the Thunderbirds. In between the rows of shamans are the Thunderbirds themselves, who also serve the storm god. In such a relationship, totems, shamans, and natural phenomena are all connected in a spiritual manner. These Thunderbird and Thunderbird shaman motifs bear similar iconographic variables to that of the central figure (the puma heads and discs).

The Mound Builders & Eagle Men

From the Gulf of Mexico to the Great Lakes, there once stood thousands of human-made ceremonial mounds. Some of these objects were pyramid-shaped, some circular, while others were constructed in tiers and geometric forms. Many of the mounds resembled animals, such as birds and reptiles. At Poverty Point, Louisiana, an early mound-building complex in the shape of a giant Thunderbird was discovered.

Archaeological excavations of the mound-building cultures, known as the Adena and Hopewell excavations in the southeastern United States, have revealed common bird-men motifs (Figures 2-3 and 2-4). These figures have similar motifs: wings and tails of birds, headdresses, heart-shaped pouches, necklaces, discs, trophy heads, and markings of forked eyes or forked mouths. The thunderbolts have been replaced with rattles (Figure 2-3B) or feathered staffs (Figure 2-4B). The discs are still prevalent (Figures 2-4A, 2-4B), but there are also

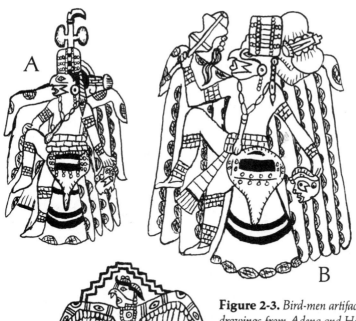

Figure 2-3. *Bird-men artifacts. Facsimile drawings from Adena and Hopewell excavations of mound-building cultures, southeastern United States.*

new and distinct differences in the motifs of these mound-building cultures.

The objects on the necklaces, for example, are known as bull roarers (Figures 2-3A, 2-3B, 2-3C, 2-4A). The heart shaped pouches in these same figures require further explanation. This pouch is a type of medicine bag. A shaman was able to perform the necessary skills for healing because he or she possessed a "heart without worry." The disc-shaped stone is known as a *chunkee* stone by Woodlands tribes. Perforated stone discs were widely used as healing objects.

Heyoka-Thunderbird Shamans

The early Eagle Men were known as Thunderbird shamans. Today they are known as Heyokas, or "contraries," especially by the Sioux. Among the artifacts of the mound-building cultures at the Adena and Hopewell excavations, evidence was found that these bird men wore false beaks. In Sioux folklore, a Heyoka is a clown-like trickster who obtains powers in dreams and visions from Thunderbirds or Thunderbeings. Power is given in obedience to a vision of lightning or a Thunderbird.

The Sioux Heyoka is defined as one who is shapeless but has wings, has no feet but does have talons, has no face except for a huge beak, and who moves counter-sunwise with a voice like thunder and the glance of lightning. The Eagle Men of the mound-building cultures possessed these same attributes. Thunderbirds have always embodied a contrary nature. In fact, the storm itself represents a psychological catharsis.

Nicholas Black Elk, a Lakota Holy Man, experienced a Heyoka calling and clarified his visions with the psychosymbolic powers of the contraries. Accord

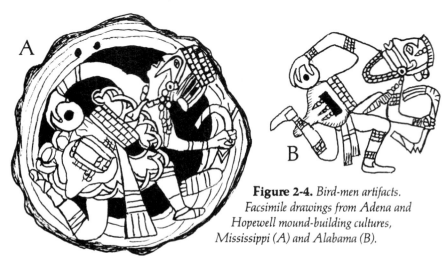

Figure 2-4. *Bird-men artifacts. Facsimile drawings from Adena and Hopewell mound-building cultures, Mississippi (A) and Alabama (B).*

Figure 2-5. *Facsimile drawing of Lei Kung, the Chinese thunder god. Note the beak-like face, wings, and human torso. The figure is surrounded by fire (indicating lightning) and drums (indicating thunder). Facsimile drawing from* Symbols, Signs and Signets *by Ernst Lehner. New York: Dover Publications.*

ing to him, when a vision comes from the west, the land of the Thunderbeings, it arrives like a thunderstorm, full of terror. When it passes, the world is greener and happier.

The Heyoka, or Thunderbird shaman, uses the powers of reversal as a form of sympathetic magic. In the past, Heyokas spoke backwards, rode their horses backwards, and performed many other absurdities, causing onlookers to laugh or become shocked. This opened people up to immediate experience—the quick flash of lightning—which has great psychosymbolic meaning and power. The subtle, clown-like antics of the Heyoka, then, are forms of shock therapy, creating a reversal of polarity. The clearing of worry, doubt, and idle mental or emotional obstructions is a necessary prerequisite for healing. When the mind is cleared, the body heals itself.

The Antiquity of Thunderbirds

We can thus trace the roots of the eagle dance to the Thunderbird, and the contraries to the Thunderbird shamans. Many theories have been proffered as to why the Incan, Mayan, and Anasazi cultures vanished. Is there a true mystery surrounding the disappearance of these cultures? Similarities in mythol ogy suggest that they simply migrated to other geographic locations, merging with cultures similar to their own.

Legends of Thunderbirds abound in the Americas. As has been illustrated, the Thunderbird legends evolved along with the migrations of aboriginal cultures into South and North America. In other chapters, we will discuss different aspects of culture, folklore, flora, fauna, and art that supply added credence to a trans-oceanic migratory route using the Polynesian island chain as a link to the Americas.

It is interesting to note that bird-men creatures have been carved in the cliffs of Easter Island overlooking the shoreline. In Polynesia, an important deity was "Punna, the Thunderbolt," similar to the storm god of the Americas.

Searching back even further into history, we find that Lei Kung was known as the Chinese thunder god, one of the 80 members of the Ministry of Thunder (Figure 2-5). The thunder god punished the wicked and was patron to the shapeshifters—the aboriginal shamans—before their migrations to Indonesia, Polynesia, and undoubtedly later to the Americas.

Conclusion

The Thunderbird is the icon of the various "storm gods" of aboriginal shamanism. Though variations emerged, the key central elements remained intact. Wherever Thunderbird lore is found, it is almost always accompanied by mention of the Feathered Serpent. In Mesoamerica, the Feathered Serpent motif represented the nations of the sun, the first aboriginal nations. Thunderbirds were the marks of the ancient aboriginal shamans. In North America, the Thunderbird clans were generally reserved for chieftains and priests and represented a totem of leadership.

PART II
Donn Le Vie, Jr.

There is something captivating about listening to legends from ancient cultures that temporarily increases our hunger to return to the natural Earth rhythm, the birthplace of all folklore and myth. In the past, the elements, all life, and the magic of the human imagination were the only ingredients necessary in order to foster a magnificent visual feast. Legend and myth both flowed with the cyclical movements of nature, devoid of any artificial time frames.

In contrast, the industrialized techno-sapien, forever tied to the hands of the clock and fragmented by the demands of a microchip culture, has no time

and ☐ ON ☐ SƎ⅄ ¿SNOⅠⅠ contemplate the holistic nature of the inner
and ˥ledge it offers. Cross-cultural legends that
recou ¿suoᴉʇɒ presence with the creation and destruction of
the Earth, as well as interpersonal and emotional conflict, appear hopelessly
lost in the world of literalism and logic.

Millions of people in modern society are trapped in an emotional and spiritual purgatory, waiting for *someone else* to release them from their self-imposed
bondage to a mundane existence. In the meantime, they occupy themselves
with delusions of power and wealth, are enslaved by alcohol and drugs, hyp-
notized by the superficial glitter of the material world, and drowning in a sea
of debt.

Goals and aspirations become the byproduct of political and media-
induced propaganda; assault rifles and semi-automatic weapons "protect" them
from their insecurities, and nuclear stockpiles and laser weapons maintain constant vigil against the "enemy" while streams and oceans, rainforests and wilderness areas continue to be sacrificed by a callous, short-term, profit-oriented
mentality.

The youth of today are cast into this cultural maelstrom, to fend for themselves at the expense of others. Social rituals, including the rites of passage from
puberty to adolescence and from adolescence to adulthood, have dissolved,
as have the mythological images that form their foundation. Few cultures today
maintain connections to their archetypal ancestry, choosing instead to sever
the nurturing umbilicus and forsaking the source of true wisdom and knowledge: the womb of mythology.

A theoretical universe is empty—a pristine vacuum in its pureness of logic,
order, and structure. But a world enlivened with the magic of myth and legend
overflows with emotion: conflict and resolution; corruption and honesty; pain
and pleasure. It is a dynamic world, where the drama unfurls on an ever-
changing stage.

The Native American nations went to great pains to protect their legends
from the inevitable dilution and subsequent extinction that followed generations of evangelical efforts to remove the "primitive" religions and replace them
with an empty rhetoric of their own. With only very few exceptions, most collections of Native American folklore have been eradicated or altered beyond
recognition. As Iron Thunderhorse has stated, one icon that has weathered this
evangelical ethnocide is the Thunderbird—the totem of leadership and the
messenger of the Great Spirit.

Even the survival of this icon is remarkable, for the church not only deci-
mated most original Native American literature and legend, but destroyed
much of ancient Mayan folklore as well. The Spanish conquest of the Yucatan

was unquestionably one of the most immoral and unjust acts that "civilized" people have ever perpetrated against their fellow humans.

Perhaps no other Westerner understood the Mayan knowledge and civilization more intimately than the Catholic bishop from Merida, Fray Diego de Landa. De Landa was tutored by Mayan nobles so that he understood their hieroglyphics and could interpret their sacred calendar. De Landa gathered from the Maya their collected writings on philosophy, science, astronomy, metaphysics, and aesthetics—and promptly destroyed them by fire in the Plaza de Mani when he suddenly decided they contained *mentiras del diablo*, "lies of the devil."

Fray Diego de Landa replaced this most incredible assemblage of knowledge with his own recollections, published under the title, *Relacion de las Cosas de Yucatan* (An account of the things of Yucatan). Although this feeble substitute manuscript contained an occasional description of Mayan folklore, ceremonies, and customs, it was replete with information on the Mayan civilization as the swords of the conquistadors felled it to its knees.

The Spaniards took no mercy on the Mayan people or their culture. They soon realized that conquering the Maya meant dismantling their highly organized society as quickly as possible. They did so by murdering Mayan nobles, priests, leaders, and teachers, and by destroying all their remaining literature. Catholic churches, monasteries, and cathedrals were built with the rubble from the schools and temples the Spaniards destroyed. Lost to the ages was perhaps one of the greatest accumulations of knowledge the Western world has ever known. The once-mighty Maya were now powerless, confused, and servants of their new masters.

Only the most geographically isolated Mayan communities escaped the heavy hand of the conquistadors. Today, in the state of Chiapas, Mexico, live the last survivors of the Mayan blood line, the Naha Lacandones. It is estimated that they number less than 500, and today their very existence is threatened by lumber companies that lust after their precious mahogany trees. New roads and an airstrip bring in tourists. American missionaries, who began their efforts in the late 1950s, have already divided the Lacandones into two factions — the "Christianized" northern group and the traditional southern Lacandones. The local mission offers medicine and emergency transportation to any Naha Lacandon who requests it; however, traditional Lacandon custom demands favors returned for favors received.

For their part, the missionaries refuse Lacandon gifts, asking the people instead to lift up their spirits to Jesus Christ. Evangelical blackmail may finish the job the Spaniards started centuries ago, and the remaining fragments of yet another rich cosmology and folklore will be lost forever.

The Thunderbird ancestry as described in Part I of this chapter represents a key element in the rich, mythological heritage of shamanic peoples. As the old gods disappear, people the world over are seeking a new mythology: the "mythology of this unified earth as of one harmonious being," as Joseph Campbell calls it. Their search has taken them through the realm of the senses, but mythology is not something born of the brain, the result of processed sensory input. Instead, it blossoms from the heart. In this way, mythology springs forth from *behind* or *within* what the senses perceive. It is the soul's universal language, and the Thunderbird ancestry is just one dialect of the soul.

Thought manifests first as language; soul, some say, manifests as mythology and legend. With mythology, language acquires vitality, each word is imbued with essence, character, and significance. In spite of cultural and temporal variations, each myth contains an underlying theme that unites all myth and legend: namely a person's interaction with nature, other people, and oneself through the use of metaphor.

Literal interpretations of sacred writings and folklore have always generated internal conflict for individuals who subscribe to those teachings. This inner struggle arises because of humanity's dual nature: the need for its mythological self to seek its true expression (or the need to understand the symbology associated with its mythological being) and its desire to follow guidelines that condemn it to a profane existence as ordained by religious dogma. No wonder humanity so often seems to be experiencing an emotional purgatory on this plane of existence!

We have become caught in a spiritual "no-man's land," struggling to somehow respond to the archetypal echoes of the intuitive self. This is where true knowledge and wisdom abide, in the nest of the Thunderbeings. We also wrestle with the logical mind, with its ecclesiastical rules and regulations that have been culturally ingrained in us. Our lost shamanic heritage provided us a direct communion with the unknowing mind that lies beyond thought, the Great Spirit, God, or any other name one wishes to use. In its place are religions that require interceders on our behalf.

Biblical scholar Lloyd Graham has called the Protestant account of the Creation "kindergarten cosmology." And yet this account has been blindly believed for two millenia. The Western mind must be trained to think in a more abstract fashion; it must seek out the wisdom in the mythological truth much as the Thunderbird ancestry provided for Native Americans.

Much of the metaphysical and cosmological knowledge absorbed by Western culture came from the Middle East. In his metaphysical ignorance, Graham writes, Western man has injected his own ego into his universe—including his ego's concept of the Creator. Graham says that only a mind incapable of metaphoric, abstract thought could promote the idea of an anthropomorphic creation; that Western man, with his limited capacity for abstraction and cosmology, was unable to fashion a Supreme Being or religion for himself. Instead, he had to import his ideology from the Middle East.

Graham's rather poignant criticism of Christianity and its creation myth should serve as a reminder for the need to preserve the legends and folklore of the creative mind and to find applications for them in our everyday lives.

The days of the Mythopoeic Age, where the ancient wisdom was shared by many, are gone. No longer are great schools of thought dedicated to the subjects of epistemology, ontology, and cosmology—reality, truth, and knowledge. Such knowledge was available to the priestly founders of Judaism and Christianity. But from it, they forged their scriptures, doctrine, and dogmas. With that accomplished, all evidence of their source material—the ancient wisdom—was lost.

The Thunderbird ancestry is still strongly rooted in Native American folklore. But those in society who have forsaken their mystical heritage still remain shackled to a literal existence, unable to realize the bliss of transcendence through the power of metaphor. As the *Kena Upanishad* so eloquently states:

> Eyes cannot see it, speech cannot describe it, nor the mind conceive it. We know not, nor can we imagine, how to convey it. For it is different from the known; and beyond the unknown. Thus have we heard from the illumined ones, who have told of it. . . . If realized here, then truth exists; if not realized here, then there is only ignorance. The wise, seeing it in all things, become on leaving this world, beyond death.

The pieces that remain today in all ancient cultures must be brought back to life. For when the magic disappears from a community, all that remains are the people: some good, some bad, some in between, but people who have lost their uniqueness and sense of wonder.

Chapter Three

ORIGINS OF THE CULTURE HERO

PART I
Iron Thunderhorse

The mythic culture hero is a popular figure with Native American tribes and varies from nation to nation; however, one such figure seems to have been known to all nations in the Americas and provides a link to the origins of the migrating shamanic tribes through the South Pacific islands. In practically all of these hero legends, a red-haired, bearded holy man brought culture to the native peoples.

In North America, legends still persist of a fair-haired, bearded culture hero who taught the Indian people such things as astronomy, the art of social order, and agriculture. The Algonquin nations of the eastern seaboard called him the Pale One. He is remembered as Paruxti, the son of Tirawa, the Sky Father, while others refer to him as Wakona.

This hero was always associated with the planet Venus—the dawn star that follows the path of the sun and is symbolic of enlightenment. A Seneca legend calls him Hea-wah-sah, "he who draws his power from the dawn star," and says that American Indian tribes would not fight at night because the presence of this "star" was so sacred.

The Dakotah nation once knew this hero as Waicomah. Among the Choctaw, he was called Ee-me-shee ("he from the winds"). The Yakima of the Northwest referred to him as Tacoma. Other Woodland tribes called him Ee-see-co-tl, or Eemeeshetotl: the Feathered Serpent Lord. He was known as lord of both the winds and the heavens. In other words, the Horned and/or Feathered Serpent was an icon well known all over the Americas.

Mesoamerica

To the Aztec and Maya Indians of Mexico, this culture hero was called Quetzalcoatl—the Feathered Serpent. He taught the people about the arts, agriculture, and culture.

Figure 3-1. *Facsimile drawing of the Feathered Serpent motif at Chichen Itza, Mexico, the Toltec empire's main complex built by Quetzalcoatl.*

At the center of Tenochtitlán stands the "wall of serpents." This wall encloses a vast area that contains various temples. Here, at one time, stood the round temple of the deity, Quetzalcoatl, and beyond the temple rose the palace of Montezuma.

At Chichen Itza, there is evidence of the worship of the Lord Feathered Serpent among the ancient Toltec. There are actual accounts of a chief named Quetzalcoatl who built the Toltec empire. This chief was defeated by his archrival Tezcatlipoca, or Smoking Mirror. Seeing what little fruit his doctrine bore, he left by the same road on which he had come — to the east. He disappeared on the coast of Coatzacoalcos.

Subsequent accounts reveal that this light-skinned, bearded god-king traveled to Cholula and subsequently to Tlillan Tlapallán, an unidentified spot on the Veracruz coast. From there, he sailed eastward, mounted on a raft of snakes (Figures 3-1 and 3-2).

Kukulcan

The name Kukulcan is translated as "Feathered Serpent" (*kukul* meaning "feathered" and *can* meaning "serpent"). Professor Michael D. Coe of Yale University and the Peabody Museum Anthropology Department believes that there were actually two rulers in the Yucatan Itza: Kukulcan I and Kukulcan II. As he rightfully recognized, these were both actual men who claimed the title of Kukulcan as a "chief of men."

Figure 3-2. *Facsimile drawing of gold disk found in the sacred Cenote at Chichen Itza, Mexico. Here, the Toltecs drive off a pair of Mayan warriors. The figure with the beard and bird headdress is probably Quetzalcoatl. Facsimile drawing from* The Maya, *by Michael D. Coe. New York: Thames and Hudson.*

The culture hero Kukulcan is equivalent to the Quiché Gucamatz, to Votan of the Tzentals, Itzamná of the Yucatecs, Bochica of Columbia, Viracocha of Peru, and Sumé and Payetome of Brazil. All were names from different dialects representing the same culture hero.

Viracocha—Peru

In the Peruvian jungles, the culture hero is known as Viracocha. This is the abbreviated form of "Con-Ticci-Viracocha-Pachayachachic," meaning literally, "the ancient foundation, lord and instructor of the world."

When the Spaniards discovered the Incan Empire, Francisco Pizarro noticed that the mass of local Indians were small and dark-skinned, but that the members of the Incan tribes were light-skinned and, in many instances, had red hair. When Pizarro inquired about these people, he was told they were the descendants of the Viracochas, an ancient tribe of fair-skinned aboriginal people.

Legends say that this race of fair-haired aboriginals built great statues and pyramids, as well as an empire stretching from Cuzco along the Pacific. The Spaniards also recorded in their chronicles that the ruling families of the

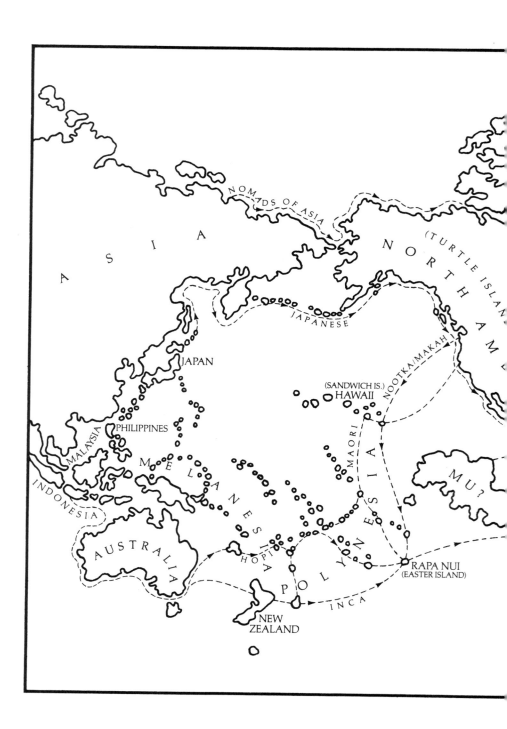

NOMADS OF ASIA

ASIA

NORTH AM

(TURTLE ISLAND

JAPANESE

JAPAN

(SANDWICH IS.)
HAWAII

NOOTKA/MAKAH

MALAYSIA

PHILIPPINES

M E L A N E S I A

MAORI

MU?

INDONESIA

P O L Y N E S I A

AUSTRALIA

HOPI

RAPA NUI
(EASTER ISLAND)

INCA

NEW
ZEALAND

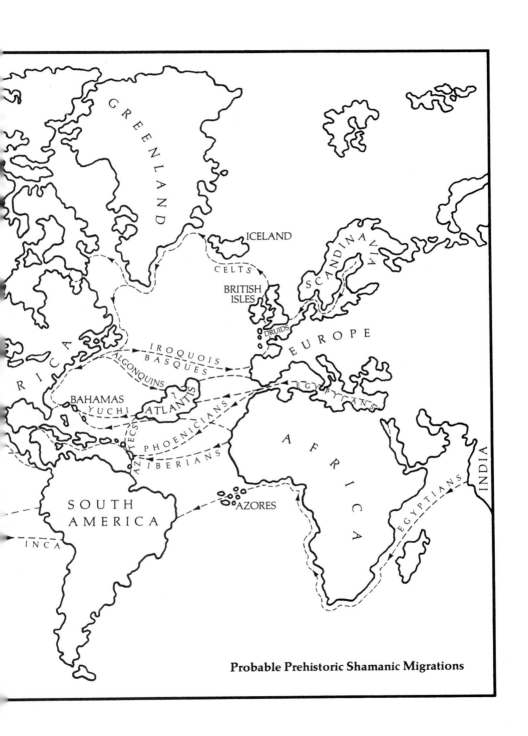

GREENLAND

ICELAND

SCANDINAVIA

CELTS

BRITISH
ISLES

EUROPE

DRUIDS

RICA

IROQUOIS

BASQUES

ALGONQUINS

EGYPTIANS

BAHAMAS

YUCHI

ATLANTIS

AZTECS

PHOENICIANS

AFRICA

IBERIANS

AZORES

INDIA

SOUTH
AMERICA

EGYPTIANS

INCA

Probable Prehistoric Shamanic Migrations

Figure 3-3. *A "long-ear" nobleman of Easter Island (Rapa Nui) with beard and feathered crown. Drawing after an artist with the Captain James Cook expedition, from* Aku-Aku, *by Thor Heyerdahl.*

Viracocha called themselves *orejones*, or "long ears," due to their custom of artificially lengthening the ear lobes with weights.

However, just as mysteriously as this race of people had come to South America, they departed toward the west, promising to return in the distant future. The Viracochans were also known to the Native Indian tribes of South America as "sons of the sun."

The Rapa Nui Connection

Rapa Nui is the proper name for what is more commonly known as Easter Island. This island is situated in the Pacific Ocean between the Cook, Society, and Marquesas Islands and the western coastline of Chile.

In the 1950s, Thor Heyerdahl conducted several expeditions to this area and sponsored an archaeological dig at Easter Island. He also conducted similar expeditions to Lake Titicaca at the seat of the old Incan Empire. Heyerdahl discovered many amazing relationships between these separate cultures. He also noticed that there were two distinct peoples still living on Rapa Nui: those who were short, with dark skin, and those with red hair and light skin.

Legends on Rapa Nui say that the first king, who sailed to the island long ago from the east on a huge raft, was of a race known as the "long-ears" (*hanau-eepe*). By contrast, the natives are referred to as "short-ears" (*hanau-momoko*). The long-eared ancestors of Easter Island are said to be the sculptors of the famous giant statues indigenous to the area. These "long-ears" also wore beards and feathered crowns (Figure 3-3). Interestingly enough, Heyerdahl's expedition also found a variety of plant life that was not indigenous to the area—plant life that has since been discovered to have come from South America or from islands closer to Indonesia.

Origins of the Viracochas

So the mystery still remains: where did these Viracochas come from? The Sandwich Islanders have a legend that chronicles the life of Wakea—the Fair God—who came to an island in the Tahitian group long ago. These people are Polynesians and were once known as the Maori. The Maori navigated from New Zealand and Australia to Easter Island. The Maori chiefs wore tattoos and topknot hair pieces similar to those worn by the Algonquin people of the eastern seaboard in America. Wakea was also associated with the Morning Star.

In Polynesia, Tiki was the first recognized man/god. Effigies in his honor are shaped like embryos to symbolize ancestry (Figure 3-4). In the North and South American tribes, the hocker motif is very similar to Tiki and is also used to symbolize ancestral clan lineage (Figure 3-5).

Figure 3-4. *Facsimile drawing of Hei-Tiki, a Maori fetus-like amulet symbolizing ancestral lineage. From* Dictionary of Folklore, Mythology, and Legend, *by Funk and Wagnalls. New York: Harper & Row.*

The Islands' Creation Connection

In Polynesia, one of the main creator gods was Ta'aroa, who was said to have been born from a cosmic egg. The Hopi of Arizona worship a Creator/sun god called Taiowa. To the Pawnee Indians, the Creator was called Tirawa. Although these names are spelled differently, the pronunciations are quite similar.

Indonesia has many beliefs, including those in nature spirits, ancestral ghosts, magical powers, and multiple-layered heavens. Kawi, the language of the Indonesian Islands, is an infusion of both Javanese and the old Sanskrit of India, which demonstrates the transmigration of Hindu and aboriginal cultures. As a result of feudalism, the aboriginal peoples were constantly being pushed out of the Old World. Apparently, they followed the island routes to new lands.

Dr. Nandisvara Mayake Thero, an expert on the Australian aborigines, says that the land mass of present-day Australia was once part of a continent that probably included Antarctica and portions of Asia and Africa. Early maps of Antarctica drawn by ancient mariners also show a different land mass than that of today; however, this is probably more attributable to archaic methods of cartography and surveying than to geological changes.

In the Melanesian Islands, we also find many legendary similarities—for example, the concept of dual souls, the Sacred Twins, the wise brother and the trickster/fool. Long-standing migrational traditions also abound. Clans are matrilineal, and legends of red-haired culture heroes, such as Sina Kwao and

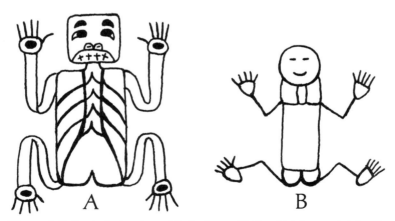

Figure 3-5. *Facsimile drawings of the hocker motif, thought to be associated with childbirth, fertility, and lineage. A) Hocker motif from the symbol of the Raven Clan moiety of the Tlingit tribe of the Northwest Coast. B) Hocker motif found at El Morro, New Mexico.*

Gwau Meo (who became powerful war ghosts similar to the Zuni war twins), introduced magic and other spiritual elements into the Melanesian culture.

The Supreme Being of the Arosi of Melanesia was Hatuibwari, who was represented as a winged serpent. The Melanesians also had three categories of folklore. The first, the *kukwanebu*, were fairy tales told during the rainy season. (This was very similar to legends told in the winter by Native Americans). Second were the *libogwo*, or historical tales. And third were the *liliu*, the sacred myths connected with ritual ceremonies.

In Melanesia, the *baloma* are ancestor spirits who visit the villagers. Likewise, the Polynesians, especially on Rapa Nui and the surrounding islands, all have underground caves where they keep the sacred possessions of their ancestors and where they receive guidance from their *aku-aku* spirits.

In Polynesia, the Sky Father was worshipped along with the Earth Mother. In Hindu tradition, the "Maya" deity was seen as the primordial Mother Goddess, and this concept evidently was carried into Polynesia.

Conclusion

The foregoing are only a few of the more obvious cultural links that suggest a migratory diffusion from the aboriginal cultures of the Old World to the aboriginal cultures of the New World. Most of the older cultures even speak of a Sacred Tree and the numerous races symbolized by its branches. At any rate, once the underlying symbolism of the culture hero is uncovered, it is easier to understand how the aboriginal shamanic tribes say that we all have the same roots.

We have followed the path of the culture hero—the Pale One, whose totem is the Feathered Serpent—backwards in time through the Southwest, Mesoamerica, South America, and though the islands that lead east and west to the "Old World" of prehistoric times. We have seen that dark-skinned and pale-skinned aboriginal peoples were interbreeding and sharing cultures.

During Thor Heyerdahl's expeditions to Easter Island, he observed an ancient two-way migrational pattern. Native peoples from Turtle Island, he discovered, had traveled toward the west, while other aboriginal tribes had journeyed east. He even discovered a type of wood reed that is native to Lake Titicaca and Bolivia growing in lakebeds on Easter Island. Art, customs, legends, flora, and fauna all demonstrate a shared exchange of life.

Art is another area of investigation that tends to suggest common roots of religious expression and cultural cohesion. Dr. Alberto Villoldo of the Four Winds Society has found evidence that demonstrates the cross-cultural art forms of Japan, Polynesia, Ecuador, and Peru. He has also discovered a possible transmigrational route whose former use is difficult to deny. The art forms

Villoldo compares are never identical but remain in close relationship. When two cultures intermix, he says, new experiences merge with the old and become transformed. The outcome of such a union results in the enrichment of each culture.

Professor Fox Tree, an Arawak Indian from the University of Massachusetts, is a specialist in the art history of China, Japan, and the first peoples of Turtle Island. For more than twenty years, he has been examining voluminous amounts of material that had been previously overlooked, misinterpreted, and even suppressed. Fox Tree's conclusions add more support to the theory that a pre-European contact existed between native nations in other parts of the world.

Among other things, his research uncovered a map reportedly used by Christopher Columbus which indicated his exact destination and how long it would take to reach it. Professor Fox Tree believes that this map was made from information provided by Native American mariners. Additional evidence is found in Fox Tree's recent discovery of a painting of a three-masted "Indian" sailing ship, dated at 500 B.C. Interestingly, Thor Heyerdahl discovered the image of a remarkably similar three-masted vessel carved on one of the Easter Island statues.

These recent findings suggest that the history books being used in our schools today may be obsolete — filled with inaccurate accounts that have been taken for granted for hundreds of years. As we gradually reclaim pieces of our prehistoric past, the evidence of our common roots grows stronger. The culture hero, the Pale One who symbolizes the victory of wisdom over ignorance, has returned.

PART II
Donn Le Vie, Jr.

Anthropology and archaeology offer more than an historical chronicle of ancient humanity. Through the study of art, artifacts, symbols, and ceremony, we also find the primal mind.

In spite of cultural conditioning, the acquired consciousness that dominates our normal waking day is still the key to this primal past. Symbology, legend, and myth have survived through the ages because of their correlation with nearly identical symbolic patterns that exist today — in aboriginal societies on the periphery of contemporary society.

A reassuring trend is developing today in the behavioral and social sciences that appears to run counter to the two-dimensional "tunnel vision" that permeated these disciplines until very recently. Investigators in these fields now appreciate mnemonic vehicles such as cave art, sculpture, language, and myth that function as bridges connecting tribal antiquity or the "essential self," with our high-tech, fast-paced culture of the twentieth century.

Greek mythology and Native American folklore bear striking parallels in character, plot, and moral. However, modern *Homo sapiens,* with their conditioned consciousness and externalized awareness, often have a hard time grasping these parallels, as well as their relationship to society's attitudes toward the contemporary hero. As repeatedly demonstrated in this book, these relationships do exist. And the relevance of their powerful symbologies has been maintained throughout the millenia—in spite of our ever-shrinking global village.

Along with physical evolution of the human brain, the mind has undergone progressive change. But remnants of its primal stages are still held deep in the psyche. The psyche, in turn, is molded by the information stored in the collective unconscious—the common psychological inheritance of humankind. On a conscious level, this information bypasses our awareness, but unconsciously, it emerges and is expressed in dreams and other symbolic forms.

In Western society, much of the symbolism woven into the tapestry of the psyche finds expression through religious tradition. For example, in a Christian society, the celebration of Christmas may produce an emotional response to the legendary birth of a god-man child, regardless of how strongly one adheres to the religious doctrine itself. Psychologists say that on an unconscious level, we have identified with a symbol of rebirth, the relic of a practice much older than Christmas or any Christian celebration.

Unlike other cyclic god-king myths, the Christian resurrection celebrates an event that was finite: birth, salvation, death, and eternal existence on another plane. It is widely held by religious scholars that this sense of finality contributed to the tradition of the egg and the Easter rabbit; that is, these symbols somehow met the need for the "recurring promise of rebirth" that early Christians inherited from older, pre-Christian fertility ceremonies.

The influence that symbols have had on socio-cultural evolution becomes more apparent as the message of re-creation unfolds. This applies to legend and especially to mythology in its most ancient form—that of the culture hero.

Mythologist and author Joseph Campbell discusses the language of myth and symbols in *The Hero with a Thousand Faces.* Cosmological mysteries, Campbell says, become manifest in human culture through art, religion, philosophy, science, technology, social behavior, and even dreams. They pour forth through the secret opening of myth, whose symbols deny order, categorization, or suppression. They germinate spontaneously from the human psyche and carry forth the essence of their own creation.

Repeatedly, the theme of the birth-death-rebirth cycle surfaces throughout myth and religion. In his introduction to *The Wisdom of the Serpent—The Myths of Death, Rebirth and Resurrection*, Alan Watts writes of death's provocativeness. According to Watts, the arts, sciences, religions, and philosophies of the world were born because of humanity's knowledge of its mortal flesh. What could provoke more thought than the idea of falling asleep and never waking up? This premise would seem to suggest a corollary: "Who and where was I before my conception?" These rhetorical questions have profound but equal weight. Our emergence from "nothingness" strongly implies that we can return from this "nothingness" again and again.

There are numerous cultural myths that relate to the cycle of birth, death, and rebirth. In spite of their separation in time and space, the essence of each myth nonetheless remains the same. In *The Forgotten Language*, Erich Fromm claims that contemporary aboriginal myths and primal myths tens of thousands of years old are written in the same language. This language escapes modern humanity's consciousness; it lies forgotten, lost to the waking senses. But in the dream state, Fromm says, we suddenly have the opportunity to become fluent in the language of symbolism. When understood, this language comes alive through the dialect of wisdom and knowledge, the myth. This is the language of self-knowledge, of our own personalities, that lies buried beneath layers of ego defense mechanisms and protective behavior. An understanding of this language would reveal much about the deepest parts of ourselves—the parts we have lost to the external world of the senses.

In the Great Sandy Desert of northwestern Australia, the aborigines have constructed a 100-mile-long track, beginning at a hole in the rock where "in the dreamtime, the Great Rainbow Snake went underground." This track is marked with various rockholes—event markers of totemic journeys—as well as by circuitous hairpin curves and dozens of meandering tracks. Each mark or track is associated with a specific place, and each place bears a relationship to the activities and ceremonies of a dreamtime ancestor.

In *The Creative Explosion—An Inquiry Into the Origins of Art and Religion*, author John Pfeiffer praises the aborigines' ability to assimilate so much information. When one stops to consider the voluminous amount of mythology involved in this one relatively small area, it boggles the imagination—especially when one realizes that this repository of mythology (which has been accumulating at least since the Late Paleozoic) was handed down intact from one generation to another. The aborigines used only memory, art, and ceremony to imprint their recollected patterns on the desert floor.

Less than a hundred years ago, mythmaking was believed by scholars to be a function of the primary stages of human cultural development, including the simple observations of lunar, planetary, and stellar movement and the cycles of fertility. Fortunately, the tidewaters of myth and symbol have changed, making room for more responsible and insightful evaluations. In his acclaimed *At the Edge of History*, William Irwin Thompson reflects on this paradigm shift by reminding us that a "mythopoeic mentality" need not be confined to pre-civilized people, but is present in all genius—from Boehme, Newton, and Kepler to Yeats, Wagner, and Heisenberg. Myth, says Thompson, represents more the imaginative reflection of reality than it does a primal stage of human development. In this reflection, the unknown and the known become linked through a systematic correlation where mind, matter, society, self, and cosmos surface in the esoteric expressions of poetry and number.

The Pythagoreans of ancient Greece, along with Plato, preserved the archaic themes that existed long before their Classic Period. According to scholar Giorgio de Santillana, the very foundations of modern Western philosophy (formerly credited to Pythagoras), can actually be attributed to Plato.

In *Mystical Hymns of Orpheus*, Thomas Taylor writes that the founder of Greek theology is reported to have been Orpheus, the first of the prophets and poets—teacher of sacred rites, mysteries, and antiquities, and from whose wisdom ". . . the divine muse of Homer and the sublime theology of Pythagoras and Plato flowed." Throughout the last few centuries, scholars have debated whether Orpheus ever really existed, but the celebrated position he held in practically every ancient mystery school would support that the theology credited to him was derived from reliable sources. Moreover, it was Orpheus, claims Herodotus, who introduced facsimiles of the more ancient teachings of Indian and Egyptian knowledge on which the Greeks built their own theologies.

The Greek mystery schools enjoyed celebrated status during the first six centuries B.C., with the likes of such members as Pythagoras, Socrates, Plato, Aristotle, and Anaxagorus. Greek mythology had no greater exponent of the birth, death, and rebirth cycle than Plato. In fact, it has been reported that if Plato had not embodied reincarnation in some of his greatest works, it would remain simply a curiosity for anthropologists and students of folklore.

Bound to mythology and legend is metaphor. People have difficulty understanding metaphor when they view it in a literal sense. Although culture heroes and mythological figures may originate in a particular locale, they are meant to be understood fundamentally in the broadest sense—as metaphors of states of mind and spirit, independent of place and time.

To combat the confusion surrounding mythology, metaphor, and history, Joseph Campbell proposes that poetic and mystical readings of mythology should replace religions (which he calls *interpretations* of mythology) as the ultimate and indisputable word of God. In this way, he says, Western culture could be purged of the "numbing banality of fundamentalist literalism."

One would wager that most fundamentalist proponents of Western Christianity do not share Campbell's view of the virgin birth as metaphor. And what of the ultimate challenge: the Genesis version of creation by God in six days versus the Grand Unified Theory of science that delineates the process leading to the Big Bang some fifteen billion years ago? According to Campbell, *both* can satisfy the quest, with observed structure, mathematics, and particle physics serving as historial support (much as the fossil record supports geology), and the biblical version serving as inspired poetry.

As evidenced by the ongoing debate between the creationists and the evolutionists, the answer to the creation question is complex and evasive. But the wisdom permeating the birth, death, and rebirth cycle has universal application in its richness of metaphor.

Let us not omit the fairy tale in this discussion, for in many cultures, only the finest of lines separates myth from folklore. Bruno Bettelheim, renowned child psychologist, presents this concept in *The Uses of Enchantment—The Meaning and Importance of Fairy Tales*. In his book, he relates how "saga" (the Nordic term for myth and fairy tale) incorporates the cumulative experience of a society and passes on that acquired wisdom to future generations. Myth carries with it spiritual force, divine presence, and superhuman heroes, demanding great tasks and deeds. The fairy tale, on the other hand, employs more humble themes and settings, and demands little effort on behalf of the listener or reader.

Solar and lunar cycles are also interwoven in cross-cultural legends. As Mircea Eliade writes in *The Myth of the Eternal Return* (Princeton University Press, 1954), the lunar cycle is nearly ubiquitous in mythology:

> The phases of moon—appearance, increase, wane, disappearance, followed by reappearance after three nights of darkness—have played an immense part in the elaboration of cyclical concepts. We find analogous concepts especially in archaic apocalypses and anthropogenies; deluge or flood puts an end to an exhausted and sinful humanity, and a new regenerated humanity is born, usually from a mythical "ancestor" who escaped the catastrophe . . .

In the "lunar perspective," the death of the individual and the periodic death of humanity are necessary, even as the three days of darkness preceding the "rebirth" of the moon are necessary. The death of the individual and the death of humanity are alike necessary for their regeneration. Any form whatever, by mere fact that it exists as such and endures, necessarily loses vigor and becomes worn; to recover vigor, it must be reabsorbed into the formless if only for an instant; it must be restored to the primordial unity from which it issued. . . .What predominates in all these cosmico-mythological lunar conceptions is the cyclical recurrence of what has been before, in a word, eternal return. . . the motif of the repetition of an archetypal gesture, projected upon all planes—cosmic, biological, historical, human.

The myth of the eternal return surfaces repeatedly across time and culture. As Joseph Campbell explains in *The Masks of God: Oriental Mythology*, the cyclical nature of the sun's daily passage, the phases of the moon, the changing of the seasons, and the organic pulse of birth, death, and new birth, represent the miraculous continuity of emergence—a fundamental operative of the universe.

Today, the legends that persist around the globe speak of a time when the gods incarnated among the population and taught them art and science. These legends say that, in the course of time, the enlightened leaders departed, promising to return in times of necessity. During this golden age, people lived in harmony with each other, spoke the same language, and were all aware of the same truths. But then came a time when the gods were not in their midst— when the people were forced to apply all they had learned in order to shape their own destiny. Instead of holding to the spiritual truths they had learned, they chose to believe in form and appearances.

Which brings us to the present day and our personal lives. "How is a person to go about finding his or her myth?" asked a young man of Joseph Campbell shortly before the professor's death. Campbell responded with a question of his own: "Where is your deepest sense of harmony and bliss?" "I don't know—I'm not sure," the youth responded. "*Find* it," Campbell replied—"and then *follow* it."

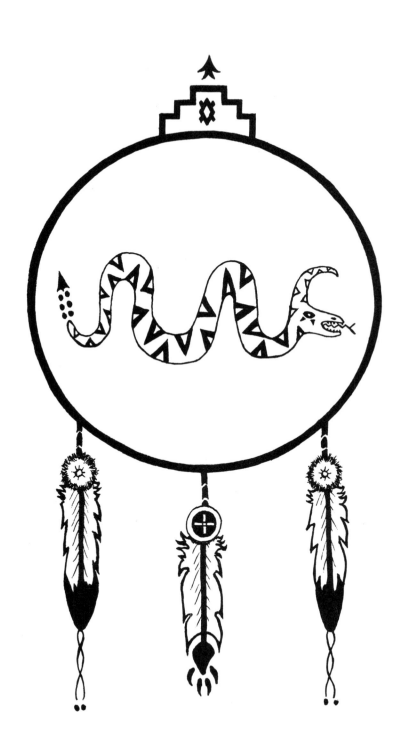

Chapter Four

THE ANCIENT PROPHECIES

PART I
Iron Thunderhorse

The ancient prophecies of Turtle Island's shamanic peoples have been a source of guidance for many generations. Like the daybreak star shining brilliantly against a backdrop of eternal darkness, the prophetic spark of enlightened wisdom shines forth from the heavens. Prophecy is the beacon that leads the insightful few from chaos to the spiritual center of mystical equilibrium.

The Great Spirit speaks to shamanic peoples in dreams and visions. Prophecies are indeed visions. And because of what they presage for the future, they are also much more. To understand the prophecies, one must see with spiritual eyes. Those who look at a forest as merely the raw material with which to build a city are viewing this natural resource through the conditioned reflexes of materialism. Behind such ideologies lie politics, financial competition, and power struggles. In the shamanic world, there is only the unseen power that depends on the interrelationship of all living things.

There were numerous prophets in the native nations of the Americas. Metacomet (also known as King Philip), Handsome Lake, Wabasha, Powhatan, Pontiac, Deganawidah, Tecumsah, Sequoya, Sitting Bull, Black Hawk, Smohalla, Goyathlay (also known as Geronimo), Crazy Horse, and Wovoka were just a few of the more well-known visionaries of the North American native nations.

In Times Gone By, the spiritual teachings of the Ojibway, relates that thus far seven major prophets have come to the Anishinabe. Each of these prophets predicted what the future would bring for their respective tribes. Each of the prophecies was represented by a sacred fire, and each fire was related to a particular period in tribal history. Thus, the teachings of the seven prophets are referred to as *The Seven Fires*, as chronicled by Brian Wright McLeod.

The first fire tells us that the Ojibway nation would rise and follow the sacred shell, that their religion would serve as a rallying point for the Anishinabe, and that the traditional ways of the Midewiwin religion would be the source of much strength.

The second fire tells us that the nation would be changed by a large body of water, that the direction of the sacred shell would be lost, and that the religion would become weak. It is also said that a boy would be born to point the way back to the traditional ways, a boy who would show the direction to the stepping stones of the Manitoulin Island chain.

The third fire tells that the Ojibway people would find the path to their chosen ground—a land in the west to which they must move their families.

The fourth fire tells of the coming of the light-skinned race.

The fifth fire relates to a great struggle that was to come.

The sixth fire tells us that during this time, grandsons and granddaughters would turn against their elders, and that the spiritual ways of the Ojibway would almost disappear.

The seventh fire tells of the emergence of a new people, a people who would retrace their history to find the ways that had been left behind. It says that the water drums would once again sound their voices, that there would be a rebirth of the Ojibway nation and a rekindling of the old fires.

At this time, it is said, the light-skinned race would be given a choice. If they chose the right road, then the seventh fire would light the eighth and final fire—an eternal fire of peace, love, and brotherhood. If the light-skinned race chose the wrong road, however, then the destruction which they brought with them to this great land would come back to them and cause much death and suffering.

Elsewhere in this book, reference has been made to the Hopi legends that also relate the story of a great flood and the migratory island stepping stones. These legendary tales are not myth; they are prophetic histories of the post-glacial rise of the Earth's sea level which forced most coastal indigenous tribes to migrate elsewhere.

The Delaware have a history called the Walum Olum, or "red score," recorded on sticks bearing carved pictographs (Figure 4-1). In their recordings, one set of pictographs illustrates the coming of the white race. Were these historical accounts or prophecies?

Researchers and scholars have referred to these pictographs as actual historical accounts, and this appears to be correct. Divination methods of the Algonquin Nations, such as the casting of bones and sticks, for example, were often used to predict the future. These prophecies were recorded on sticks or birchbark scrolls for future verification.

The Hopi prophecies have received much attention in recent years. Hopi prophets have revealed that the present world cycle will end in the "Great

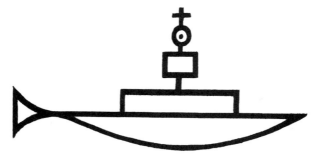

Figure 4-1. *Facsimile drawing of one of the carved stick pictographs known as the Walum-Olum. With this particular piece, an explanation reads, ". . . persons floating from the east, the Whites were coming."* From America's Fascinating Indian Heritage. *Pleasantville, NY: Reader's Digest Books.*

Purification." It is believed that this period of purification will bring about widespread destruction unless people change their ways. During this period, which many believe we are now entering, it is said that the Hopi guardian twins of the north and south poles will leave their stations, causing the world to tremble. We have seen the warning signs already around the perimeter of North America: earthquakes in the West and Southwest, volcanic activity in the Northwest, polluted air and water in the Northeast, and environmental destruction in the South. Although there will be many natural disasters worldwide, the Hopi believe that the mid-North American continent will be safe.

Many scientists who were once skeptical of the possibilities of polar shifts or polar wandering are now doing research in the field of plate tectonics and geomagnetics. More than 170 geomagnetic reversals have occurred over the past 80 million years. Scientists believe the next shift will occur as early as the year 2030.

The Maya of Central America believe that the present Earth cycle will end between December 21, 2011 and June 6, 2012. During this period, they predict, an interesting planetary alignment will occur. Venus will pass in perfect alignment between Earth and the sun, with the transit lasting approximately eight hours. Venus is the only planet in the solar system that rotates in a retrograde direction—in other words, from west to east. This "reversal" from the ordinary pattern is the sign of the contrary. For centuries, our ancestors have associated Venus with the culture hero, the bringer of peace and tranquility to a cycle previously dominated by chaos. Could this be why Venus was so reverently charted by Mayan skywatchers?

The Hopi prophecies also speak of the "lost white brother," *Pahana,* the culture hero who is the equivalent of Mesoamerica's Feathered Serpent. Pahana surfaced with the people of the underworld and possessed great wisdom. He promised to return with many blessings for the Hopi as he set off on his journey to the east. The prospect of this "second coming" has been met with great anticipation, because prophecy states that all fighting will cease in the light of the great knowledge and wisdom he will bring.

Several times in the past, the Hopi have mistakenly placed their faith in the wrong Pahana, such as when the Spaniards came to their land centuries ago. The Maya and Aztecs had similar prophecies and were mistaken as well. Perhaps their error lies in believing that the Pahana was one physical person or group of people, rather than a psychosymbolic metaphor for the spirit of enlightenment.

In all the "lost white brother" legends, this mysterious culture hero initially came from the west and traveled east. This is consistent with the legend of Feathered Serpent. Similarly, the planet Venus always rotates from west to east and is known as the Morning Star or Evening Star, depending on the time of year it is observed. Could Pahana be the planet Venus, the deified personage of the "son of the sun," the offspring of Father Sun who follows in an opposite direction and returns every 5,125 years to restore balance to the world?

In most of the legends and prophecies of the Native American shamanic tribes, the Sacred Twins play an important role. To the Algonquins, the twins were Wolf and Gluskabe (turtle); to the Iroquois, they were White Hare and Wolf; to the Winnebago, they were Flesh and Stump. In the Plains, they were called Lodge-Boy and Throw-Away-Boy. In the Zuni nation, they were known as the War Twins.

In all of the twin legends, we find the epitome of opposite characters: good versus evil, corruption versus honesty. One twin is usually strong and clever, the other weak and stupid. In most tribes, the twins are also personifications of the sun and moon.

Wherever we find the benevolent culture hero, we always find his sly counterpart, the tyrant. In Mesoamerica, the counterpart to the Feathered Serpent is Lord Smoking Mirror, Tezcatlipoca. Lord Smoking Mirror is the patron of war, the underworld, and darkness. It appears that tyranny sometimes endures longer than honesty, but the lost white brother always returns and brings stability to the people. The Mayan prophecies say: "All moons, all years, all days, all winds reach their completion and pass away. So does all blood reach its place of quiet, as it reaches power and its throne."

Another perspective on this theme is given through the use of color. The color white has always been synonymous with peace, wisdom, and the way of compassion. It also signifies white magic. The peace star is the sign of the culture hero, the Pahana. This is the planet Venus, the bringer of all things to the center. The peace star motif of the Lakota (Figure 4-2) is interpreted to mean: "In this design, all directions come together in harmony at the center. They stop each other, thereby stopping conflict to create peace."

The great Indian prophets of Native America all spoke of a time when the people of the four races and the four directions would join together at the Tree of Life—at the center—to become as one nation. Many believe this period is beginning now. The period of purification is the final test of readiness for those who will find true peace within themselves. Those who do will perform the work necessary to bring the nations together.

Many of the Native American shamanic prophecies predict a time when the sons and daughters of the colonizers would come to the Indian people and ask for guidance in bringing balance to Mother Earth. This would occur after many had realized the destruction of a significant portion of the environment. Nicholas Black Elk foretold this many years ago. Wallace Black Elk, a contemporary Lakota shaman, also received a vision similar to that of Crazy Horse, in which the central element was the Tree of Life, the provider of shelter for all people.

Figure 4-2. *Lakota Sioux Peace Star motif. Facsimile drawing taken from Prairie Edge catalogue, Rapid City, South Dakota.*

Conclusion

Don Eduardo Calderón, an Incan *curandero* (Peruvian folk healer), says his visions show that the sacred knowledge of the ancestors must be revealed and shared if the planet is to survive. His visions also reveal that the new shamans and caretakers of the world will emerge in the West—on Turtle Island.

New medicine societies are surfacing all over Turtle Island. Along with the good, there are drawbacks because of persons selling the sacred ways or otherwise exploiting the spiritual prophecies. Be that as it may, there is evidence all around us now demonstrating that the time of purification is upon us. As Wallace Black Elk says, the Tree of Life is also the Tree of Knowledge. That knowledge is shamanism, and it springs from the oneness of the shamanic roots.

One theme of this book is the attempt to re-establish the lost mysteries of Mother Earth and Father Sky by revealing the symbolism behind shamanic art, mythology, legend, philosophy, and practice. The ancient prophecies are a living legacy. They are the very leaves of the Great Tree of Life.

PART II
Donn Le Vie, Jr.

The Toltec culture has been credited with the first use of the name Quetzalcoatl, the Mesoamerican Feathered Serpent. It is perhaps here that the greatest conflict occurred with respect to cultural, philosophical, and religious differences between the beneficent Quetzalcoatl and the malevolent Tezcatlipoca. In many conquered Mayan cities, the Toltecs continued their warlike tendencies and even subjugated the Mayan population, serving as the "lords of the New Order." This domination continued for approximately 200 years, until the Aztecs came sweeping through the Yucatan Peninsula from the north.

Quetzalcoatl undoubtedly appeared in more than one "incarnation." There are numerous accounts of a great mythological being who energized the religious fervor in Mesoamerican peoples. This being also seems to have been an historical individual who appeared several times during different cultural periods. Many priests and kings claimed the title of Quetzalcoatl—supposedly only those of kind heart and deed who had attained enlightenment and achieved total clarity of vision. But no doubt there were many who abused both the title and the power.

The Aztec religion is an enigma. Part of it embraced a philosophy characteristic of a more refined social structure, receptive to gentle influences, while the rest expressed a belief in undiluted rapaciousness. One can only surmise that perhaps some external influence pulled the Aztecs away from their original monotheistic simplicity. Instead, they worshipped thirteen principal gods and no fewer than two hundred subsidiary gods—deities who presided over everything from the seasons to various human occupations.

The Aztecs have also been credited with introducing the ritual of human sacrifice and corrupting the original benign teachings of Quetzalcoatl. Human sacrifice, though impossibly cruel by contemporary standards, has been practiced throughout history by many cultures; however, few could rival the fervor with which the Aztecs participated in it. Estimates run as high as fifty thousand sacrifices annually.

Quetzalcoatl's prophecy of his return unwittingly set the scene for the arrival of Cortez in 1519. The Spanish conquistador himself met the image of the fair-skinned, dark-haired "god-king" the Aztecs had been awaiting. To further impress the people, Popocatépetl, the "smoking mountain" volcano, became active on the eve of his arrival. Cortez, of course, wasted no time revealing his true intentions, bearing a crucifix in one hand and a sword in the other.

But what of Quetzalcoatl's promise to return? In the return of Venus, the Morning Star, we see the planet absorbed by the light of the sun, absorbed into the One. Yet even this oneness presages the beginning of another departure, another cycle. The ancient Mesoamerican Indians had a deep sense of cosmic and spiritual cycles, some of it left with them by the last mythical Quetzalcoatl. This became confused with some of the historical Quetzalcoatls and, around the time of Cortez, no one really knew quite what to look for. At least one version of the return has Quetzalcoatl appearing again at the end of the "ninth hell" and the beginning of the first of the "new heavens." Even today, some people living on the Yucatan Peninsula whose bloodlines were relatively untouched by the Spanish conquest have carefully preserved such legends and teachings.

The Mesoamerican vision and prophesy of hope, its vision of the return of light and of the connectedness of all life, are as fine and sophisticated as any other spiritual teaching. The Feathered Serpent and the ascent to the heavens from matter are not only hopeful in terms of an avatar's return, but are hopeful for all people on a spiritual quest as symbols of the return to life through spiritual rebirth.

According to Carl Jung, animals are universally associated as symbols of transcendence. The Feathered Serpent is a figurative representation of emergence from the depths of the ancient Earth Mother, a "symbolic denizen of the collective unconscious" that embodies humanity's striving to attain its full potential.

Snakes and lizards are transcendent symbols combining aquatic, aerial, and terrestrial aspects in a vertically structured cosmology. Entwined serpents, such as those found on early Grecian stone pillars (topped with busts of gods called "herms," from the god Hermes), are frequently associated with fertility. But this is a spiritual fertility—a fertility of deliverance and healing.

The underworld serpent's acquisition of wings provides the means for transcendence. The underworld snake consciousness passes through the medium of earthly reality and ultimately, through its winged flight, attains the reality of the transpersonal. This is the power of the Greek god, Mercury; the winged horse, Pegasus; the winged victory statue; and the various winged dragons that appear throughout classic literature.

Transcendence, or liberation, is not a process in and of itself; it is only the third of three levels of initiation, the other two being submission and containment. By passing through each of these three levels, an individual can better reconcile conflicting elements of his or her personality. The result, then, is a balance that allows for a metamorphosis that leads to *self*-mastery and becoming fully human.

According to Joseph Henderson, author of *The Wisdom of the Serpent*, the serpent wisdom is symbolically represented by its lidless eye. Henderson states that man has projected his own unspoken desire to obtain from the Earth a knowledge that escapes him in ordinary daytime consciousness. Essentially, this is the knowledge of death and rebirth, a knowledge that remains elusive until some transcendent principle surfaces from the shadows of the unconscious and reveals itself to the conscious mind.

Even the Bible acknowledges the serpent's ability to shed, along with its skin, constricting attitudes and ideas. As Matthew 10:16 admonishes, "Be ye . . .wise as serpents, and harmless as doves."

Other references to the serpent/transcendence theme include the ancient Chibcha legends of Colombia, which associated the serpent with highland lagoons. The origin of the El Dorado legend—the mythical city of gold—has its roots in Colombia. In truth, the term "El Dorado" originated with the Chibcha ceremony in which a chief covered his body with a vegetable gum and sprayed gold dust onto the adhesive coating. The chief then dove into a lagoon from a raft to offer the gold on his body to the gods. This ritual appears to be one of transcendence: a symbolic shedding of the skin, a metamorphosis.

In their greed, the Spanish conquistadors and those who followed searched for a literal El Dorado in the Amazon jungles, when all the time they carried the real treasure within themselves. Imagine how different the history of the Americas would be today if this knowledge of the figurative had been understood in 1519. The translation for "El Dorado" is "gilded man." Its misinterpretation is yet another example of people searching outside themselves for gratification, happiness, and reward—the byproduct of Western civilization. Even Voltaire's Candide could not resist the temptation to gather up the gold, emeralds, rubies, and diamonds that covered the ground during his visit to El Dorado. "Where are we?" he exclaimed. "The King's children in this country must have an excellent education, since they are taught to show such a contempt for gold and precious stones."

Iron Thunderhorse has discussed the need for using spiritual eyes to understand the potential behind what the senses perceive, to use the power in visions as a window into the soul. As he reminds us, visions provide the window through which we can view the freedom that awaits us on the other side of the thin veil, the reality that whispers to us from the other shore.

Many investigators have been successful at temporarily peeling back the mental cataracts that obscure our vision into the reality beyond the senses. So can we all. But such a feat demands setting aside expectations and the linear, logical thinking that Western society has ingrained in us over the centuries. It involves opening up to new perspectives—perspectives that promise freedom from the neurotic bondage we have allowed ourselves for so long.

Jung eloquently stated that the purpose of theology is not to demonstrate the existence of light, but to bring vision to blind people who are not aware that their eyes can see. Modern people need to be taught how to see. And the first step is to remove the stygian reality perceived by our senses. Once we take this step, we will be on the path to inner vision.

Chapter Five

MYSTERIES OF
THE FEATHERED SERPENT

PART I
Iron Thunderhorse

Throughout the indigenous nations of the Americas, a common symbol can be found that weaves many cultures and societies together: the Feathered or Horned Serpent. Embodied within the iconography of these seemingly simple yet contrasting elements lies an ancient body of relationships designed to maintain balance between humanity and the natural elements.

In its quest for a more civilized way of life, humankind has seriously disturbed the balance of nature's cycles. Some tribal elders say that many of the people are not yet ready to obtain the wisdom of the ancients, as they do not have the compassion and unconditional love necessary to make use of such knowledge. Yet many elders now recognize more and more people tearing down the old, worn-out boundaries devised by previous generations. This is leading to an increasing awareness that will soon cause the elders to open the door a little wider for those with a sense of responsibility and reverence.

Harmonic Convergence demonstrates, on a global scale, that a renewed collective ethos has re-ignited the spiritual flames of many like-minded people who feel the need to bring harmony back to the world. Harmonics is the key to our future, and the purpose of this study is to reclaim the ancient way of nature's harmony.

The Serpent

The serpent, when seen as the foundation for the more complex Feathered and Horned Serpent motifs, is an ancient symbol representative of energy itself. The serpent was noted for peculiarities which later contributed to the many psychosymbolic analogies associated with the serpent/energy theme.

Aboriginal peoples discovered, for example, that a serpent sheds its skin regularly; so the serpent symbol includes the notions of resurrection, renewal, and cyclical regeneration. Serpents also lived in the water. They sought refuge in caves, among rocks, in trees, and in many other accessible areas. Their adaptive traits gave them status as creatures who held the power of the four sacred elements: fire (energy), air (tree serpent), earth (land serpent), and water (water serpent). The powers of the serpent could cure or cause illness in all other creatures, so its apparent ties to life and death strengthened the symbolism of spiritual resurrection.

In the Orient, the serpent is the favored symbol of the life force called kundalini. It is associated with the raising of the spiritual fire within. Like a serpent, the primal energy winds its way up the spinal column, threading its way through the seven chakras, the spinning wheels of energy associated with certain nerve ganglia (also referred to as miniature brains associated with psychic development). The ancient symbol of the caduceus (Figure 5-1) is derived from this phenomenon. It is symbolic of the magnetic bipolarity of human spiritual power. One side is "solar," or active, while the other is "lunar," or passive.

Ancient teachings reveal that a serpent cannot stand erect of its own accord. By analogy, a serpent needs a tree to wind its way up toward the world of spirit (Figure 5-2). Thus, the spine represents a tree on which the spiritual fire can ascend. And thus comes the association with the Great Tree of Life. Unless it has a vehicle in which it can ascend, a serpent is doomed to isolation in the lower worlds. Likewise, a body without spiritual animation is a meaningless heap of chemical compounds. Without spiritual life, nothing can exist; hence, the combined symbols of the entwined serpent and the staff, or Tree of Life.

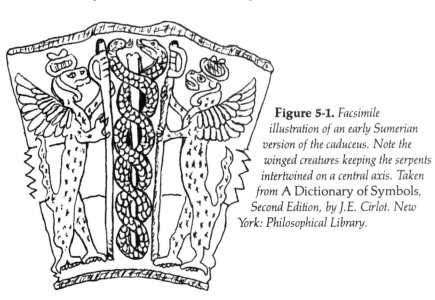

Figure 5-1. *Facsimile illustration of an early Sumerian version of the caduceus. Note the winged creatures keeping the serpents intertwined on a central axis. Taken from* A Dictionary of Symbols, Second Edition, *by J.E. Cirlot. New York: Philosophical Library.*

Figure 5-2. *Facsimile illustration of serpent spiraling up a tree. This is the symbol of the ancient art of geomancy.*

Cycles of the Serpent

One arcane symbol associated with the serpent cycles is the ancient *ouroboros*—the symbol of a serpent biting its own tail. This basic symbol later developed into the dragon—a type of mythic monster that was part snake, part bird, and part Earth monster. According to the *Dictionary of Symbols*, it was seen as a primal being symbolizing the "primeval anarchic dynamism which preceded the creation of the cosmos and the emergence of order."

The *ouroboros* is to be found in the *Codex Marcianus*, a second-century manuscript based on ancient premises. The meaning of this particular symbol encompasses all cyclic characteristics such as unity, multiplicity, evolution, involution, birth, growth, disease, and death.

The motif of the serpent as a symbol of time cycles in the pre-Columbian Americas is evidenced by a close examination of the Mesoamerican codices, such as the *Codex Dresdesis* (known more commonly as the *Dresden Codex*). In Figure 5-3, for example, we find the serpent motif mixed with the rain god, Chac, which symbolizes the lengthy torrential rainy season in the jungles of the ancient Maya.

Figure 5-3. *Chac, the Mayan rain god, emerging from the jaws of the Feathered Serpent. Notice this includes the* ouroboros *motif, i.e., the cycle which returns to start anew. Facsimile drawing from the* Dresden Codex.

Figure 5-4. *At right is a typical use of the* ouroboros *symbol, including the number "18" written in bar and dot form and the water lines associated with the torrential rainy season. Chac, the rain god, stands to the left of this symbol bearing two torches, probably to denote the intervals of sun before and after an 18-day (or week) rainy period. Facsimile drawing from the* Dresden Codex.

In Mesoamerican iconography, the *ouroboros*, rather than the older form biting its tail (Figure 5-4), was depicted as the circular curvature wherein the tail and the head (beginning and end) of a serpent met, or intersected.

The psychosymbolic significance of the serpent cycle is indicative of self-fecundation, a self-sufficient natural organism — a nature a la Gaia, which continually follows a cyclic pattern, returning to its own beginning.

The Balanced Cycle

Another peculiarity of the serpent return cycle is the combining of certain cycles. In many instances, in the Orient as well as in Mesoamerican and North American iconography, the *ouroboros* is depicted as half-light and half-dark. The conjunction of light and dark represented the union of earthly impulses (the serpent element), while the celestial impulses represented the bird element. The synthesis of these two resulted in the birth of the dragon, or Earth monster.

Our ancestors were always observing the natural order of seasonal and cosmic cycles. In doing so, they discovered how these cycles somehow merged and nourished all life forms, balancing out previous cycles in a continual flux of interacting combinations.

The Maya were experts at observing these cycles. What has been commonly referred to as "calendrics," or the science of prediction by the calendar, is actually a ceremonial repository of various cycles. Astronomers assume there were scientific reasons for such heavenly observations and preoccupations. However, Dr. Michael Coe cautions us that the Maya were predominantly astrologers, not astronomers, and the existence of pre-Columbian astronomy would be difficult to prove.

The principal cycles of night and day, month and year, are the forces of the sky that most commonly influence biological life and psychic vibrations on Earth. The return of the dualistic solar/lunar cycles is the essence of the half-light, half-dark aspect of the *ouroboros* symbol. I have observed this all over the Americas. It is the equivalent of the Oriental yin and yang symbols, which, when combined, give birth to the symbol of wholeness: Tao.

An interesting association of this merging of cycles is described once again by J. E. Cirlot, an authority on ancient symbolism whose expertise has proved to be invaluable in many fields of study. An interesting analogy can be observed between the merging of polarity cycles with the changing or adapting psyche. In folklore, the underworld is associated with the dying moon whose horns are seen in the quarters and is symbolized as the crone or hag. This is the waning cycle. The upper world is the realm of the nascent sun. This waxing period of growth and fertilization is symbolized in folklore as a tiger, serpent, child—anything with vitality. The child emerging from the serpent's jaws represents rebirth, the unfolding of a new cycle from the ever-present cycle of fertility in nature.

Emergence & Re-emergence

The theme of re-emergence, like the shedding of a serpent's skin, is repeatedly evidenced in the symbology of Native American and Mesoamerican philosophy. In the state of Ohio, for example, we find the Great Serpent Mound (Figure 5-5), an effigy-type earthen mound attributed to the ancient Adena Indians (*circa* 500 to 900 A.D.), whose culture thrived during the Early Classic

Figure 5-5. *Facsimile illustration of the Serpent Mound in Ohio, denoting cyclic regeneration and a self-fecundating cosmos.*

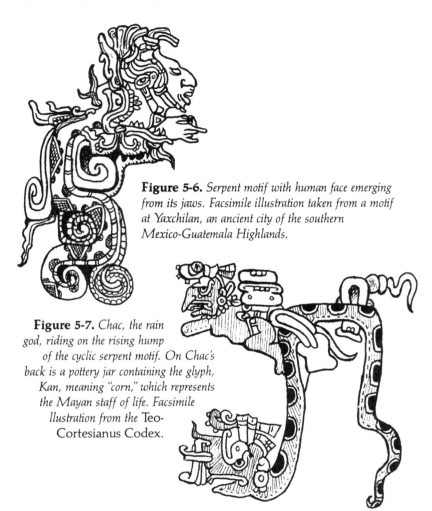

Figure 5-6. *Serpent motif with human face emerging from its jaws. Facsimile illustration taken from a motif at Yaxchilan, an ancient city of the southern Mexico-Guatemala Highlands.*

Figure 5-7. *Chac, the rain god, riding on the rising hump of the cyclic serpent motif. On Chac's back is a pottery jar containing the glyph, Kan, meaning "corn," which represents the Mayan staff of life. Facsimile llustration from the Teo-Cortesianus Codex.*

period of the Mayan ceremonial center of Tikal. The serpent mound was definitely not a burial or ceremonial mound like other earth-mound structures previously encountered. It is, instead, a kind of talismanic herald to the spirit forces; it honors the natural cycles. It is easy to identify the mound's symbolic meanings. The serpent's tail (the source) begins with a slowly unfolding spiral (the birth), then progresses in an undulating pattern. The curves and dips along the serpent's back correspond to the waning and waxing fluxes of the moon. The mouth of the serpent gives birth to a new seed, or cycle, waiting to unfold.

In Mesoamerica, we find the astro-calendrical emergence symbols of the *ouroboros* and the deity-in-serpent's-jaws combined. Mayan iconography offers

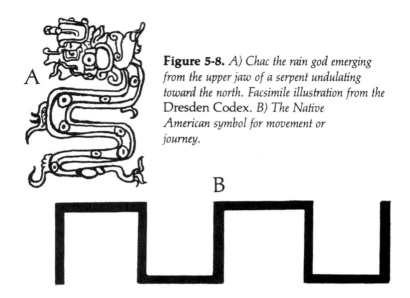

Figure 5-8. *A) Chac the rain god emerging from the upper jaw of a serpent undulating toward the north. Facsimile illustration from the* Dresden Codex. *B) The Native American symbol for movement or journey.*

many examples of this combined motif (Figure 5-6). In such cases, it is possible that the *ouroboros* depicts the returning cycles, while the deity depicts the identity of the particular cycle referred to or recorded.

In like manner, the undulation of the serpent without the emergence symbol was used to denote a cycle in progression, and the appropriate signifier might be used as a rider (Figure 5-7). Also, when used to portray an upward rise or downward fall, such a cyclic symbol could very well depict the high and low points of periods of torrential flooding and other such cycles (Figure 5-8). To miscalculate such cycles would undoubtedly have spelled disaster for these people.

The Dragon/Serpent Monster

In the Orient, serpent and dragon motifs are interchangeable. There are subterranean and aerial dragons, as well as aquatic and earthly ones. In cultures where it appears, the serpent/dragon motif almost always denotes conjunctions and cyclic emergence. The ancient Gnostic notion of a universal dragon can also be found in many cultures as an inducement to overcoming hardships. The hero either slays or is devoured by the dragon.

A close observation of certain Mesoamerican Feathered Serpent motifs shows a striking similarity to those of certain Oriental dragons (Figure 5-9).

The Oriental symbolism of the cosmic dragon enables the cosmological mapping of three worlds, with the forces of nature depicted in their cyclic patterns. The underworld, the heavens, and Earth are joined by envisioning these raw powers. Thus, an intermediary is created between the extreme polarities which links the cosmic forces into a triadic pattern of planes: the upper level of spiritual phenomena, the intermediate level of earthly life, and the underworld of subterranean forces.

The two-headed dragon motif is also familiar in Mayan hieroglyphics. In its sacred iconography alone, the two-headed dragon has certain peculiarities, which we will analyze elsewhere. But for now, a primary focus can be presented. Usually, the two-headed dragon represents either a turtle-like or alligator-like figure and appears in the form of an elaborately decorated stone altar.

In Mesoamerica there exists a mythical character known as Tlaltecuhtli, which is a post-Mayan name for an earlier character found in Olmec and Mayan iconography. This character is depicted as an earth monster, a toad or turtle-like amphibious creature with great tusks and claws. Equipped with a head on each end of its body, it was thought to swallow the sun in the evening and disgorge it at night. Generally speaking, the double-headed motif represents the Earth, with the heads serving as entrance and exit points. This is representative of the gateways to the upper worlds (heaven/sun) and lower worlds (ancestry/moon).

In the Orient, it was a dragon that delivered the legendary mystical trigrams, known as Pa-Qua, to a famous emperor. There, dragon cults have also been associated with ancestor worship and with the art of geomancy, *feng-shui*.

Figure 5-9. *Facsimile drawings showing similarities between A) Oriental dragon head and B) Mesoamerican dragon/ serpent head.*

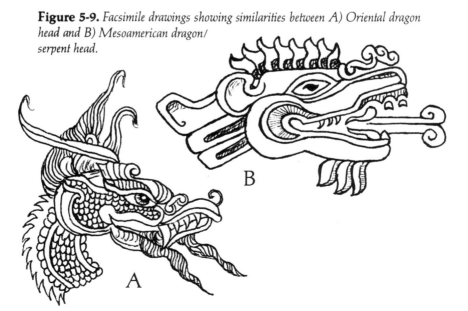

The Mayan Ethos

The Mayan Indians were a shamanic people who perceived a cosmos with three divisions: an underworld with nine layers; the Earth, with three layers and four directions; and the spirit world with thirteen layers.

The vehicle used by shamanic peoples such as the Maya to obtain access to these other worlds is quite clear. At the center of the world (*axis mundi*), the four sacred roads meet. This is the place of conjunction where the Tree of Life and Knowledge grows. It is interesting to note that the three divisions of tree symbolism also correlate with the three main worlds: roots = underworld; trunk = earth; and foliage = spirit world. The Sacred Tree depicts in symbolic form the inexhaustible process of life—birth, growth, and decay.

At the Temple of Inscriptions in Palenque, in the Mexican state of Chiapas, a secret vault with a hidden stairway was discovered that led to an elaborately carved sarcophagus. Within the vault were found the skeletal remains of Lord Pacal Votan.

The ornate carvings on the lid of the sarcophagus, measuring twelve feet high, seven feet wide and weighing five tons, constitute a beautiful ideogram (Figure 5-10). Its outside edges, right and left, are inscribed with nine astronomical signs called skybands, for a total of eighteen celestial symbols. Its upper and lower edges are inscribed with three faces, each with one hand curved upward in front of the mouth. This is the Native American sign which means "to speak." These are most likely the faces of shamans who are calling to the lords of the day (the spirit world) and lords of the night (the underworld).

The bottom of the central ideogram shows a fantastic facial symbol, its lower jaws exaggerated with huge teeth. The jawbones are marked with spots, an emphasis in iconography denoting a bone or death. The upper jawbones are also highlighted in this way yet, above the nose, the face seems to be fleshed and alive. The forehead bears the popular *kin* glyph (thought to denote the sun, time, or day) and a headdress with the "triadic" symbol.

Lord Pacal Votan himself sits crucified, root chakra attached to the headdress center, facing upward as if floating or in ecstatic motion. Behind him is a four-sectioned cross or axis whose right and left sides bear elaborate serpent's heads with grotesque figures emerging from their jaws. Dr. Linda Schele of the University of Texas at Austin interprets this as the dying sun as it slips into the jaws of the underworld.

My interpretation is as follows: The word "Pacal" is translated as "hand shield," and the word "Votan" is Tzental (lowlands) Mayan dialect for "Feathered Serpent, Lord of the Light." Therefore, this ruler's full name would be translated as "hand shield of the Feathered Serpent." The name Votan signifies that this ruler was considered an incarnation of the Lord of Light, much like the Incan rulers.

One Mesoamerican tale about the Feathered Serpent in the original creation myth says that there were four previous worlds to the currently passing fifth world (also called the Fifth Sun). The Feathered Serpent was a "Sun" during one of his previous incarnations. According to legend, he journeyed to the underworld, Mictlán, where he brought back the bones of previous worlds. Sprinkling his own blood over them, he turned them into human beings. This is analogous to the theme of resurrection within the psyche.

Thus, as I interpret this ideogram, the Feathered Serpent's hand shield enacts his own reincarnation as the "son of the sun" and he travels to the underworld to gather the bones of his ancestors. To do so, Pacal Votan crucifies himself at the base of the Tree of Life that flowers at the world's axis. This sacrifice to the sun on the Tree of Life is the foundation for the sacred Sun Dance, known throughout Native America as the dance of ultimate sacrifice.

Metaphysical Elements of the Underworld

The grotesque face below Pacal Votan is the ideogram for the underworld monster (probably Tlaltecuhtli), a toad-like creature with great tusks. This ideogram definitely has tusk-like protuberances extending from the lower jaw, engulfing Pacal Votan on both sides.

Both the *Popol Vuh* and the *Chilam Balam* (sacred shamanic books of the Maya) relate that the four crossroads represent the entrance to the underworld. The Maya call this junction, "*Cahib Xalat Be*," where the red, black, white, and green roads intersect. This also may be connected to the four elements.

The symbol of bones as a determinative element should be noted here. Bones commonly represent the indestructable psyche, the nature of life everlasting—hence, a belief in psychic resurrection. The jawbone is also an interesting symbol. Jaws hold the teeth in place, and teeth constitute the fortified outer wall of protection.

There is, moreover, a tradition in the Polynesian Islands which should be interjected here. The Maori natives hold two types (or levels) of esoteric knowledge, each with exoteric implications. The first is called "upper jaw" knowledge, which pertains to the period of genesis, the origins of the world and humankind's population of the world. The other type is known as "lower jaw"

Figure 5-10. *Lord Pacal Votan sacrifices himself on the Tree of Life, re-enacting the Mayan creation myth as the Feathered Serpent journeys to the underworld to bring back the bones of the ancestors. Facsimile drawing of sarcophagus lid at the Temple of Inscriptions, Palenque, Mexico.*

knowledge and relates to the histories of the individual chiefs as well as the clan lineages from the time of the departure from their homeland up to the present.

We have seen previously how shamanic roots tie the Polynesian cultures to our own native culture in the Americas. Accordingly, there is something to be learned from the Polynesian symbology. When Pacal Votan re-enacted the myth to bring back "the bones of people of the previous worlds," he was literally bringing back their wisdom, their ancient arts, and their sacred practices. This is exactly what we need to do today.

Another element to consider is the face above the jawline of this Earth monster which remains in the flesh, in the now. As Manly Palmer Hall, esoteric philosopher and founder of the Philosophical Research Society, states, each element contributes to the implementation of the ancient precepts: The eye represents divine awareness; the ear, divine attention and interest; the nose, divine longevity and vitality; the mouth, divine protection and commands. These are the precepts that will bring order to the chaotic Earth monster.

At the monster's forehead is a symbol known as the *kin* glyph, which represents the sun. This symbol also denotes time and day. Yet, esoterically speaking, its particular positioning at the third-eye chakra is unmistakable. This is meant to symbolize the enlightened state. And directly above it is a headdress, consisting of a band crowned with the triadic symbol, denoting the heavens.

The side of the ideogram to the viewer's left is definitely from the aquatic kingdom and represents the lunar aquatic nature—the subconscious mind. The opposite side is a leaf/flower blossom, symbolizing the flowering/solar nature—the conscious mind. In the center is an upright pillar or tree. This symbolizes the primal, superconscious mind, a reciprocal point of balance. Here dwells the exit point upward, through which the Tree of Life and Knowledge lead to higher worlds.

The reader should also note that the central figure on the astronomical band to the left is the symbol for the moon, and that the central figure on the right is the glyph for the sun. Hence, the solar and lunar natures and their esoteric analogies to the right and left sides of the brain are doubly significant.

Students of the *Popol Vuh* will notice that one side of the Tree of Life was associated with the sun and the other side was associated with the moon. The lunar aspect is associated with the subconscious, the solar aspect with the conscious, as well as with life and death, knowledge and wisdom.

Behind Pacal Votan is the symbolic Tree with its four sacred directions and its *axis mundi*. It is covered with eye/mirror symbols that collectively form a scale-like design, which I interpret to mean awareness. Like the thousand-petaled lotus of the Oriental, this Sacred Tree opens up new inner eyes and mirrors of awareness once a proper balance is achieved.

The Tree of Life is also an excellent symbol for the spinal column, which holds the "foliage" of the seven chakras. Once the solar and lunar sides become centered, their newly merged power enables a person's ultimate awareness to unfold via the uppermost summit of the Tree, the crown chakra.

At the top of the Tree, we find a quetzal bird with a grotesque face. The re-birth of the ancient roots of Quetzalcoatl is evidenced by the inserted mirror/scale motif within the bird's tail. The spiral curls inward to signify involution. The grotesque face of this bird is that of the Mayan god, Bolon Dz'Acab, patron of lineage and descent. The literal meaning of his name is "nine generations." He is thought by some authorities to be the Mayan equivalent of the Lord of Darkness, Tezcatlipoca (Smoking Mirror). He bears a huge eye at the position of the third eye which looks down as a mirror image of his profiled physical eye.

The combination of the quetzal bird and the Lord of Darkness might be seen as a successful flight through the underworld and spirit world, combining both shadow and light. Pacal Votan seems to have fulfilled ancient prophecies as a reincarnation of the legendary culture hero/deity. This makes sense, for in Mayan philosophy, the cycle of everlasting life ultimately resulted in deification. This also shows the connection between ancestral worship and the divine heirship of Mayan rulers.

The Ceremonial Bar Motif

The ceremonial bar is the common term given to the Mayan motif of the double-headed dragon. It is depicted with a thin snake-like body connecting the dual dragon heads, usually in an artistic manner to form a kind of "linked chain" image. On the ideogram of Pacal Votan's sarcophagus (Figure 5-10), this ceremonial bar has an upward arch. In other ceremonial bar motifs, it is depicted in a short, straight line without the usual links (Figure 5-11), and in most cases, it is shown in a drooping downward arch (Figure 5-12). Generally, the ceremonial bar is held in the arms of a Mayan nobleman or priest-like figure. In the jaws of each serpent can be seen the emerging head with a grotesque face.

As discussed earlier, the two-headed dragon denotes the Earth monster. The emergence from the jaws of the Earth monster represents the birth and death of a particular star or planet in deified form. Psychologically, it makes sense that the Earth as a living form should have two heads in order to allow other living celestial forms to appear and disappear — in other words, to pass through it. If it were depicted with only one head, these forms would logically never reappear.

The head in the dragon's jaws is none other than the "Roman nose" deity of the Maya, properly called Itzamná — the supreme creator god. Translated literally, his name means "iguana house." Iguana house was the embodiment of creation. The root words *itzam*, meaning "iguana," and *na*, meaning "house," were also used for the word "floor" which could be seen as the Earth's surface. Itzamná was the god of creation, the sky, the Earth, and the father of sciences and the arts. He was also the father of the Feathered Serpent.

Another common symbolic representation to note is the intersecting of serpent and tree. Also, the undulating path of a serpent in the sand or through water is likened to the passage of time, as the path of the Creator along the celestial ecliptic. In this sense, Itzamná is akin to Father Time, the creator god, the Earth god, who represents the intersecting conjunctions of all time cycles.

Figure 5-11. *This particular bar motif does not bear the usual links between the wrists. Even the patron god of lineage, seen on the outer right- and left-hand sides, looks like an infant here. Perhaps this signifies the birth of a particular cycle. Facsimile drawing from Stela N, Copan, Honduras.*

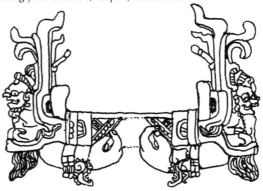

Figure 5-12. *Ceremonial bar motif with drooping links. Notice how the hands are bound as if the person were handcuffed. Perhaps this indicates imprisonment to the cycles of nature. Facsimile drawing from stela "P" at Copan, Honduras.*

Can we further substantiate this assumption? One early method of record-ing time consisted of marking notches or lines on a stick, rock, or bone to rep-resent the passage of days. In this system, the curvature of a horned moon between notches signified one complete lunar cycle or month. In the Indian nations of the Americas, it was common to depict the passing of a solar year as a straight line with a circle on the end. To record the passing of more than one year, these lines with circles were attached to a horizontal axis (Figure 5-13).

Figure 5-13. *Facsimile drawing of a pictograph showing how Indian tribes recorded time. This figure represents three years.*

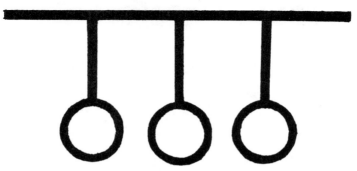

If we look at the ceremonial bar that intersects the Sacred Tree on the Pacal Votan sarcophagus (Figure 5-10), we see that each link has an intersecting line with a circle attached. It could be that each of these denotes the passage of a certain cycle, such as an approximate year of the *Tzolkin*, the ceremonial and sacred almanac cycle of 260 days, or a year of approximately 365 days to total 52 years. On the other hand, it may just represent the passing of the sacred cycle as it emerges and re-emerges.

Itzamná was thought to be the most ancient form of the Feathered Serpent. In sacred Mayan cosmology, deities had many interdependent but individu-alized variations—clearly a reflection of the unfettered shamanic psyche in full bloom.

Cycles, Balance & Imbalance

We have just explored the meaning of the motif of the "double-headed time cycle band that passes Earth" (my interpretation). This was usually held in the arms of a priestly or lordly person, probably a ruler whose obligation was to keep the sacred balance. Many of these images are carved on giant stelae—stone slabs or pillars. These huge sculptures have records inscribed on all sides, with information on cycles as well as the status, lineage, and deeds of various

Figure 5-14. *Astronomical band. Here, the ceremonial bar motif shows a probable imbalance in a cycle, or the death of one cycle heralding a new one. Facsimile drawing from Stela 10 at Serbal, Guatemala.*

rulers. They are probably markers denoting the cyclic balance within the Great Cycle of the Serpent as each ruler in turn assumed the responsibility for harmonic balance and record keeping.

In order to maintain the harmonic balance of fertility in his land, a ruler had to keep the sacred laws; otherwise, his people might not survive. If an imbalance was too severe, then a ruler had to devise counterbalances to prevent a popular revolt.

In one stela at Serbal, Guatemala (Figure 5-14), we notice a ceremonial band of astronomical signs. The sign at the extreme left resembling the letter "W" is the sign of Venus — undoubtedly the Morning Star symbol. The belt worn by this ruler is also decorated with astronomical signs, identifying him as a keeper of the sacred balance. The bar he holds is tilted slightly upward to the left and downward to the right. The downward end has no open jaws, but the inverted figure appears to represent the "long nose" god of Mayan lineage.

The upward part of the bar signifies the return cycle in abstract form; however, note that the jaws of the serpent do not contain the emergence character. Perhaps this is a record of someone who failed to keep the laws that had been passed down through the sacred lineage.

In short, then, the ceremonial bar can be seen as a form of scale used to weigh the cosmic balance on Earth in relation to the underworld and spirit world.

The Manikin Scepter & Lineage

Another common motif which has baffled observers is the Manikin Scepter motif. This is a doll-like figure with a handle that terminates in the form of a serpent (Figure 5-15A).

In its ithyphallic form, the Manikin Scepter was a fertility wand representing the flow of vital energy. The scepter face of Figure 5-15B is Bolon Dz'Acab, the patron of all lineages — in this case, the royal lineage of the universe. What is usually characterized as a long nose is actually the upper jaw of the serpent. Note the curvatures in the upper jaw of the Manikin Scepter's face and the serpent's upper jaw below it.

In most cases, the face and body of the Manikin Scepter are similar to those of previous illustrations; however, one curious inscription at Palenque (Figure 5-16) shows a child with the umbilicus leading to the jaws of a serpent.

These Manikin Scepters all have fanciful third-eye decorations, which authorities now agree represent the Smoking Mirror motif and the equivalent of Tezcatlipoca, Bolon Dz'Acab. Since Smoking Mirror is the patron of the priesthood, I believe this is a way of saying that this deity's consciousness is of the other worlds.

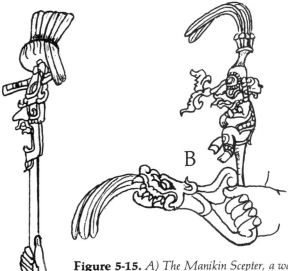

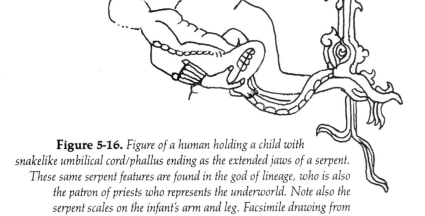

Figure 5-15. *A) The Manikin Scepter, a wand-like stick with a head on one end. Note the open mouth and the Smoking Mirror motif at the third-eye chakra of the head, and the serpent's head at the lower end of the scepter. B) Manikin Scepter with a full body of the god of lineage. Note the phallus and blooming third-eye motif. This is the wand of fructification and sacred lineages. Facsimile illustrations of artifacts from Quiriguá, Guatemala.*

Figure 5-16. *Figure of a human holding a child with snakelike umbilical cord/phallus ending as the extended jaws of a serpent. These same serpent features are found in the god of lineage, who is also the patron of priests who represents the underworld. Note also the serpent scales on the infant's arm and leg. Facsimile drawing from stucco relief sculpture at the Temple of Inscriptions, Palenque, Mexico.*

There are four aspects of Smoking Mirror, but for purposes of this discussion, only two aspects are relevant. The White Smoking Mirror was regarded as the alter ego of the Feathered Serpent and was the guardian of the western entrance to the underworld where the ancestors lived. Another variant of the Manikin Scepter shows the head of Smoking Mirror on a staff. His mouth is open as if speaking, and his third-eye awareness indicator is in full bloom. An interesting analogy that survives to this day among American Indians is the "talking stick." Holding this stick gives an individual in a circle the authority to speak uninterrupted until the talking stick is passed on.

Thus, I interpret the Manikin Scepter as a talking stick used by the royal Mayan priesthood. When it was held, it probably signified that the bearer was a priest who had consulted with the ancestral Tree, and that the priest's words were those of the Tree itself.

The Horned Serpent Motif

The Horned Serpent (Figure 5-17) is prevalent in all corners of Turtle Island: in the pueblos; in the Northwest, where it is known as Pal-aht-ki-sum to the Pit River Madesiwi Indians and as Sisiutl to the Kwakiutl, Nootka, and Tsimshian tribes; at Zuni, where it is called Kolowisi; and at Segi Canyon, Arizona, where it is called Baho-li-kongya.

Two-headed serpents, such as the Eskimo Pal-rai-yuk and the double-headed Horned Serpent of the Coast Salish, also verify these as common motifs throughout the Americas. Usually there are signs that relate to fertility along with these horned symbols. Thus, a cycle of fertility and vital energy flows through the cosmologies of all the natives of the Americas.

Figure 5-17. *A typical Horned Serpent motif found in Native American iconography.*

Figure 5-18. *These additional facsimile illustrations (not referenced in text) reveal the many forms of the Feathered Serpent motif found throughout the Americas. A) Feathered Serpent from pottery stamp, Zamora, Michoacán, Mexico; B) Feathered Serpent from pottery stamp, Piedras Negras, Veracruz, Mexico; C and D) Zuni Plumed Serpent; E) Prehistoric Horned Serpent at Puye, New Mexico; F) Casas Grandes Plumed Serpent; G) Winged, Horned Serpent from Alabama; H) Winged, Horned Serpent from Arkansas.*

Conclusion

The Feathered Serpent is a primary symbol of the cycles of the heavens, while the Horned Serpent is a primary symbol of the cycles of the underworld and the moon. Together, they represent the older lunar and solar zodiacs and the collective omens seen in the jaws of the two-headed serpent, Earth.

The eternal struggle of the natural forces of the sun and moon has analogies everywhere: yin/yang; serpent/eagle; ego/id. Without a center of gravity or balance, these forces are competitive and antagonistic. A center, such as the Earth, the *axis mundi*, the Tree of Life, or the superconscious, brings about a balance of forces that results in harmony.

PART II
Donn Le Vie, Jr.

Time: a never-ending series of events; a human-made label to measure change; the separation of experiences. Traditionally, in Western culture, time is expressed in two different ways. It can seem to "flow" like an eternal river, or it can appear as a succession of moments with three major divisions: past, present, and future.

As we have seen, the serpent motif used as a time symbol is often evidenced by its undulating form, which signified movement and journey to the Mesoamerican and North American Indian. When used as a calendrical sign to highlight certain cycles, the symbol more closely resembles that of a snake. The deity accompanying the symbol is the determinative element. For example, the Feathered Serpent is used to denote solar and lunar cycles; when displayed as a dragon, it symbolizes the merging of sky and Earth. The Horned Serpent represents subterranean currents, underground rivers, moon cycles, and earthly connections with the underworld. Obviously, the natural characteristics of each element serve as mnemonic triggers of association.

In a later chapter, Iron Thunderhorse will address Earth currents and the use of carved Earth monster altars to channel these currents. He will also discuss the fertility-sanguinity lines that flowed through the many nations and explain how the ancient art of geomancy can be revived to neutralize the Earth imbalances presently facing mankind.

Regardless of the shape or structure of the serpent motif, it embodies the universal theme of nonlinear time; that is, the perception of time as cyclic. But the cyclic nature of the universe is not just associated with time. The classic study found in Mircea Eliade's book, *Shamanism*, entitled, "Shamanism and Cosmology," mentions universal shamanic themes. One of these is the Tree of Life. In a cosmological sense, the Tree of Life ascends from the center of the Earth, the umbilicus, and represents the continual regeneration of the cosmos, the "inexhaustible spring" of universal life.

Eliade also recognizes the shaman's knowledge of harmony within the dualistic forces of the universe. The shaman knows that the creation of the world is a result of the conflict generated between polar opposites: the lower regions of the Tree of Life, as symbolized by the serpent and the waters (the feminine); and the upper regions of the Tree of Life, as represented by the bird (the masculine). As a result of the conflict, the Tree of Life is destroyed. Thus, the "archetype of all creative human activity" suffers destruction for the purpose of being born again.

Destruction and creation. Birth, death and rebirth. To everything there is a season. Even from the Tree of Life can the notion of time be perceived as cyclic, from the cyclic nature of life and the universe itself.

In a 1987 issue of *Shaman's Drum* magazine, an article entitled, "Tree of Life May be Dying" referred to El Tule, the mythic Tree of Life in Santa Maria del Tule in Oaxaca, Mexico. The Mexican Indians' 2,000-year-old national symbol showed signs of dying from pollution.

According to the legend of these Indians, Quetzalcoatl abandoned the Earth because of his disappointment with the conduct of humanity. They believed that his promised return would be a sign for the dawn of a New Age—an age of enlightenment. Some legends suggested that Quetzalcoatl would return from El Tule in a "flaming shower of sparks" on August 17, 1987. His failure to do so at that time would be a sign that humanity was not yet ready for an age of enlightenment. The death of El Tule suggests that in spite of the arrival of the New Age, some people are destined to remain in the lower realms of awareness.

At any rate, Venus/Quetzalcoatl, the Morning Star of enlightenment, rises in the east, and the shore where the ocean meets the dawn sky—the mouth of the dragon—is symbolic for the New Age. When the old cycle was over, it was said, Venus/Quetzalcoatl would return reborn in the jaws of the dragon.

In *The Gods of Mexico*, author C.A. Burland writes that according to legend, Quetzalcoatl had sinned and was forced to leave the world. After rising into the sky, he was drawn into the light of the sun and disappeared. For four days, Quetzalcoatl journeyed through the underworld. Following another four-day period, he returned to the upper world on the ninth day. This disappearance and reappearance of Quetzalcoatl coincides perfectly with the periodic eclipse of Venus by the sun.

McFadden further relates that Quetzalcoatl prophesied that the Tree of Life would wither and die, symbolizing the end of one age and the beginning of another. Therefore, the death of the Tree represents the rebirth both of a new cycle and of the Tree of Life itself.

In 1986, Iron Thunderhorse became involved with a project that consisted of correlating the various Thunderbird symbols found throughout literature. He traced the Thunderbird origins back to Tiahuanaco and the Incan empire, concentrating on the relationship between the Feathered Serpent and Thunderbird motifs in all native cultures. To celebrate Quetzalcoatl's return, Iron Thunderhorse was guided in the construction of a remarkable mask of Kukulcan.

This paper mache mask was sent to the XAT Medicine Society in Nashville, Tennessee for use in its first ceremony celebrating Harmonic Convergence on August 16-17, 1987. From there, the mask was sent to the Algonquin Medicine Society in Vermont, where the second ceremony was conducted. It then traveled to Brown Bear Mallot, and the Alaskan Medicine Circle held the third celebration on Sheep Mountain, a power spot in the Alaskan north country. The mask was finally sent to the Metis Medicine Circle in California for the fourth ceremony.

"Thus," says Iron Thunderhorse, "the mask of Kukulcan traveled counterclockwise—like the Heyoka—activating the power of the Feathered Serpent nations. The new clans, as prophesied, and all sacred directions of Turtle Island, will become a circle of one nation awakened to the new dawn."

Only within the last several centuries has humanity severed its ties with the cycles of nature through mass migration to the cities. Only in relatively recent years has humanity lost touch with the elements that respond directly to shifting natural forces. Still, the ancient cycles and rhythms of time are woven throughout our consciousness.

A good example of this is the concept of reincarnation. The belief in reincarnation undoubtedly gained impetus from the simple observation over countless generations that the nature of life on Earth is cyclical—a wheel of birth and rebirth, just as surely as spring follows winter. The evidence was observed daily: a new moon replacing the old; the night yielding to the birth of a new dawn, even the sun being resurrected above the morning horizon. But this seemingly irreversible, rhythmical "passage" of time was in need of a practical record-keeping process. This came about in the form of ancient calendars, which received added significance through religion.

Besides the Mayan Tzolkin, one of the most widely studied of these calendars is the impressive structure of Stonehenge, in England. It appears that Stonehenge's three-phase construction timetable spanned 900 years, from 2600 B.C.

to 1700 B.C. The feat of building Stonehenge and the associated megalithic observatories has been called the technological equivalent of landing a man on the moon and returning him safely back to Earth.

There are differences of opinion today between astronomers and archaeologists as to the purpose and function behind some of the not-so-obvious properties of Stonehenge, especially the ring of 56 marker holes that form an outer circumference around the complex of stones.

The renowned astronomer Fred Hoyle has one insightful speculation on the Stonehenge circle. He suggested that, by moving two marker stones around it at different but appropriate rates, the circle was used to predict when the sun and moon would be close enough together for eclipses to occur. One stone, representing the sun's path, must be moved two places every 13 days, taking 364 days for a full circle. Hoyle thought that midsummer and midwinter calibrations were necessary so that the year would never be more than half a day off from 365 days. The stone marking the moon's 27.3-day orbit had to be moved two spaces every day. Adjustments to this lunar stone could be made every new and full moon. The Stonehenge circle, in Hoyle's view, is a fine working model of the ecliptic—the plane in which the planets orbit the sun.

One more factor that requires consideration is the movement of planetary bodies above and below the ecliptic. (Because of such movement, eclipses do not occur monthly, but only at specific times during the year.) By using a third stone in the circle and moving it three holes each year, even eclipses can be predicted when all three stones are aligned properly.

The question then arises: How did Stone Age people record the passage of thirteen days to coordinate the movement of these stone counters with the proper rhythm? Again, Hoyle provides an answer. He explains that in a circle subdivided into thirteen parts, and with a stone to move one place each day, one could keep track by moving the principal markers in the large circle each time one of the 56 small circles, or hole markers, has a stone in position 1 or position 7.

But the coincidences and similarities associated with the Stonehenge megalithic features and the Mayan Tzolkin matrix demand more than casual investigation. The significant numbers at Stonehenge are one, seven, and thirteen. These are the same numbers of importance for the Tzolkin, where the number one signifies unity, the number seven represents the mystical center, and the number thirteen refers to the movement of all things. According to José Argüelles in *The Mayan Factor*, the numbers seven and thirteen:

> . . .are the key numbers in the Mayan matrix. . . .Taken as a grand calendar, the Tzolkin describes the Mayan Great Cycle, or Hologram of Time. . . .In speaking of the Great Cycle, the word calendar should be

taken advisedly. Hologram of Time is much more in keeping with the Mayan perspective. That is, just as the Tzolkin is the Universal Harmonic Module accommodating all permutations of movement and measure, so the Great Cycle should be understood as the hologram of civilizational possibility, providing the harmonic calibrations that link terrestrial evolutionary process with the galactic program.

According to Argüelles, there is no escaping the cyclical concept of time—even on a galactic scale. But which of the cycles contains the greatest significance to us? Using relative comparisons, the galactic synchronization suggested by Argüelles dwarfs any other approach. But when we consider absolute semblances, is not the cycle of spiritual birth and rebirth of equal, or perhaps even greater, significance for us?

The Mayan sacred books, the *Chilam Balam of Chumayel*, affirm a monotheistic doctrine, a great deity with a timeless quality. They also verify the cyclical concept embodied within the Mayan calendar. A Mayan Nahua chanting poem speaks of the east as "the place where the light emerges"; south is called "the place where death comes"; west is referred to as "the region of the holy seed ground"; and north is "the land of thorns." In this poem, one can see reference to the perpetual recreation of life. The seed is ground in the west, and the seeds of revival are planted with the light from the setting sun. Rebirth takes place when dawn surfaces in the east.

Western society continues to see "yesterday, today, and tomorrow" as progressing in a single, one-dimensional, unidirectional line. This concept of time implies a horizontal structure to the universe and reality. The shamanic peoples' perception of time was ever-changing, possessing both eternal and vertical, non-linear concepts. The Indian concept of time progresses without the need for engagements with the future. The concepts of "future" and "past" remained an extraordinary enigma to the Indian. The concept of cyclical time will remain equally puzzling and inferior to Western society so long as it perceives from an ethnocentric position, using itself as the standard by which all things are to be measured.

No doubt the most prominent symbol depicting human-beast relationships and time in pre-Columbian history was the snake or serpent. The serpent, ordained to dwell on the Earth and subject to the forces governing its earthly existence, eventually found liberation through union with the quetzal bird—the treetop forest dweller who was capable of transcending the limitations of time and space. So too can each one of us.

Chapter Six

MOTHER EARTH & FATHER SKY MYSTERIES

PART I
Iron Thunderhorse

The symbol of the Horned Serpent is an ancient composite motif for the mysteries of Earth power or geomancy, while the symbol of the Feathered Serpent is an ancient composite motif for the mysteries of sky power or astromancy. Our ancestors knew that the cycles and motions of the planets exerted an influence on the cycles and motions of planet Earth.

Many of the mysteries associated with the shamanic arts of geomancy and astromancy have been lost, dying with the elders who guarded and practiced them. However, traces of these arts are still visible to those who listen to the voices of the Earth spirits in the rocks, trees, ancient power spots, and all of nature—especially where shamanic people once lived and worshipped. These places talk to me and have been my most trusted and faithful teachers. When I need answers, the ancient spirits whisper to me their mysteries.

Our ancestors believed we came from the stars and will return there. Legends of Star Man, Star Woman, Star Husband, and Star Boy are widely known in Native American tribes. The Algonquin family of nations was known as the Great Star Nation, after the star Sirius B, which has been called the Dog Star. The Algonquins knew it as the Wolf Star. The Pleiades is another kindred constellation. The Passamaquoddy were known as the People of the Dawn Star, and the Skidii Pawnees' entire culture revolved around star lore.

Similar teachings of migrations from other lands to Turtle Island come from various locations in the Pacific and Atlantic, during pre-glacial flooding periods. The teachings also say that, at one time, the Earth was inhabited by one people not yet divided. These people have sometimes been referred to in stereotypical terms, such as "pagans" or "barbarians."

Lineages of the Earth Mother: Nature's Guardian

Archaeological evidence of the past few decades overwhelmingly contradicts the contemporary assumption that eastern Mediterranean civilizations were dominated by male gods from early prehistoric times. The oldest traces of ceremonial artifacts are invariably female.

As archaeological discoveries continue to reveal, the Mother Goddess represented the most ancient spiritual practice that had definite connections to fertility and the life-creating forces of nature.

The oldest figurine of the Mother Goddess, discovered in Austria, dates back to approximately 30,000 B.C. (Figure 6-1). Another figurine from Czechoslovakia has been dated at 20,000 B.C. (Figure 6-2). On the island of Malta, artifacts of the Mother Goddess date back to the Neolithic Period, between 4,200 and 2,000 B.C. These figurines show the Mother Goddess with large breasts and other over-exaggerated features that signify her as the nurturer and the bounty of generous provisions.

In many areas, the Minoan Earth Goddess is shown with bare breasts (the nurturer) and holding coiled serpents in each hand. Since early recorded history, the serpent has been associated with healing and with the cycles of nature and the moon. The symbol of the snake shedding its skin is an allusion to the

Figure 6-1. *Drawing of Mother Earth Goddess figurine, Australia, dated approximately 30,000 B.C.*

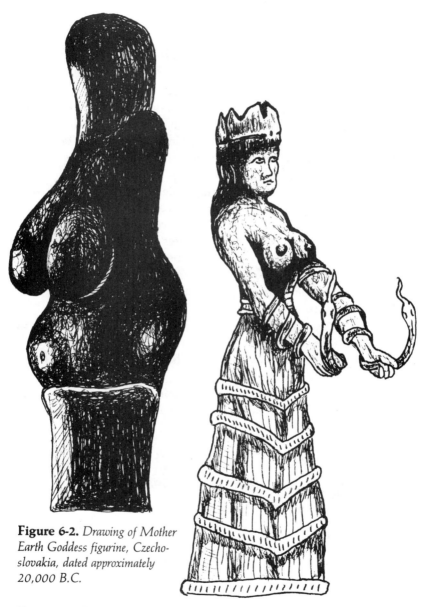

Figure 6-2. *Drawing of Mother Earth Goddess figurine, Czechoslovakia, dated approximately 20,000 B.C.*

Figure 6-3. *Drawing of Earth Mother Goddess with bared breasts, holding two snakes. From figurine found at Knossos, isle of Crete.*

shedding of the uterine lining during the woman's moon-time cycle. It is also a psychophysiological re-birth process imitated by the Earth Mother, as the "fertility lining" of Mother Earth's womb is shed at the solstices and equinoxes.

The Labyrinth: The Mother Earth Symbol

The 1901 archaeological study led by Sir Arthur Evans at the palace of Knossos on Crete noted that the palace itself represented a pattern of the mythical Cretan labyrinth. Here, the Mother Goddess of nature reigned supreme (Figure 6-3). On the isle of Malta, the hypogeum ("under the earth") alludes to a subterranean labyrinth. Early Neolithic dwellings were first built below ground out of massive stone. These were the sacred temples and shrines of the Earth Mother, who is nature herself.

An aerial view of the prehistoric ruins at Mnajdra on the Isle of Malta reveals a striking design of intersecting circles in a maze-like effect that was partially above and partially below ground (Figure 6-4). The same view of a prehistoric dwelling on the Canary islands shows striking parallels (Figure 6-5). Similar dwellings have been uncovered in Jordan and Zimbabwe, in Africa.

When viewing these two examples, one recognizes their similarity to the many stone cliff dwellings of the early Anasazi and to the Native American pueblos of the Southwest (Figure 6-6).

The etymology of the word "kiva," or the ancient pit houses of the Southwestern pueblos, reveals that this word means "old house," and some observers believe these underground dwellings may have been the original houses of indigenous Americans of the Southwest.

The people of Easter island have subterranean places of worship where they believe the spirits of their ancestors dwell. In these places the people keep

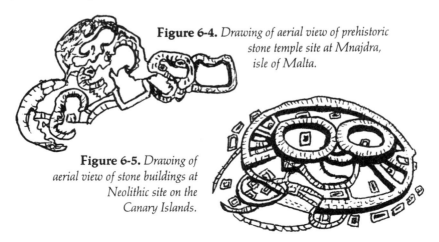

Figure 6-4. *Drawing of aerial view of prehistoric stone temple site at Mnajdra, isle of Malta.*

Figure 6-5. *Drawing of aerial view of stone buildings at Neolithic site on the Canary Islands.*

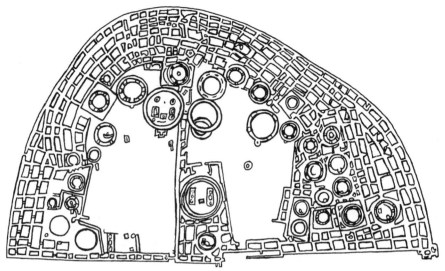

Figure 6-6. *Drawing of aerial view of Pueblo Bonito, Chaco Canyon, New Mexico.*

ancient artifacts. As Thor Heyerdahl's expeditions speculated, these locations may also have served originally as dwellings.

In Polynesian island folklore, there are male and female teachers who pass along original earthly knowledge. The esoteric name for this knowledge means "cave-of-many outlets."

Aztec and Mayan legends relate that the ancient ancestors came from the original seven caves called Chicomoztoc, also known as Aztlán. The legends of the Melanesian island chain speak of ancient ceremonies coinciding with the harvest season when spirits of the ancestors come from underground to visit the villages. This is unquestionably similar to the ceremonies of the Hopi Kachinas—ancestral spirits who return each year from their mountain cave homes to bring fertility back to the tribe.

Frank Waters' classic study, *The Book of the Hopi,* noted a significant relationship between the legends of emergence and the Mother Earth symbol (Figure 6-7). Waters states that there are six such symbols of ancient origin—one circle and five squares ranging from four to six inches in diameter. Carved on rocks and wood, these symbols are used in the kiva during Wuwuchim ceremonies at the Hopi village of Walpi.

The square-shaped symbol is commonly referred to as T'apu'at, which means "Mother and Child" and represents spiritual rebirth from one world into another. The circle symbolizes the Sky Father, the giver of life, and the universal

Figure 6-7. *Hopi Mother Earth symbols. Facsimile drawings from* Book of the Hopi, *by Frank Waters. New York: Penguin Books, 1984.*

pattern of creation which flows to the four cardinal directions. To follow this natural order is to obtain a spiritual balance or rebirth.

The aboriginal Aranda tribe of northern Australia participate in a cere-mony, conducted by their shaman, around a ground painting called *ilbantera.* This painting consists of a series of light and dark concentric circles and is their "place of emergence." The Aranda believe that all life emanated from this place. To the Australian aborigines, the place of emergence is the entryway to the "Other World": the womb of Mother Earth from which all the other earth spirits were born.

In the last decade, a sacred place of the Juaneno Indians at Long Beach, California, on Rancho Los Alamitos, was saved from possible destruction. This ancient rock altar and earth pit at Dana Point was the site of ancient puberty ceremonies where young women enacted the mysteries of the Earth Mother as life-giver and nurturer (Figure 6-8).

The Native American tribes have a female goddess who personifies the attributes of Mother Nature in her changing role associated with the seasons. She is known to the Navajo as Estsanatlehi, the Woman Who Changes. She is wife to the Sun Father and never remains in one condition, and is thus a proper matron for the fertility cycle.

Figure 6-9 depicts the Sleeping Earth Mother Goddess, found on the Isle of Malta. Several observers have expressed the opinion that the presence of the

Figure 6-8. *In many Native American puberty ceremonies, the girl lay in a pit dug just below the surface. Herbs and incense were placed over her body, and she was heated underneath by hot rocks.*

Figure 6-9. *Drawing of Sleeping Earth Mother figurine found on the isle of Malta, from the Neolithic Period.*

Earth Mother Goddess may have been indicative of a dream cult. It is probably more accurate to understand the sleeping mother figurine in her role as Changing Mother. In the winter she and her mate, Father Sun, hibernate. This is the period when solar and lunar powers are rejuvenated. Changing Earth Mother is a reflection of Grandmother Moon, whose cycles wax and wane, controlling the growth of crops and the tides. The serpents carried by the Earth Mother are symbolic of the tides, the currents and healing/rejuvenating power. The Aztec Earth Mother also personifies these attributes (Figure 6-10).

Lineages of the Sky Father: Celestial Guardian

Many of the Indian nations in the Americas have legends and ceremonies relating to the sun. The Zuni *pe'kwin*, or sun priest, the Chumash sun shrine and *kakunupmawa* ceremony, and the Natchez sun chief are all evidence of this time-honored tradition. Many chiefs considered themselves to be the "son of the sun." This belief dates back to early Incan influence and perhaps even beyond. However, the Incan philosophy presents a very good point of reference for the deeply rooted metaphysical principles that lie at the core of shamanic tradition.

The Incas built their sacred capital city at Cuzco. In the Quechuan dialect, this word means "navel of the world." Rapa Nui, the native name for Easter Island, also carries the same translation. The Sapa Inca, or supreme Inca ruler, personified the "son of the sun." The entire Incan empire was called Tahuantinsuya, the Land of Four Quarters.

The four geographic divisions were maintained by four *apus*, or prefects. These were chief advisors to the Sapa Inca. Each one presided over one of the

Figure 6-10. *Drawing of stone sculpture of the Aztec goddess, Coatlicue, also known as Mother of the Moon. This figure includes two snakes with human hearts, hands, and skull—all important aspects of the Aztec religion.*

four great provinces—Antisuyu, Chinchaysuyu, Cuntisuyu, and Collasuyu—and the four provinces were oriented at the four cardinal points of the city.

The center of the city fed the social and religious order though lines of kinship. A system of connecting links, also known as *ceques*, functioned as royal lineage to the great "sun." On these long, straight lines were placed *huacas*—the sacred shrines.

The entire system of *huacas* constituted a sacred solar and lunar calendar. A schematic diagram by Gary Vescelius, an Incan scholar, illustrates the intricacies of the calendrics of this system. Each shrine corresponds to the waxing and waning cycles of the moon as it also coincides with the solar cycle (Figure 6-11).

Astronomer Dr. R.T. Zuidema researched this system in depth and discovered that, according to old historical accounts, there were about 328 *huacas*. He calculates that this figure represented the time it took the moon to complete twelve circuits in the solar year. The thirteenth moon represents the beginning of a new solar year. One 1534 account he studied mentions that the Sapa Inca divided the population of Cuzco into twelve key groups and assigned each of them the name of the month and the duties related to the year's progress through the calendar. Each moon cycle is 27⅓ days long; 12 x 27⅓ equals 328—the number of huacas in the Incan empire's domain.

Inti Raymi

Each year a special ceremony took place in which the Incas celebrated the sun's life-giving force interacting with the beginning of the seasonal fertility cycle controlled by the moon goddess. This was called Inti Raymi, the "feast of the sun," and was celebrated each year during the Moon of Hard Earth (Cusqui Quilla) in June. (Because it is south of the equator, Peru's winter solstice occurs in June rather than December.)

At the proper time, a calculation was made whereby the sun could be viewed from the vantage points of certain towers as it drew near. Everyone fasted for the purification that was necessary to bring about a proper renewal.

Chicha, a sacred beer made from fermented corn, was drunk by the Sapa Inca, who passed the refreshment on to the precepts. The Sapa Inca then went to the famous Coricancha—the "Temple of the Sun"—where he sat in one of

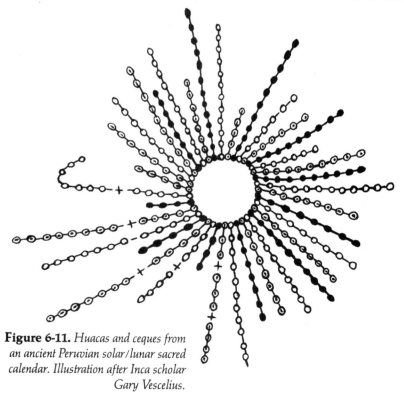

Figure 6-11. *Huacas and ceques from an ancient Peruvian solar/lunar sacred calendar. Illustration after Inca scholar Gary Vescelius.*

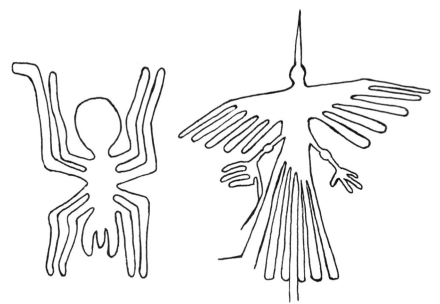

Figure 6-12. *Spider and bird motifs. Facsimile drawings of aerial views of the Nazca lines, Peru.*

two benchways to await the first rays of the sun's new year. Thus, a symbolic ray of life flowed from the sun to the royal family on Earth.

Interestingly, the Incas were noted for their almost unbelievable agricultural feats. Their knowledge and wisdom of the seasonal fertility cycles were unparalleled.

The Nagual Lines

A study of Figure 6-11 reveals the abstract pattern of the sun with its rays spreading out over the entire Incan empire. The famous desert drawings seen from the air at Nazca, Peru also reveal many patterns (Figure 6-12). These lines are associated with certain constellations. In most cases, they are known as *nagual* lines.

The concept of the *nagual* is deeply rooted in Mesoamerican folklore. A *nagual* is a kind of alter ego. It is believed that when a baby is born, it has a companion spirit in animal form. The child and its *nagual* animal spirit are so closely linked that if one becomes ill or dies, the other will come to the same fate.

Among the Maya, the *tonalpouque*, or astrological diviner, would cast a newborn child's horoscope to determine its name and destiny. The *tonalamatl* were hand-illustrated books that set out the basic auguries of each day of the sacred calendar so that parents might consult it and determine whether or not

Figure 6-13. *Drawing of totem pole from the Northwest Coast region of North America.*

a child's birth date held positive or negative influences.

To determine a child's true guardian spirit, the father would sprinkle ashes on the ground at night near the newborn baby. He would then examine the ground on the following morning and observe what animal tracks were visible. Thus, he identified the child's *nagual*.

Various nations and cultures also became associated with certain animals to represent the people as a whole. In modern society, this term is referred to as totemism. In the Algonquin Indian dialect, it means "my kin" (*nto'te•m*). The totem concept associates a clan or gens group with an ancestor—usually an animal or star—as its protector or guardian spirit.

In essence, then, nagualism and totemism are similar concepts. The totem poles of various tribes identified clan lineage with ancestral guardian spirit animals. Parts of totem poles also identified status and achievements, as well as various folk tales (Figure 6-13).

In areas where good carving trees were scarce, totems were honored by building large earth mounds in the shape of the clan's animal totem. This practice can be observed in various forms all over the Americas. Many legends speak of the first humans, or ancestors, as giants who lived with giant animals.

The Lakota nation has a system of lineages called the *tiospaye*. Hereditary patriarchial leaders kept their lineages whole through relations and marriages designated according to heredity. Ron Goodman's publication, *Ethnoastronomy of the Lakota*, explains that the Lakota used the constellations both as a calendar and as a map. The stars pointed to particular places where the Lakota were to gather and make camp at certain times. The Akicita Warrior Society was responsible for this precise designation. Each year the seven tribal bands of the Lakota camped together at a council meeting. Each camp's position imitated one of the seven stars in the Pleiades cluster, believing that this constellation was their true home in the stars.

Boundaries & Lineage

Just as our four-legged relatives mark their boundaries, we humans also identify and mark our territories. In Mexico, archaeologists have uncovered over one dozen "colossal heads" of sculpted stone, ranging in height from over four feet to more than nine feet. These sculpted heads have been found at the Olmec centers of San Lorenzo, La Venta, Tres Zapotes, and Cerro de las Mesas.

The heads all have similar features, such as slanting, puffed eyes, obese facial features, thick-lipped mouths with downturned corners (possibly to indicate a baby's cry), prominent jawlines, and heavy necks. Ignacio Bernal, a leading Mexican scholar on indigenous cultures, reveals that these distinct features in Olmec art depict the combined features of a baby and a jaguar.

Figure 6-14. *Facsimile drawing of Olmec colossal head, from Monument 1 at San Lorenzo, Honduras.*

The colossal Olmec heads are indeed a combination of jaguar and baby features. But this concept goes beyond an aesthetic ideal. Earlier, we discussed the concept of the *nagual* and of a baby having an animal guardian soul; however, an entire people could also have a tribal guardian. In Mesoamerica, the jaguar was the personification of the rainforest jungles. It was also a symbol for the shamanic priesthood. The eighteen famous books known collectively as *Chilam Balam* were the sacred prophecies of this priesthood. *Chilam* means "prophet" and *balam* translates as "jaguar." The Olmec people adopted the jaguar as their totem, and the giant heads indicated the tribal *nagual*: half jaguar, half human. This medicine was their protection from harm.

It appears that these giant stones, then, were boundary markers, similar to totem poles, identifying the ancient clan of the jaguar *nagual* (Figure 6-14). These totems and boundary markers may have also been positioned as power spots to further enhance the distribution of geological currents in the earth. This systematic practice is referred to as geomancy.

Archaeoastronomy: Earth Meets Sky

The ancient ceremonial centers were places of power—places that very possibly tapped into geological features that accumulate energy. The Chinese form of geomancy is called *feng-shui*, meaning "wind and water." Wind is active and water is passive, the yin and yang of nature. One can surmise that a similar form of geomancy was performed by natives in the Americas. A close Cherokee brother of mine is a well-known rainmaker who also practices dowsing, a form of geomancy that has been passed down to him through the generations.

Cuzco, the legendary location of the center of the Incan empire, reveals a form of geomantic divination. According to legend, the first "son of the sun" drove a rod of gold into the Earth where two rivers met. The rod vanished, and at this spot Manco Capac built the Coricancha.

The Incan capital is unique for yet another reason. Dr. E.C. Krupp, an astronomer, explains that the alignment of these two rivers reflects the celestial alignment of the Milky Way. Because the axis of the Milky Way is skewed relative to the Earth's rotation, its orientation shifts; hence, it seems to run in two criss-crossed intersections about twelve hours apart. (It is interesting to note that in the Andes, the Milky Way is known by several names: Spirit Trail, Trail of Flowers, and River of Spirits.)

The Hopi rely on the zenith and the nadir to position their kivas and to coordinate their important ceremonies. The spiritual leaders know when to begin certain prayers and songs by looking directly up through the kiva skylight and recognizing the passage of certain stars and constellations. The Navajo also recorded these in their sand paintings in order to observe the positions of certain stars as a signal for conducting the proper ceremonies.

Conclusion

Today, our land is being mined, stripped of its trees, and polluted with toxins and nuclear waste. Our rivers are full of human-made chemicals. The air is polluted with smog. Acid rain and a fractured ozone layer threaten our existence and the well-being of the planet. All of these ills are attributed to the "greedy ones," as the prophecies have foretold. But prophecy also speaks of a time when the children of the greedy ones would come to the shamanic people for help. This time is now upon us.

The prophecies reveal that when Earth and sky meet, this land once more will become a living paradise. In other words, when we begin to bring back the ancient ways of Earth and sky (geomancy and astromancy) and the ways of the shamanic peoples, there will be no need for differences. Our diversity will be channeled into the Tree of Life and Knowledge, bringing balance and harmony back to the world. Unborn generations depend on this. Earth and sky are one. They are our providers.

The greedy ones who are destroying the world today use money and force to take what they want from the land. They do not ask our primal ancestors. But there will come a day when all the dollars and weapons on the Earth Mother's skin will not be enough to stop the chain reaction that has begun to take place. Every empire reaches its zenith, then perishes, just as the shooting star drops from the sky. To live as true human beings means to exist in harmony with Mother Earth and Father Sky and all our relations—from Grandfather Rock on the Earth to Grandmother Moon in the heavens. Let us all pray and work together for balance. The end of the era of greed and the beginning of the era of harmony are now on the horizon.

PART II
Donn Le Vie, Jr.

Investigating the meaning of symbols requires a differentiation between symbols of a "cultural" origin and those of more "natural" origins. Cultural symbols link a particular society with its eternal truths. Such symbols are often associated with religious denominations, ideologies, and philosophies. For the most part, cultural symbols are the products of conscious development, and have undergone numerous changes throughout history. As a result, their collective images become the accepted property of technological societies.

On the other hand, natural symbols are a by-product of the psyche, representing a variety of themes that relate to essential archetypal images. Symbols are the language of the unconscious. Dreams, with their rich symbolism, have free reign over the unlimited expanse of the unconscious. It was Jung's opinion that the unconscious serves the conscious mind as a great guide, friend, and advisor.

As a symbol, the Earth Mother, or Great Mother, as she is sometimes called, has many characteristics that vary in definition and form. The most obvious include those of a personal, familial kind: mother, grandmother, and so on; and secondarily, any women with whom one has a relationship. Less obvious examples include figurative mothers, such as those found in mythology and legend, and the figurative mothers who awaken marvel and devotion within: a country (". . . stand beside her and guide her. . ."); the universe and nature (Mother Nature); the Earth (Mother Earth), oceans, mountains, and forests. The Earth Mother archetype, however, is most often associated with fertility.

The Earth Mother archetype can carry negative as well as positive connotations. For example, Quetzalcoatl succumbed to the evil power of the Great Mother when he failed to resist the temptations of the flesh. Early primordial versions of the legend reveal that demons brought Quetzalcoatl a "harlot" named Xochiquetzal, who later announced herself to be none other than the goddess of harlots, equivalent to the Great Mother. In this legend, the seduced Quetzalcoatl becomes Xochopilli, the prince of flowers. The metaphor expresses Quetzalcoatl's regression, his new identity as the son and lover of the Mother Goddess. Realizing his disgrace, Quetzalcoatl laments:

> Our Mother
> The goddess with the mantle of snakes,
> Is taking me with her
> As her child.
> I weep.

In one form or another, the creative spark of human spirit that always seeks expression lies harbored in the symbolic imagery of the unconscious. And what of creativity—where does it originate? Can we correlate it with the intuitive flash of insight that suddenly "appears" in the conscious mind? Are highly creative people more receptive to or more in touch with the symbolic imagery of their unconscious than others?

The great French mathematician Poincare credited several mathematical insights to sudden pictorial "revelations" that emerged from his unconscious. The nineteenth-century German chemist Kekule, searching for the molecular structure of the hydrocarbon benzene, dreamed of a snake biting its own tail— the *ouroboros* symbol. He interpreted the dream to mean that the symbol for the benzene molecule was a closed carbon ring.

Symbols serve as triggers for the mind, helping it to contend with or assimilate images that agitate, stimulate, inspire or evoke something beyond the obvious. They influence, to greater or lesser degrees, the processes of intuition, emotion, and perception. This is exemplified in Plato's *Republic*, in which Socrates is guided by Plato to propose specific instructions to rulers, soldiers, and all humankind:

> They are to be told that their youth was a dream, and the education and training which they received from us, an appearance only; in reality during all that time they were being formed and fed in the womb of the

earth, where they themselves and their arms and appurtenances were man-ufactured; when they were completed, the earth, their mother, sent them up, and so, their country being their mother and also their nurse, they are bound to advise for her good and to defend her against attacks, and her citizens they are to regard as children of the earth and their own brothers.

Connection to the Earth Mother is an ancient but basic relationship we all share with this fragile planet. Few cultures experience this relationship as deeply as the Native Americans. Mystical ecology, Hopi metaphysics, geomancy, restoration, and preservation are just a few solutions they offer to help heal our ailing Earth Mother.

These are solutions of the present — action that can be taken today. But what of tomorrow and the days after that? How do we assure that nature's sacred balance — the connectedness of all things — can be safely maintained in the future? Perhaps the ancient wisdom excerpted from a speech given by Chief Seattle more than 125 years ago provides a clue:

You must teach your children that the ground beneath their feet is the ashes of our grandfathers. So that they will respect the land, tell your chil-dren that the earth is rich with the lives of our kin. Teach your children what we have taught our children, that the earth is our mother. Whatever befalls the earth befalls the sons of the earth. If men spit upon the land, they spit upon themselves.

Form and energy, matter and spirit. In themselves, matter and spirit are indifferent; both are capable of good or evil. As concepts, both are relative; however, they also represent genuine opposites that make up portions of the physical and psychic universes. Existence of any kind demands their presence. Even in their most absolute extremes, one cannot exist without the other. This truth is manifested in the yin and the yang. The yin embraces within itself the potential of the yang, and vice versa. Matter incorporates the seed of spirit, and spirit the seed of matter. Birth and rebirth, the great cycle continues.

Chapter Seven

THE HIDDEN LANGUAGE OF SHAMANISM

PART I
Iron Thunderhorse

Many scholars have declared that native shamanic nations of pre-Columbian America had no written language. This is a monumental error. In fact, there existed a body of shamanic languages that was practically universal, ingeniously pieced together like an interlocking mosaic. It could be found in beaded pieces of clothing; on painted shields, robes, tipis, and parfleches; proudly applied in the form of body paint; on cliff and cave walls and bones of ages past; and on feathers, twigs, stones, and artifacts. In these places we find the hidden languages of shamanism.

All languages use similar modes of communication which are unique to the human species. Early humans spoke in guttural grunts and used simple gestures. To clarify many of their observations, simple pictographs were developed. As time progressed, and the prehistoric mind developed a deeper understanding of the world, these pictographs became more complicated and abstract. Picture symbols evolved into ideograms, emerging from mere objects into expressions of complete ideas and abstract concepts. Eventually, an exalted form of language developed called hieroglyphics, or "sacred writings." These writings embodied the expression of long-standing beliefs, practices, mythologies, legends, and histories—all in highly evolved metaphysical formulae that took centuries to develop.

Gestures & Signs

Since prehistoric times, gestures have been used as a means of communication between people and cultures. Gestures are a type of body language used by both humans and animals.

Anthropologists have scrutinized the structure of the various forms of communication among present-day shamanic tribes and have confirmed the universality of many forms of gestures. In the Native American nations, these gestures became a means of communication between tribes with different dialects or languages. Sign language as a means of intertribal communication developed right along with spoken languages, and it was just as sophisticated.

Communication of ideas relied on two separate systems of transmission: sight and sound. If the sounds were not understood, a gesture or sign was used to communicate the message. If the sign or gesture was not understood, a picture, symbol, or pictograph was used to convey the intended meaning (Figure 7-1).

The Universality of Pictographic Symbols

Lavan Martinou, a contemporary epigrapher specializing in Native American pictographs, calls attention to the fact that many rock art scholars insist on an exclusively artistic interpretation and function for petroglyphs. The basic premise for this conclusion relies on the fact that unusual or unique symbols occur with great frequency in a particular geographic area.

There were, however, localized symbols used by certain tribes. For example, the Utes did not symbolize prayer feathers, kachinas, or other ceremonial objects that were not a part of their culture. Conversely, the Hopis *did* incorporate these symbols into their art/communication forms, for these things were indigenous to their society. In most cases, non-Hopi societies still recognized the significance of such symbols, even though they had no need to depict them.

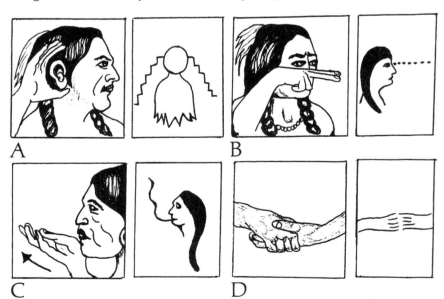

Figure 7-1. *Sign language on the left, with corresponding pictograph on the right: A) to listen; B) to see; C) to speak; D) peace.*

Figure 7-2. *A Hopi seed jar. The symbols tell of the Hopi creation myth. The center opening is the sipapu—the place of emergence. Hands reaching out from both sides indicate living things coming into the world. Below center is the vulva—the womb of Mother Earth. The lines signify the spirits of the unborn entering the world. At top center is the eye of the Great Spirit, centered in the four corners of an abstract eagle's head, with the wings of spirit on both sides. Facsimile drawing from a* National Geographic *illustration.*

Dan Lewis, an elder of the Mojave tribe, writes that the pictographic language used by Native Indian tribes was an ancient writing system used all over the Americas and, therefore, universally understood. The meaning of every mark within each pictograph was exact. The pictograph, then, was the exoteric writing system. Ideograms were more complex symbols used to illustrate the esoteric elements of culture, such as those found in legend, folklore, and mythology.

The exoteric nature of the pictograph made it the language of the masses. Conversely, the hidden knowledge incorporated in the esoteric ideogram meant that it was to be shared by the secret societies of shamans and medicine people.

Art & Craft as Language

Art in shamanic tribes served a multifold purpose. It was a visible expression of spiritual philosophies that were a way of life. Art, culture, and spirituality were not separate expressions; they were interrelated and interdependent (Figure 7-2).

A good example of this relationship can be found in bead and quill work. The wampum belts of the Algonquin and Iroquoian tribes were not used as trade items in pre-contact times. These items were ceremonial records used to

Figure 7-3. *Facsimile drawing of a beaver pelt that records the mnemonic indicators of a seventeen-year period. Each year was remembered by recording an outstanding event that occurred during a particular winter. From Iron Thunderhorse's collection of pictographic files.*

commemorate significant tribal events. Color as well as symbology was used to tell a particular story (Figure 7-3).

Buffalo robes were used to keep mnemonic records which were painted on one side. Plains tribes used pictographs to record tribal histories on clothing items and passed these items on to the keeper of tribal accounts. Oral traditions also accompanied the visual archives. These pictorial robes have sometimes erroneously been referred to as calendars, when their real purpose was to serve as a mnemonic history of the tribe (Figure 7-4).

Certain robes recorded personal histories and even served as epic autobiographies. One such account is the now-famous robe of Standing Buffalo, a

Figure 7-4. *Facsimile drawing of the George Washington belt. More than six feet long, this belt records the covenant of peace between the original thirteen colonies and the Iroquois nations. From* Akwesasne Notes, *the newspaper of the Mohawk Nation.*

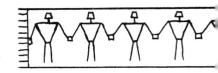

notable Sioux war chief of the middle 1800s. The war shirt of Mato Topa (Four Bears), chief of the Mandans, is another example, where details of his many exploits on the war path have been incorporated in pictograph form.

Body Paint

Originally, native tribes in the Americas painted the exposed portions of their bodies to protect themselves from the elements. The origin of the term "redskin" is derived from the early Europeans, who applied it to the Delaware Indians, an Algonquin tribe, because of their practice of wearing a vermillion-colored body paint made from berries, animal fat, and herbs.

Ceremonial body paint has been erroneously categorized as "war paint" by non-Indian accounts. Although body paint was used in war, it was also used for important ceremonies. It was a visual representation of an individual's medicine or magic (Figure 7-5).

The Language of Feathers

Feathers were also used in communication, and the manner in which they were displayed had both exoteric and esoteric significance. Single feathers, such as the coup feather, were given as a reward for certain accomplishments (Figure 7-6A). Other arrangements, such as the Indian scout headdress (Figure 7-6B), the dog soldier headdress (Figure 7-6C), and the sundance headdress (Figure 7-6D), as well as the traditional tribal chief headdress, depicted special social status.

Esoteric elements also conveyed certain exploits or feats. For instance, a warrior who had been severely wounded in battle or who had suffered much was recognized by a split feather (Figure 7-6E). A feather with a band of beads in the center signified the number of enemies slain in battle. A feather cut in a sawtooth pattern might signify the status of a medicine man (Figure 7-6F).

The Language of Blankets

The intricate designs woven into blankets also conveyed messages or stories. Navajo blankets, for example, reveal personal and tribal lineage and serve as a means of passing on tribal icons that functioned as visual prayers. The Sioux and many other tribes incorporated legends and prayers in their blankets, using certain totems, animals, and symbols for various clan lineages (Figure 7-7).

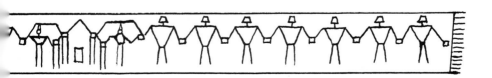

Figure 7-5. *An example of facial painting and personal symbology. This original drawing by Iron Thunderhorse depicts a personal initiation into the mysteries of the Lodge of the Wolf-Raven. The ideogram shows Iron Thunderhorse wearing a wooden wolf-raven headdress carved in the style of the tribes of the American Northwest Coast. The wolf symbolizes the teachings of Earth wisdom and the paths to knowledge, while the raven symbolizes medicine power or magic. The circles painted on the face represent the sacred hoop, cosmic consciousness, and the entrance to the heavens. The lightning bolt signifies Iron Thunderhorse's medicine visions, and the dots represent the sacred hailstones which are the marks of all Thunderbeings.*

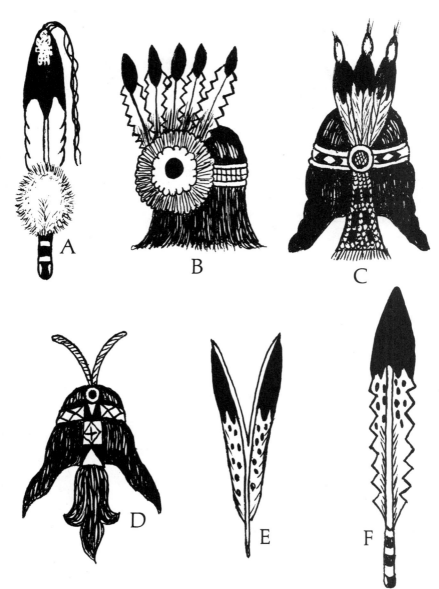

Figure 7-6. *Illustrations of the various meanings behind the wearing of feathers (see text).*

Figure 7-7. *Facsimile drawing of the Lakota Sioux symbol for the* onikare, *or sweatlodge. This and many other figures represented visual prayers and served as an abstract but powerful means of communicating culture. From Iron Thunderhorse's collection of pictographs and symbols, as given by Lakota spiritual leaders.*

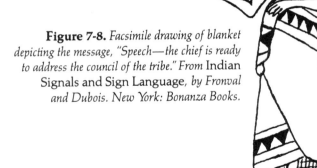

Figure 7-8. *Facsimile drawing of blanket depicting the message, "Speech—the chief is ready to address the council of the tribe." From* Indian Signals and Sign Language, *by Fronval and Dubois. New York: Bonanza Books.*

The Omaha nation developed a system of identification based on the manner in which the blanket was worn. To wrap a blanket around the body and over the left shoulder signified the ardor of youth. Draped over the left shoulder without being wrapped around the body, the blanket signified a person's readiness to run from impending danger. A blanket drawn across both shoulders with the arms hidden inside it conveyed the status of an elder. To wear a blanket over the head and shoulders, using the hands to hold the edges at the neck, signified a state of rage. Wrapping a blanket from mid-chest level to the ground, leaving both shoulders bare, was a signal that a chief or tribal orator was about to speak (Figure 7-8).

Trail Signs

When a Native American set out to hunt, gather medicine, or travel, signs were left on the trail that indicated what direction was being pursued. When entire bands or tribes were on the move, scouts were assigned the duties of choosing the best trail to the intended destination.

Natural features, such as unusual rock formations, areas with brush or other types of vegetation, and branches or notches carved into the bark of trees served as trail markers. The language of reading trail signs was an art everyone understood. A small rock placed on a larger rock meant "this is the way." A clump of tall grass, knotted as it stood leaning to the right or left meant "turn this way." A combination of objects and symbols was also used to communicate the proper direction to follow as well as more complicated messages (Figure 7-9).

Generally speaking, a tomahawk or arrow painted red signified war. A broken arrow placed across a trail and in full view was a warning not to proceed any further, with serious consequences implied. If a bundle of sticks was left piled in front of a tribal member's lodge during the night, it was a gentle reminder to make good on a debt owed.

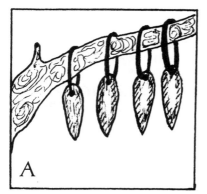
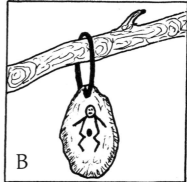

Figure 7-9. *Such signs as these combined symbols and natural elements to serve as ancient billboards. A) "The river is full of fish." B) "Our village is starving—help!"*

Indian Signals

To communicate over great distances, the Native Americans used mirrors and smoke to send signals, not unlike Morse code. With smoke signals, one cloud meant "caution," two clouds revealed that "all is well," and three clouds translated as "help."

Figure 7-10. *Facsimile drawing of a pictograph showing the Sioux way of saying, "Brave takes prisoner."* From Indian Signals and Sign Language, *by Fronval and Dubois.* New York: Bonanza Books.

The drum was a means of communication similar to the modern walkie-talkie. It usually announced great events or the onset of war.

Arrows were used to send messages over great distances. Blazing arrows shot high in the night sky from a cliff or mesa contained their own significant meanings, often determined by the particular height or trajectory of the arrow.

The Metaphysics of Written Languages in the Native Americas

History reveals that systems of written language develop in much the same way and contain universal elements. Among Native Americans, each sign represented a word, idea, or action, much like the Chinese, Korean, and Japanese written languages. Petroglyphs are carvings inscribed on rock surfaces and can be either pictographic or ideographic. Pictographic glyphs represented the language of everyday events (Figure 7-10). Ideographic glyph writings became the written language of the shaman. Abstract or symbolic glyphs represented esoteric or metaphysical concepts.

Some homonyms were used in Mayan and Aztec hieroglyphic writing. Homonyms are words with the same sound but with different meanings, such as those found in rebus writing (Figure 7-11).

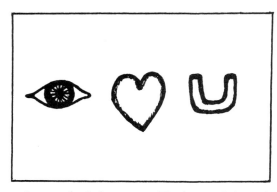

Figure 7-11. *An example of rebus writing. The three symbols together represent the message, "I love you."*

Figure 7-12. *Facsimile drawing of a pictograph attributed to the Delaware Indian creation myth, the Walum-Olum. This pictograph says, "Friendly people with great possessions in boats. Who are they?" From* America's Fascinating Indian Heritage. *Pleasantville, NY: Reader's Digest Books.*

Some American Indian ideographs indicate that hieroglyphics in North America developed to a very significant degree (Figure 7-12). Some scholars believe that the Aztec ideograms nearly, but not quite, evolved into an actual phonetic system.

William Gates, who developed an outline dictionary of Mayan glyphs, verifies that Mayan writing was originally ideographic. Many of the Mayan glyphs used for pictograph writing include associated elements. Elements added to the left of a main glyph are prefixes; those added to the right are suffixes; above the main glyph are the suprafixes; and those placed below are called subfixes. Added elements placed within the main body of a glyph are called "infixed."

Linda Schele, an art historian with the University of Texas at Austin, has made significant progress in deciphering the exoteric verbiage of the Mayan elite. Professor Michael D. Coe of Yale University suggests that as much as 85 percent of all Mayan inscriptions are now understood. As to the undeciphered hieroglyphics, these are shamanic abstractions and metaphysical concepts that science has trouble understanding.

The Mesoamerican Problematic

The fifteen percent of the inscriptions left undeciphered in Mesoamerican Indian nations are shamanic ideograms reflecting the mythology, ethos, metaphysics, ceremonies, customs, and folklore of various periods, tribes, and nations.

The ideographic inscriptions of the Mayas can be found on architectural panels, pottery, codices, and other artifacts. In other cultures, such as the Mesopotamian, Egyptian, and East Indian, very similar ideographic styles were developed. Although the symbols were not identical, similar methodologies and archetypal elements are common to all indigenous peoples' ideographic writing systems.

Egyptian hieroglyphics were highly ideographic and advanced in form. The Egyptian system was so sophisticated, in fact, that the artistic panels built into the architecture often reflected complicated geodesic formulae. This method of inscribing knowledge onto temple walls was also a common characteristic of the Mayan Classic Period.

Figure 7-13. *A) Drawing of a Chinese sculpture in the "right palm forward" pose. B) Representation of a Mayan sculpture in the "left palm forward" pose.*

The Mayan Gesture Language

We have seen in this chapter how sign language was and is closely associated with picture writing. Mesoamerican cultures, especially the Mayan, also enjoyed a very sophisticated system of sign or gesture language which enhanced their ideographic communication. This system is very similar to the Hindu dance forms known as *mudrās*.

As my own research into this area has developed, its parallels to the Hindu and Polynesian gesture systems are too striking to disregard. The following examples are just a sample of a larger, more detailed study of the Mayan gesture language which is presently in progress.

In other chapters of this book, we discussed the strong diffusion of culture that occurred along with the migrations of shamanic tribes into the Americas. Gesture language seems to have been part of this diffusion.

To begin our study of gesture language, we will compare sculptures from Buddhist and Mayan artists. The sculpture in Figure 7-13A depicts the Buddhist holy figure, Maitrey, from the seventh century. The left hand faces upward, palm out, in the *wu wei* gesture, meaning "fear not," while the right hand (now missing), faces downward with the palm forward in the *shik-yuan* gesture, signifying "the wish is granted."

In Figure 7-13B, we see the Mayan corn god, Ah-Mun, making the same gestures, but with opposite hands. In certain ancient languages, words were spoken in terms that were often reversed; however, the message remained the same. Therefore, we could interpret this Mayan sculpture as signifying, "The wish is granted, so fear not." Since Ah-Mun was the Mayan god of maize, the sacred staff of life in Mesoamerica, it is safe to assume that prayers were constantly offered to this deity for the perpetuation of the crops. The deity, then, is depicted using symbolic gesture language to acknowledge the faithfulness of the supplicant.

The Mayan stelae sculptures bearing ceremonial bar motifs generally show the hands bound as if they were shackled. The hands, when bound, are all in similar positions, with the thumb and forefinger touching. In the Hindu dance gestures known as *mudrās*, this position is known as the Padmakosa hand—the lotus form. The Hawaiian hula dance hand gestures have similar positions.

The Sacred Dance Gestures

In the Hindu culture there exists a system of sacred dance. The Natya Shastra is the most comprehensive text on this subject, containing 37 chapters. These dances involve tales of gods and goddesses and generally relate to the Vedic scriptures, which are approximately 4,400 years old.

In the Hindu tradition, dance was regarded as a panacea for all the ills and woes of the world. Those who worshipped god through dance were assured of redemption. The *mudrās* and *hasta-mudrās* are stylized hand gestures that allow the dancer to express any object, event, or emotion. The gestures are never used in isolation from the rest of the body, but they are the main attraction and the main message.

The Natya Shastra involves 31 single-hand poses and 27 combined-hand gestures. Also used in these dance forms are *navarasas*, nine basic emotions or sentiments expressed with facial gestures. These are love, valor, compassion, contempt, wonder, fear, repulsion, wrath, and peace. (We have already noted that the Mayans had similar expressions.)

Figure 7-14.
*Facsimile drawing of
Mayan sculptured panel
at Palenque, Mexico.*

Costumes were an important part of the Hindu dance called *aharya*. Certain Mayan paintings, such as the famous murals of Room 1 at Bonampak, Mexico, exhibit strong resemblances to these costumes. These murals display definite gesture language, in what appears to be a concerted contemplation of events. Mayan paintings at Uaxactun, pottery paintings from the Yucatan, as well as the codices, also exhibit a definite form of gesture language.

There is also a Hindu form of seated dance. In the Balinese culture, this is called *rabyar*. The dancer never rises from the floor or from a seated position on a raised platform. This dance uses the torso, arms, hands, facial expressions, and body movement. The Hindu form includes several varieties of *bhangas*, or bends of the body from the vertical: *abhanga* (slightly bent); *samabhanga* (equally bent); *atibhanga* (greatly bent); and *tribhanga* (thrice bent). Each *bhanga* holds special meaning.

With these basic descriptions in mind, note the Mayan deity in Figure 7-14 from a sculptured panel at Palenque, Mexico. In this great panel, we see a figure seated on a platform, arms facing forward and behind the body, with hands in different gestures. The right leg is hidden behind the dais, the raised platform, and the left leg is exposed in front. A two-headed jaguar flanks the seat. As previously mentioned, the jaguar in Mesoamerica was associated with the underworld and with shaman priests. The underworld connected the shaman to the ancient teachings and to ancestry, hidden cures, and secret knowledge.

This particular sculpture is strikingly similar to Buddhist and Hindu sculptures that express various aspects of the metaphysical, including cosmology, the pantheon, and the world of esoteric mysteries.

In Buddhist belief, Manjusri was an "Adi Buddha," the personification of wisdom. He was depicted as seated on a leopard. In this Mayan sculpture, the jaguar is the wisdom of the underworld. The dual heads signify the past and future. The position of the priest's leg behind the platform is symbolic of what has already transpired, and the exposed leg is symbolic of what is yet to come. The priest gazes into the past so that the future can be met in a state of enlightened awareness. The seat itself is similar to the lotus-dais observed in many Oriental sculptures. The petals of the lotus are worked into the sculpture.

The Sacred Dance: Pantomime as Language

In Mesoamerica, supplication to the pantheon of respective periods was a way of life. Ceremonies were richly accented with sacred dances. In fact, many of the Mesoamerican sculptured panels depict the dances, ceremonies, and mythology of the shamanic people of this area.

Sacred dances are a means of expressing personal transformation—a metamorphosis expressed through pantomime which shifts the dancer from

Figure 7-15. *Facsimile drawing of Maori facial tattooing. From Iron Thunderhorse's collection of pictographic files.*

Figure 7-16. *Facsimile drawing of Mayan figures showing men's faces tattooed with jawbone designs. This was also the Polynesian symbol for the sacred "lower jaw" knowledge, and evidence suggests that this practice found its way to the Yucatan from Polynesia. Drawings from lintels at Yaxchilan, border of Guatemala and Mexico.*

the mundane world to the realm of the sacred. In Mesoamerica, there were dances for war, peace, victory, joy, rain, hunting, crops, fertility, and to show reverence for the hidden forces. From the Dance of the Condors of the Ayarachi tribe in Cuzco, Peru, to the shuffle dance of the Plains Indians; from the ancient ceremonial dances of the Hopi to contemporary "fancy" dancers, a sacred language of the spirit is unfolded.

In Japan, the term *saragaku no no* refers to the enactments of sacred mimes. A mime had five divisions of skill to master, each displaying a different psychosymbolic form of metamorphosis. Even the famous hula dances of Hawaii were not always used to entertain. The "true hulas" were given to the Hawaiian natives at the beginning of the world from the gods, Noke Akua Mai, and were regarded as a holy way of communicating with them. During this dance, the *kumu*, or hula priest, is accompanied by two groups of *ho'opa* who keep time with drums or hollowed-out logs, while the *olopa* (the performers) use hand gestures to express the sacred teachings.

Tattoos: Pattern Language

The Arioi society of Polynesia is a spiritual society that performed pantomimes of mystery plays connected with the deity, Oro. The Arioi were considered divine messengers of the gods and were arranged in seven class orders, each with its own collection of body tattoos. The higher the social status, the more elaborate the tattoos. With highest-order members, most of the body was covered with tattoos.

The Maori of New Zealand used tattoos to express and pass on tribal lineages, folklore, and culture (Figure 7-15). Tupal Kupa, one of the last Maori Arawa nobles, was a keeper of the tribes' sacred knowledge. Using his own facial tattoos as mnemonic aids, he was able to speak for many days on various aspects of culture and genealogies.

Facial and body tattooing was once very common in South America and Mexico (Figure 7-16), as well as among early mound-building cultures and in the eastern tribes of the United States. The Algonquin tribes of the Northeast and Southeast wore elaborate tattoo patterns. A close examination of the work of early European artists who captured the lifestyle of the Algonquin tribes (such as the water colors by John White, reproduced as engravings by Theodor de Bry), reveals the once-widespread use of facial and body tattooing in North America. In 1950, Thomas Hariot wrote about how the Algonquin Secotan tribe wore tattooed markings on their backs to show their geographic territory in symbolic form. For Native American tribes, tattooing was a rite of passage and was used in many initiations of personal development.

Conclusion

Modern language consists mainly of verbal speech and the written word, and is most often used to convey mundane messages. The ability to convey deep expressions of culture, spirit, ancestry, transformative experience, and rites of passage has been replaced by television and other technological inventions. Violence, hypocrisy, and stereotypes can be viewed on all major networks and in most forms of contemporary literature.

In the pre-Columbian Americas, shamanic tribes used symbols, pantomime, and art, as well as many other means to convey the meaning of their existence. It is therefore a serious mistake to conclude that Native Americans had no written language. All native tribes of shamanic origins communicated in forms that were written—in everything they experienced. However, contemporary humanity's fixation on hard science and its own superiority has created a veil that tragically separates most modern people from the rich and hidden languages of shamanism.

PART II
Donn Le Vie, Jr.

Over the centuries, Western socio-cultural influences have altered the original meanings of many words. Oftentimes, as a society violates or changes the meaning of a word, that violation becomes ingrained into the existing linguistic code.

For example, with reference to the realm of magic, two words immediately come to mind. One is the word "occult," which means "hidden" or "kept from view." Only through ignorance—perhaps by ecclesiastical design—could such a benign word become perverted with "evil" connotations.

Another word that has been much maligned is the word "mystical." Like the word "occult," "mystical" should not suggest anything strange or "of the dark side." It is a derivative of the Latin, *mysticus*, meaning "of mysteries," and is defined as "having a *spiritual* meaning or reality that is neither apparent to the senses nor obvious to the intelligence." The term "mystical" suggests a symmetry and unity to our life through which the very quality of our being is expressed.

In this chapter, Iron Thunderhorse describes the "occult" languages of shamanism, as well as the power of imagery to convey certain messages. Images on rock faces and in caves served as psychosymbolic triggering devices to spark an observer's receptivity to the message—whether that message was for healing, for a successful hunt, or for more negative purposes.

The mystic/shaman fully realizes what indispensible tools the mind and inner faculties are, and how journeys to other realities can be employed to cure or send diseases—and even to steal or retrieve souls. The Yanomamo Indians of South America, for instance, believe that the souls of young children are not firmly rooted within their bodies and that any loud crying or yelling could cause the soul to flee or be captured by a malpracticing shaman. If a child becomes seriously ill, it is the duty of the tribe's shaman to retrieve the stolen soul of that child.

Western civilization has placed too much emphasis on the rational faculties of humanity—on our left-brain nature. We are able to understand the functionality of things both great and small in and of themselves; however, we fail to integrate this knowledge into the overall scheme of existence. Science has become so restrictive today that modern humanity suffers from a type of starvation of the soul.

On a subconscious level, humanity is striving to balance its rationality with something beyond the purely scientific. To do this, we need to extract the essence that integrates us with the universal. We are not just observers, we are participants. For example, a Vivaldi violin concerto is not music by itself. The sound we hear interacts with our consciousness (via the organs in the ears) to produce what we call "music." We cannot simply "listen" to music. We become part of the music experience because our conscious mind has taken the sounds generated by the musical instruments and turned them into an experience enjoyed by our entire being. Our consciousness has extracted the essence from the sounds produced by the instruments and momentarily integrated us with the universe. We were always participants in the music, but our consciousness needed to gently remind us of our participation. In the depths of space, we can detect phenomena that occurred hundreds of millions of light years ago, but, as Einstein pointed out, our position as observers is relative. We are not on the outside looking in; each one of us has a place on the universal mandala.

Mystics from a variety of ancestral and cultural upbringings share common bonds—bonds that defy labeling. The spiritual sphere from which these people operate concerns itself with the vitalizing universe, devoid of religious rhetoric. This is one of the many reasons Native American mysticism has experienced a resurgence in recent years. It offers its followers the purity of a direct relationship with the universal mind, the Great Spirit.

Western traditional religions today have taken the concept of the soul and replaced it with the ego. Followers of charismatic and fundamentalist religious leaders expend more energy with relationships concerning these individuals then they do with the Christ-consciousness itself. As ego becomes inflated, so does the perception of personal power. The truth is that personal power is unnecessary; the mystical, transcendental experience belongs to all of us.

All too frequently—and unfortunately all too typically—Western philosophy equates mysticism with myth, and myth with fantasy. The late Joseph Campbell wrote a great deal about the metaphoric nature of the language of myth, and his writings give special consideration to the relationship between cross-cultural mythology and Jungian psychology. Campbell's book, *The Inner Reaches of Outer Space*, speaks of the transformation of human experience and vision through which mythology gravitates toward "a realization of transcendence, infinity, and abundance."

Campbell's central conviction is that the purpose of the mystic and artist is "recognizing through the metaphors an epiphany beyond words." However, the societal purpose of mythology, he says, is to enclose the mind, to fuse a local culture together by presenting images that "awaken the heart to recognitions of commonality. . . ."

One must understand that the "worlds" and "gods" so frequently mentioned in mythology and metaphysics are not literal; they are simply used as symbolic points of reference for states of being attainable by everyone. Similarly, a metaphor, when taken literally, is a lie. If one attempts to give literal meaning to a metaphor, the richness of its true meaning will escape one's grasp.

We see the dangers, then, in taking things too literally. For many years, literalism has permeated the fields of religion, anthropology, philosophy, and psychology. Most of these disciplines have made progress in the deeper understanding of humanity only by utilizing metaphor to peek through the mask of literalism.

Similarly, literal interpretations of shamanic languages, practices, and art have often prevented significant insights into the rich splendor of aboriginal existence. Only when we can capture the true essence of aboriginal language, mythology, and art through metaphor will we fully appreciate the magnitude of its mystical achievement.

Chapter Eight

THE SACRED FIRE

PART I
Iron Thunderhorse

A central theme in shamanic art is the accumulation of the Sacred Fire within. This is a metaphysical concept which includes reference to the magnetic and solar energies flowing throughout our Earth and atmosphere. But its deeper meaning relates to activation of certain perceptions within the psyche.

The indigenous nations of the Americas shared a secret doctrine of metaphysical lore which is similar to other shamanic cultures, yet which maintained unique variations. (For example, the American Indians developed their own systems of yoga and meditation.) The following diagrams demonstrate how highly advanced the natives' esoteric rites of passage once were. This is the secret, unwritten history of the Native American holy men and women—the Shining Ones.

Myths, rituals, and shamanic glyphs are primarily mnemonic aids which facilitate psychic transformation, or the passage through various stages of consciousness. The first ideogram (Figure 8-1), is a representation of a rock painting at Medicine Rapids, Saskatchewan. In this diagram we see a bear shaman with an apprentice, two vertical serpents, and a Thunderbird. The initial theme is esoteric. The bear shaman's internal state imitates the vertical serpents. Only the right hand is prominent. The tongue of the apprentice is extended. Unlike his benefactor, his internal nature is solid.

In shamanic hierarchy, the bear ally is the initiatory totem which passes on the esoteric rites. The bear spirit was thought to be able to communicate with the shaman and to instruct him or her in the ways of nature's mysteries.

The bear shaman depicted has a body which is opened up (analogous to being receptive). But here, the two vertical serpents are the clue—the real determinative of the glyph.

The dual serpent motif represents the esoteric nature of the Sacred Fire, known in other parts of the world as kundalini, chi, ki, or prana. This Fire is fun-

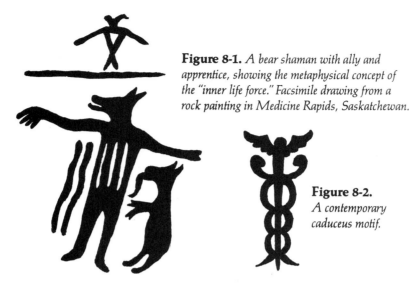

Figure 8-1. *A bear shaman with ally and apprentice, showing the metaphysical concept of the "inner life force." Facsimile drawing from a rock painting in Medicine Rapids, Saskatchewan.*

Figure 8-2. *A contemporary caduceus motif.*

damental to all shamanic tribes. It rises from the base chakra to the crown chakra at the top of the head. These serpents are bipolar manifestations of the psychic energy which animates all life. One is active, the other passive, and together they twine around the spinal column, which represents their common conduit. In Egypt and Greece, Hermes, the god of wisdom and learning, held the caduceus, a representation of a staff with two entwined snakes and two wings at the top, symbolizing this same force (Figure 8-2).

In the esoteric schools of Hindu lineage, the spine is known as the "stick of Brahma." It is composed of two etheric, winged serpents, each with five coils encircling a sacred rod. The serpents represent the active and passive energies of kundalini in the nervous system, the serpent fire. The wings signify the conscious flight into higher planes of consciousness which is achieved by the development of the Sacred Fire.

Thus, I feel this bear shaman is showing his apprentice his mastery over internal Sacred Fire. The Thunderbird above is another determinative. It shows that when the serpent fire has risen to the upright position, it leads to the exhilaration of spiritual flight into the otherworld, which is analogous to astral travel. As previously mentioned, the Thunderbird is said to cause lightning with his eyes, and winds and thunder with his wings. Therefore, this is predominantly a fire symbol—a symbol of the attainment of higher consciousness.

In the metaphysical doctrine of polarity, the right hand is active while the left is passive. Hence, the bear shaman is illustrating the activation aspects of the Sacred Fire rites. In this diagram, the neophyte is dwarfed by his giant benefactor, indicating that he has not yet absorbed the esoteric doctrines. The extruded tongue symbolizes the tasting of wisdom, the sweet nectar of the spiritual world, and represents the emulation of one who has acquired wisdom.

Even today, the Sacred Fire plays an important role in most Indian tribes. In the Huichol culture, the first shaman being is called Tatewari, "the ancient one who is the fire." It is Tatewari who protects and "transmits the traditions of long ago." Huichol shamans call the Sacred Fire *kupuri*, the "life energy force," and they believe that it is captured within the sacred peyote. Similarly, the Natchez built their entire society upon the "eternally preserved fire," also known affectionately as "the honored and sacred fire." In fact, mastering this fire has been the prime objective of shamans the world over.

The next ideogram, Figure 8-3, is of a rock painting from the Menomini Territory at Manistique, Michigan. This peculiar ideogram shows a headless body surrounded by a second pair of hands, with an umbilical-like extension protruding from the navel area and ending in a cluster of tentacle-like appendages under the being's head. When the Sacred Fire is cultivated and an experienced person seeks to indulge in a special type of emotional elasticity for clairvoyant perceptions, he or she consciously transfers awareness from the crown chakra down the spine to the area of the solar plexus.

Lawrence Gallante, an American master of T'ai Chi Chuan, recounts this special technique in his book, *Tai Chi: The Supreme Ultimate*. He explains that in the study of *zazen*, the Sacred Fire is cultivated and stored in the solar plexus. While the conscious mind is focused on this center, one's awareness is projected

Figure 8-3. *Rock painting illustrating unusual aspects of the Sacred Fire (see text). Facsimile drawing from ideogram at Manistique, Michigan.*

through the navel like a spider's web, where it attracts other forms to it like an etheric magnet. The solar plexus in Zen is called the *tan tien*.

Curiously enough, Mircea Eliade, the brilliant religious scholar, also wrote of this transference of consciousness from the brain to the solar plexus in *The Forge and the Crucible*. He acknowledged the process as the "embryo of immortality." Carlos Castaneda, the anthropologist who apprenticed under the Yaqui sorcerer don Juan, also noted this alchemical process.

To esoteric practitioners, alchemy is actually a psychosymbolic process of internal chemistry. In his book, *Tales of Power*, Castaneda is instructed by don Juan to use his bubbles of perception as "clusters" of feelings which he can assemble anywhere, anytime, at will. What we see in the above ideogram is a cluster of feelings consciously extended from the navel. Esoterically speaking, the navel is the seat of the will. The "cluster" here resembles a circle of tentacles much like the elongated appendages, or "feelers" on the heads of certain invertebrate animals. The being's head is also a determinative, indicating that the thought processes have been transferred through the solar plexus in a conscious manner.

It is interesting to note that the solar plexus is also referred to as the "little brain," or "solar brain." Through this center, the shaman releases power in order to seek out and experience states of non-ordinary reality.

The so-called "silver cord" (which clairvoyants see as an etheric umbilical cord) is associated with astral travel and traveling clairvoyance. Oriental mystics depict this cord protruding from the navel (some diagrams also show an eye centered in the navel), while those in the West show the cord protruding from the brow, or third eye chakra.

In their book, *The Projection of the Astral Body*, Sylvan Muldoon and Hereward Carrington expound on the "various brains" of the human being. They write of four principal psychic centers, resembling spheres of nerve ganglia, that serve as miniature brains. In various esoteric schools, these centers are five or seven in number, and are major nerve centers attached to the astral body parallel to the spinal column at intervals from the base of the spine to the brain. According to these authors, the greatest storehouse of condensed energy is located in the solar plexus.

The next ideogram is a drawing called Bara Maloca ("communal dwelling") taken from Gerardo Reichel-Dolmatoff's, *The Shaman and the Jaguar* (Figure 8-4). Anthropologist Reichel-Dolmatoff explains that this drawing is made by the Desena Indians from the Vaupés region in Colombia—a people who used hallucinogens to establish direct contact with the spirit world. The ideogram shows a being with raised arms and hands and whose body is transluscent from the groin to the head. The upper portion of the body is phallic, with a central

Figure 8-4. *Ideogram showing aspects of the Sacred Fire as perceived by the Desena Indians (see text). Facsimile drawing of an ideogram at Vaupés, Colombia.*

core resembling an upraised arrow. Both the inner phallic core and the auric envelope surrounding the entity are highlighted with closely packed dots representing energy.

This image is also familiar to me. It is not merely the image of a spirit ally seen in trance, but the image of the spirit within a shaman who has just ingested a sacred plant (such as datura, peyote, coca leaves, or some variety of mushroom). The image illustrates his experience of rapture from the Sacred Fire activated by the hallucinogen. Much like Lawrence Gallante's description of a rapture beyond physical pleasure, this shaman image tries to express the ineffable.

In his extraordinary text, *The Marriage of the Sun and the Moon*, Dr. Andrew Weil, a researcher into non-ordinary states of reality, mentions that certain mushrooms carry the word "phallus" in their botanical names—primarily because of their resemblance to the human male sex organ. But, says Weil, the energy created by certain hallucinogenic mushrooms is like the fire contained within the sperm itself.

As mentioned earlier, there are a variety of ways to induce the Sacred Fire within, from meditation, fasting, and physical exertion to hallucinogens, ecstatic dancing, and long periods of intense ritual.

Bearing these things in mind, the Desena ideogram can be interpreted in the following manner: The sacred hallucinogen (probably mushrooms) is ingested, which raises the phallic sperm/fire from the genitals to the top of the head (in the direction of the upraised arrow). I believe this is a psychosymbolic expression of the spiritual rapture that transcends sexual bliss. This feeling of exhilaration is illustrated by the density of the dots (energy), the force of excitation and apprehension. This energy is felt both inwardly and outwardly, as it can be seen emanating through the aura. The raised arms and hands denote the exalted status this ceremony held in tribal culture. Similarly, in Egypt, the hieroglyph of raised arms depicted the invocation of the Ka—the vital energy or Sacred Fire.

In essence, this shaman has achieved a state of personalized fire in which he has actually become the embodiment of the mushroom, the phallic/fertility essence now shared by the microcosmic recipient and the macrocosmic provider. This process is similar to the psychic combustion and turbulence experienced by shamans in their flights of transmutation.

The next ideogram, Figure 8-5, is a yarn picture from Huichol, Mexico, now in the private collection of Joan Halifax. In the lower center of this image is a *takwatsi*, or medicine basket, bearing the design of abstract Sacred Fire at the base with the antler motif at the center. Antlers represent the attainment of wisdom (whoever wore an antlered mask or headdress was considered a wise person), which is centered in the fire, the spirit.

The central circle here is the sacred hoop of life, of *kupuri*—the fiery life force likened to the sun. At its core is another medicine basket bearing the image of Tatewari, "the first shaman called Grandfather Fire." Tatewari represents the spiritual perfection of the enlightened sage. On his head is a set of antlers, the tree of good and evil in the midst of polarity and diversity.

The lowest centered antler motif symbolizes the Great Tree of Life and the *axis mundi*. Tatewari here represents the equilibrating spirit. The single burst of *kupuri* from the center of the crown chakra symbolizes both a state of spiritual equilibrium and the center of the universe.

On both sides of the image are appendages of *kupuri* energy forming an

Figure 8-5. *Facsimile drawing of yarn picture by a Huichol Indian crafter illustrating esoteric concepts of the Sacred Fire.*

abstract halo. On the right we find the masculine (phallic) symbol of the sting-ing scorpion surrounded by the blue waters of the feminine unconscious. On the left side we see the feminine corn symbol in a field of red, symbolizing the fiery conscious mind.

In the upper central portion, we find two offering bowls. One depicts the sacred peyote, with an abstract "fireburst" inside the six-tufted button. The other shows two extended jawlines of the active and passive serpents with a horizontal line of equilibrium between them. A flash of wavy *kupuri* connects the two and is a determinitive in this ideogram suggesting that the ultimate goal of the peyote ceremonies, as of Tatewari, is to harness the opposing currents of life energy and fuse them into spiritual equilibrium. Finally, the many po-larized elements in this image demonstrate that the feminine and masculine aspects nurture one another into maturity.

The next ideogram, Figure 8-6, is another yarn picture from Huichol, Mex-ico that is also in the private collection of Joan Halifax. Starting at the bottom center, we find the eight-tufted peyote button in a field of *kupuri* fire, indicating the eight cardinal points and intercardinal directions. To the right and left are censers which burn copal, a tropical tree resin. Above this are twin five-starred peyote buttons, and above these are two candles which symbolize individu-alized light—a light akin to that of the hermit's lantern in the Tarot.

This entity has the sacred *kupuri* emanating from its sides and shoulders, indicating feeling. The prominent heart area indicates that enlightenment comes from the heart. (Ask any peyote eater why he or she eats the plant and

Figure 8-6. *Facsimile drawing of yarn picture by a Huichol Indian artist illustrating a Sacred Fire ceremony.*

Figure 8-7. *Facsimile drawing of a painted Sioux buffalo hide. The figure on the horse is probably that of Crazy Horse. From the Musée de l'Homme, Paris, France.*

the answer will be, "because it gives you heart.") In the esoteric doctrines, the heart is also the seat of the emotions, just as the generative organs are the seat of the physical nature and the brain is the seat of the intellect.

I recently found an interesting discourse on chakras in Volume 27 of *The Divine Life*, written by Sri Swami Jyotirmayananda. Mantras are letters or words that, when focused on certain chakras, release latent psychic energies. Concerning the heart chakra, Jyotirmayananda writes that the language of the heart is an astral sound heard only by those who have become attuned to its current.

On the head of this entity is a type of headdress showing the luminous spirit activated by the peyote. This spirit is androgynous. The straight and wavy lines denote electric and magnetic (solar and lunar) manifestations.

The next ideogram is a detail from a painted Sioux buffalo hide currently in the Musee de l'Homme, in Paris (Figure 8-7). This scene centers around a medicine man and chief. This chief holds not a war club or a bow or a lance, but the Native American portable altar—the pipe. His feathered headdress is very large and pronounced. Like the halo, it is a symbol of profound enlightenment and wisdom. The feathers denote spiritual flight capabilities and, when arrayed around the head like the rays of the sun, are indicative of the shining Sol Invictus.

Through the ages, the headdress has been seen as a type of crown indicating the attainment of perfection, as well as invincibility. Druids, Viking Drottars, and Tibetan lamas in the Ban-po tradition, to name just a few, also wore such "sun-rayed" crowns. With such powers, this shaman's enemies are rendered powerless to harm him. Notice the drooping headdresses and crowns of the other figures, thinly etched and non-distinct. The enemies' power literally wilts in the presence of this great chief and shaman.

What individual was actually this powerful in the Sioux tribe? I believe it to be Chief Crazy Horse. Crazy Horse was known for his prowess as a war chief, but he was also a highly respected holy man, as was his father before him. His extraordinary powers of clairvoyance and spiritual strength are illustrated in this pictograph. Here he is shown as enlightened and fearless, drawing the spiritual blood of his enemies and mocking them.

Notice the horse he rides and how it seems to float as if in a frenzied dance. It is known that Crazy Horse had the power to affect people and horses when he went into a trance. Horses are known for their clairvoyance and are sensitive to the spiritual fire in humans. The name Tashunké-Witko (Crazy Horse) refers to one who is endowed with the ecstatic bliss, and the horse is symbolic for the vehicle of the esoteric doctrines. In her book, *Bury My Heart at Wounded*

Figure 8-8. *Anasazi rock painting showing esoteric aspects of the Sacred Fire. Facsimile drawing from Petrified Forest National Park, Arizona.*

Knee, Dee Brown speaks of Crazy Horse's amazing ability to enter the trance state, the "real world," and the supernatural effect it had upon his horse. No other person of the Sioux nation within the same time frame had this type of spiritual fire.

The last ideogram in this essay is an image taken from an Anasazi rock painting in Petrified Forest National Park, Arizona (Figure 8-8). This early image of the Anasazi shows the same Sacred Fire phenomenon: arms and feet spread; the extended male sex organ; and the usual associations with rapture. In the absence of inscriptions, such early images have been found in many corners of the Americas, suggesting a consistent and close association with the ageless mysteries.

Conclusion

Like so many ideograms of this type, esoteric elements lie at the core. Once the keys are known, many of these ideograms can be strung together like Indian beads. Though many such symbols are unknown to the uninitiated, the shaman knows their meanings instinctively. The reason for this is that the shaman is the wounded healer—one who has suffered the pains of the second death and survived the pangs of rebirth. Thus, he or she feels these elements from the repository of personal experience.

PART II
Donn Le Vie, Jr.

Much of the power inherent in any religion relies on its symbology. The essence of an entire philosophy can be captured by one symbol: the cross for Christianity, the Star of David for Judaism, the compass and square for Masonic teachings. But what are the roots of symbology? And how did symbols attain such importance as vehicles of social, religious, and cultural information? We find the answers in the relationship between art and the "significant experience"—the transformative power of art, ritual, and ceremony and their effects on the psyche that contribute to the Sacred Fire experience.

From prehistoric times, humans living together as family and tribal units have shared many characteristics—the more aboriginal their existence, the greater their number of basic problems. Information critical to a group's survival has to be gathered from as many sources as possible. In the absence of a common language, how is all this critical information conveyed and preserved?

Basically, the need has always been addressed through rituals, story-telling ceremonies, and other mnemonic systems. Cro-Magnon Man, as well as Australian aborigines and other contemporary primal cultures, incorporated secrecy and the cover of darkness into their ceremonies.

Anthropologists have understood that secrecy in societies with esoteric knowledge has long been associated with power, but they erroneously assume its use is primarily for the purpose of controlling other group members or holding an advantage over rival units. Proponents of this materialistic viewpoint reflect the short-sightedness of science, which often fails to see beyond the obvious. Investigators in all fields of science should commit to memory the ancient but sound Sufi advice: "If you hear hoofbeats, expect to see horses—but watch for zebras."

Selective membership in ancient societies had a two-fold purpose. One was to protect the integrity of the teachings themselves, for if secret information ever found its way into the wrong hands, the teachings could be corrupted.

The second purpose was to shield certain members of the group from the conscious-altering effects of the esoteric knowledge. Those who are unprepared to receive certain information have been known to suffer emotional and mental disorders; hence, secrecy was and is still used to prevent injury to the psyche. The Sacred Fire can reveal itself through this information overload—especially through the symbolism found in art, ceremony, and ritual.

Consider the insanity suffered, reportedly, by the Jesuits as they attempted to understand the *I Ching* from a Western intellectual viewpoint. The German translation by Richard Wilhelm of the *I Ching* has been established as the leading version. Jung's association with Wilhelm allowed him to draw upon Wilhelm's knowledge of the noncausal sense of "patterning" which plays so important a role in ancient Chinese thinking and in the principle of synchronicity.

In the 1949 English translation of Wilhelm's German version of the *I Ching*, Jung wrote the introduction to convey the spirit of its method to Western culture. Only in recent years has the collective unconscious of humanity been transformed enough so that esoteric knowledge can be made available to the world at large. The proprietary nature of sacred rituals, ceremonies, and social functions has always been powerful medicine. Only recently has it become in the best interests of all concerned to share such information, though not everyone will be receptive to what is revealed.

As a hierarchy of information was gradually established in primal cultures, top secret information was likely accessible to only a select few, while the more mundane information was disseminated to an increasingly larger part of the population. Imagine the effect on the mind of an individual when he or she was allowed access to privileged information. The uniqueness of such an experience must have created a much deeper state of concentration, attention, and retention.

This contributes to what I call the "significant experience." Significant experience can be thought of as reverse manifestation, in that an event or experience occurs first and later is re-introduced to a person's consciousness, usually through symbolism. For example, a rite of passage for a young aborigine boy could be termed a "significant experience" — especially if noise, ritual, music, chanting, or dancing accompanied the event. Undoubtedly many things seen, heard, and experienced during this ceremony will bypass the conscious mind until some later moment, when perhaps a sound or symbol opens the floodgates and the conscious mind becomes inundated with memories of the event. Shamanic art, as Iron Thunderhorse points out in this chapter, fans the Sacred Fires of the psyche — to elevate into the conscious mind the significance of certain experiences, rituals, and ceremonies.

This "significant experience" concept involves some complicated neurophysiology, but at its most basic level it deals with the mind's incredible capacity for sensing novelty. We tend to downplay the mind's ability to sense novelty. We casually call it a coincidence and usually think nothing more of it. When no causal connection can be demonstrated between two sets of events that yield some particular significance, it is clear that a type of meaningful relationship exists between them.

Let me give a personal example. My wife and I were in Albuquerque, New Mexico, shopping for turquoise rings. We had seen literally hundreds of rings, but didn't buy any until we entered one shop that had jewelry cases full of unusually colored turquoise stones set in silver. The rings were deeply set in a styrofoam base so that only the top of each ring was visible. One oval-shaped ring captured my attention to the exclusion of all others. When the sales person removed the ring from its foam-lined tray, I could see that each side of the silver ring was embellished with a Thunderbird icon. The fact that the title of this book is *Return of the Thunderbeings*, that my co-author is a Thunderbird shaman, and that no other ring in the store was adorned with a Thunderbird icon added even more to this significant experience — or "meaningful coincidence," as Jung would call it.

It is perfectly correct to say that this was a coincidence. However, we must include the word "meaningful" inasmuch as the intersection of events had a definite significance. This brings us to the threshold of Jung's synchronicity principle and its role in igniting the Sacred Fire within, which will be discussed shortly. But let us return to discussing the novelty detector.

Each species has its own special novelty detector. Whether this is hearing, sight, smell, or some other sense, no species can survive without it. Through evolution, the human species' built-in novelty detector has become more and more sensitive and fine-tuned. Collectively, our significant experiences serve as a "reference manual" to alert our senses or engage our memory to life-threatening or life-enhancing situations. With roots deep in the subconscious, the significant experience contains elements of both archetype and instinct.

When novelty is purposely created as a cultural stimulant, it serves as another vehicle for elevating memory of an event above mundane experience. Such a feat in this day and age is a difficult undertaking. Technological advances and revolutionary breakthroughs in every field that were not even conceivable ten years ago now tax and, in some cases, exceed the brain's capacity for absorbing and understanding. In addition, our senses are bombarded daily with non-informational distractions in the form of inane television programming and other devices vying for our undivided attention. Cultural and technological advancement occurring at this pace serves as a social anaesthesia for the human mind's novelty detector.

On the other hand, primal humans had nothing to distract them from their daily survival activities—no books, no radio, no television. Their only formal source of "novel" information came from public and private rituals, which opened up the channel for communications of the utmost social significance.

As mentioned by Iron Thunderhorse, the Sacred Fire represents activation of certain perceptions within the psyche. The psyche contains a remarkable capacity for knowledge that we are not conscious of. Esoteric knowledge represents indirect and symbolic perceptions of a dimension of reality that can be attained through no other method. Such esoteric teachings acquired through ritual, ceremony, and art contribute to our understanding of the elusive but elemental realities of human existence.

Theoretical physics recognizes a universe of many dimensions, where each of these dimensions may require some interpretive principle capable of responding to its unique inherent qualities. One interpretive principle, called synchronicity, was pioneered by Jung for examining alternatives to cause and effect. In addition to theoretical physics, Jung refers to many esoteric teachings of prescientific times as indicators of humanity's intuitive acceptance of the presence of the synchronicity principle in the universe.

Synchronicity, says Jung, enables us to understand esoteric teachings. In his book, *Jung, Synchronicity, and Human Destiny* (Julian Press, 1973), Ira Progoff relates a most important property of synchronicity:

> Synchronicity can become a master key for opening the door to teachings regarding the nature of human destiny that have heretofore

been closed to us. In this regard, Synchronicity has the special merit of being not only a key to the occult dimension of life, but a key that has the experience of modern science behind it.

As we have seen, shamans live in close relationship with their unconscious and often experience parapsychic events. Laboratory studies by J.B. Rhine indicate that something other than cause and effect is involved in parapsychic phenomena. Rhine's experimental results with parapsychic events went beyond the probability factor, suggesting that these phenomena cannot be explained away as mere chance or oddities of nature.

The clairvoyant perceptions and the Sacred Fire experience can be explained, I believe, by synchronicity. In order to understand the process behind the occurrence of parapsychic events, we must be aware of a concept called the "dynamic balancing process" by which the psyche functions. According to Progoff, when consciousness intensity is increased on one side of the psyche, it is correspondingly deepened on the other side. Through this "descending" process, the capacities of psychic awareness are expanded. This awareness seeks expression directly through the unconscious because it bypasses the sensory processes. It is knowledge that has arrived by *bypassing* conscious awareness.

Sacred Fire (termed "numinosity" by Jung) is a metaphor for describing the aura of great light and warmth that is affixed to the archetypes when they become immediately manifest in a powerful human experience. This experience of numinosity is accompanied by tremendous psychic intensity.

Combine fasting, chanting, and dancing for days at a time with some visual experience, and the stage has been set for the significant experience, the meaningful coincidence, numinosity, and synchronicity. When the mental level has been lowered sufficiently to cause an increase in the psyche's sensitivity to some archetypal pattern, the shaman becomes empowered to perceive and understand the reality which exists beyond time and space.

None of our senses can match the power of sight. Imagine "hearing" the Mona Lisa or "smelling" a sunset. Without vision, many of the images conjured up within our consciousness lose their true impact and importance. Conversely, the images in our conscious mind take on special significance when transmitted by vision. This is because the mind's eye solidly bonds to an experience, allowing it to be incorporated into memory for recall and reflection — and into the cavernous subconscious, where it is likely to become manifest in ways not immediately apparent.

Even more important, the information and memory of non-ordinary states (such as experiences perceived in the mind's eye of the shaman while in trance) form the basis for much of the art that Iron Thunderhorse has just explained.

The habitual use of the third eye, or *shanta ishta* ("eye of the heart") as it is called in Sioux, is a discipline that transforms the entire being.

In this chapter, Iron Thunderhorse provides the reader with several examples of shamanic art that portray the Sacred Fire within. Often, the uninitiated eye tends to take in no more than the face value of what is sees, failing to receive the psychosymbolic messages hidden within each glyph, ideogram, and brushstroke. With training and practice, however, all of us can begin to look more deeply into the body/mind relationship and reach a deeper understanding of the process of psychic transformation.

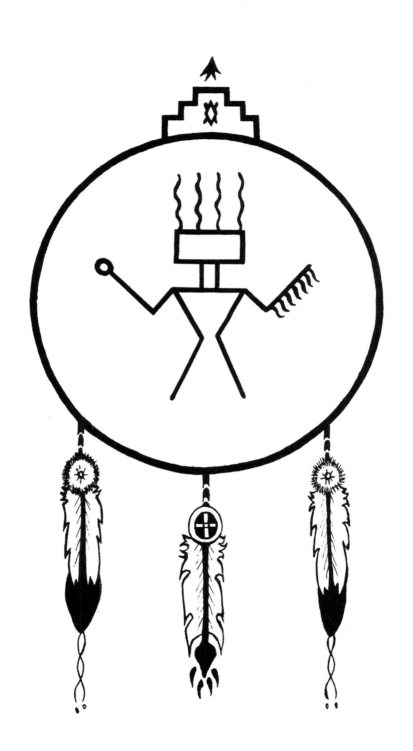

Chapter Nine

THE PATHS TO POWER

PART I
Iron Thunderhorse

In the shamanic nations of the Americas, the "paths to power" are common themes in the process of attaining spiritual perfection. The path a person chooses to achieve personal power often leads the seeker over unfamiliar ground—many times through a psychic wilderness with strange and awesome landmarks. These obstacles are different for each person. Yet, despite cultural diversity, the collective symbols for such perils and for the respective paths themselves are very similar all over Turtle Island.

In most tribal nations, there were secret societies that assisted an individual to self-mastery: adolescent societies for young girls and boys; adult societies for attaining specialized skills on the medicine path; and spiritual societies of many variations which directed a person on a particular path toward oneness with the spirit world (Figures 9-1, 9-2, and 9-3).

The Secret Lodges: Protectors of the Sacred Power

To the aboriginal Indian mind, everything that existed in the world of form was animated by a living force. To the Sioux, this force was known as *wakanda*. The simple realization that "life is power" set the would-be shaman on his or her path in search of understanding. The number and diversity of secret lodges or societies of the Indian tribes in the Americas attest to the specialized training given to medicine men and women. It was the task of these secret lodges to reveal the paths of power to the neophyte, in much the same manner as the Celtic, Teutonic, and other Eurasian shamanic tribes did.

Adolph F. Bandelier, the pioneer of archaeology in the American Southwest and person for whom Bandelier National Monument in New Mexico was named, wrote a magnificent novel, *The Delight Makers*, based on the culture of one of these lodges. Similarly, the Midewiwin, or Grand Medicine Society of the Ojibwa Indians, was studied extensively by Colonel Garride Mallery. In

Figure 9-1. *Facsimile drawing of an Acoma shaman-dancer wearing feather headdress. Here the feathers symbolize spiritual attainment, but in some instances (such as in Figure 9-3) feathers denote bravery in war. The feathers of certain birds such as hawks and eagles also signify a warrior's excellence in battle.*

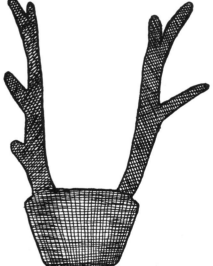

Figure 9-2. *Facsimile drawing of an antlered copper headdress excavated from the Hopewell burial mound culture in Ohio. This was probably a ceremonial headdress. Similar headdresses have been found in numerous Indian burial mounds.*

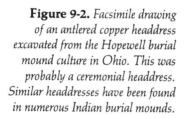

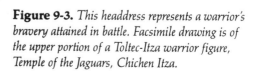

Figure 9-3. *This headdress represents a warrior's bravery attained in battle. Facsimile drawing is of the upper portion of a Toltec-Itza warrior figure, Temple of the Jaguars, Chichen Itza.*

Figure 9-4. *Hands manipulating a sacred talisman. Facsimile drawing from* Dreams: Visions of the Night, *by D. Coxhead and S. Hiller. New York: Crossroad, 1976.*

the Seventh Annual Report of the Bureau of Ethnology, W.J. Hoffman reports that certain Midewiwin initiatory rites were discovered recorded on birch bark scrolls these people left behind.

The *Popol Vuh* is a sacred book of the Quiché Maya Indians that held the basic teachings of a secret order of the Mayan priesthood. In 1967, Ralph Roys wrote his magnificent account of *The Book of Chilam Balam of Chumayel*. This collection of native chronicles from the Yucatan describes "an order of 'Jaguar priests' renowned for their abilities as prophets."

Similarly, L. Taylor Hansen's book, *He Walked the Americas*, reveals many American Indian stories. One of these pertains to a ritual that was performed in a labyrinth, used in the initiation of a secret society. All through the American interior, painted hand symbols and other hieroglyphic markings can be found.

As a final example, in a mythical recreation known as the Navajo Nightway Chant, a teacher recreates a nine-day ceremonial wherein all the mysteries or visions of the Yebitsai (Grandfather of the Gods) are imparted to the neophyte by means of a set of drawings and a sacred talisman manipulated by a set of hands (Figure 9-4). In such a manner the basic tenets of all shamanistic lore were passed on by word of mouth, hand signs, or mystery ceremonies. These are the roots of Indian sign language.

The Call to Power

The initial call to power is a sense of purpose leading in one of two directions—either the path of light (sun) or the path of darkness (moon), which reveal the higher and lower mysteries, respectively. Although one may inherit the call to power, one does not inherit power itself. Many work, pray, fast, dream, or dance for it, but for some, it remains forever elusive. Not everyone is ready to become a master of the power.

The path choice begins on unsteady ground—at the crossroads where the cosmos is disorderly; where power moves freely, unhampered, untransformed.

Figure 9-5. *Spider and cross motif. Facsimile drawing of motif inscribed onto a shell gorget, excavated from the Temple Mound culture, Mississippi.*

The diagram in Figure 9-5 shows a spider-and-cross motif inscribed onto a shell gorget, excavated from the Southern Death Cult (also known as the Buzzard Cult) which existed in the latter part of the Temple Mound culture, circa 1450-1650 A.D., in the Mississippi area.

In esoteric symbolism, the cross and spider have similar meanings. There are Native American legends of Spider Man, for example, whose web of power connects the heavens with the Earth. The mystery schools of Hindu philosophy have a similar teaching in which the gods connect the upper and lower worlds by means of web-like fibers. The universe is thus held together by threads of connecting force.

Similarly, in the Hopi creation myth, five creatures enter the upper world from their ancestral cave dwellings, one of which is Spider Woman. There is no light in the world at that time, so she tries to produce light by spinning a mantle of pure cotton. This mantle gives forth some light but not enough, so a deerskin is produced and forms a shield case that is painted in turquoise. This produces a brilliant light. Hence, the sun and moon are created—the light of the diurnal and nocturnal periods. This story also represents how the darkness of the mysteries leads to eventual illumination and is a vital link in the esoteric tradition concerning the spider's connection with the psyche. J.E. Cirlot, for example, explains that the spider symbolizes the central point of the universe—the turbulent realm of chaos from whence the Wheel of Life, the spider's web, originates.

Next we turn to the symbol of the cross, a universal symbol with numerous variations. The vertical line in the cross connects the earth with the spirit world. However, the horizontal line bisecting the vertical denotes a conjunction of opposites, connecting the spiritual principle with the worldly principle. Thus, the cross is a symbolic reference to suffering, struggle, and martyrdom.

The cross was a common symbol among the American Indians. The Aztec rain goddess carried a cross in her right hand and Quetzalcoatl was said to have taught the Toltecs the sign and the ritual of the cross. His scepter resembled a crosier, and his robe was trimmed with red crosses.

The cross represents the intersection of opposite poles wherein evil meets good, love finds hate, passive joins active, and spirit mingles with form at a central point of balance. When these opposing poles of light and darkness converge, they become compounded into the four primal corners of all creation.

The Roles of Light & Darkness

In all societies, there are good and bad deities, and this was true in the Americas as well. For example, the chief Aztec deities were the beneficent Feathered Serpent, Quetzalcoatl, and his arch-rival, Smoking Mirror, Tezcatlipoca.

Evil is sometimes known as being "two hearted"—for example, someone saying one thing but meaning another. Evil is exploitation and mindlessness. Evil is Smoking Mirror, who is locked in rivalry with his counterpart, the Feathered Serpent. The Feathered Serpent is the representative of the single heart—love, peace, and understanding.

In early Aztec mythology, this dual aspect was worshipped as the "creator gods" phenomenon. The masculine aspect of the creative principle was known as Ometecuhtli, and the feminine aspect was Omecihuatl. Both resided at the highest level, the place of duality, Omeyocán. This plateau of existence was known as the thirteenth celestial level.

The four sons of these two forces were associated with the four cardinal directions, each with its own identifying color. And each was worshipped as having the dual aspects of the Feathered Serpent and Smoking Mirror at its particular cardinal point. With this mythic dualism, the Aztecs personified both good and evil for the purpose of self-integration; that is, they believed that knowing the limits of both would ensure equilibrium.

The story of the Feathered Serpent and Smoking Mirror is in essence the story of the psyche's unfoldment—the blossoming of the soul as it harmonizes the dual polarities into unity. This story speaks of the liberation of consciousness through suffering and demonstrates that the dark side of our personalities is equally important as the light side.

This dualism was even incorporated into Aztec recreation. For example,

Patolli, an Aztec dice game, was dedicated to the "divine two." The game employed 52 squares on a cross-shaped board for four players, under the watchful eyes of the divine two, illustrated on the board's double-sided playing area.

Figure 9-6 shows players intoning invocations to the gods for success. Beans marked with spots were used as dice (odd and even), and colored stones (round pieces of jade) were used as markers. The 52 squares, in their odd and even configurations, served as a type of divination board to calculate the flux and reflux of the divine two in their sacred calendar round of 52 years.

The "primordial two" registered their influence everywhere in the pantheon of the Americas. Mesoamerican cosmology has its dualistic aspects as well. Here, the planets were thought to be messengers of the two, and by careful observation of the cyclic conjunctions of these messengers, the priesthood could readily "predict" both periods of peaceful harmony and of catastrophic conflict.

The Crossroads: Center of the Cosmos

The great cross or crossroads symbolizes the conjunction of the paths of power. One is the feminine-passive, represented by the lunar sphere of the night. The other is the masculine-active, symbolized by the solar sphere and ruled by the day.

Figure 9-6. *Facsimile drawing of Aztec dice game players invoking the gods for success. From a photo by Timothy Kendall in* Atlantis: The Eighth Continent, *by Charles Berlitz. New York: Putnam Publishing Group, 1984.*

Figure 9-7. *Facsimile drawing of the Iktomi Spider People design of the Lakota Sioux. From pictographic files of Iron Thunderhorse.*

Humankind is neither good nor bad, but a combination of both. "Know thyself," the ancient oracles advised. There comes a time when the paths of one's own dual nature meet; a time when one comes face to face with one's own worst enemy and best friend—oneself—as one stands at the center of the cosmos.

When opposing forces meet, there is a general clash if the meeting is resisted; a peaceful surrender if accepted. Nevertheless, the crossing of paths denotes a meeting of opposites. Plato, in *Timaeus*, tells how the demiurge joins the broken parts of the world soul by means of two sutures shaped like St. Anthony's cross.

The acquisition of sacred power often occurs in the midst of an ordeal, a crisis, or an encounter with death. For the shaman, the entrance to the otherworld lies through the gates of total disruption, for out of chaos comes order.

Many ancient American and Mesoamerican Indian temples were positioned to align with the four cardinal points of creation to form a cross of polarity. In the cosmology of Mesoamerica, the Earth was a cube, from the center of which grew the Sacred Tree. The Earth was held in place by the deities of the four cardinal directions. The Iroquois knew these four powerful beings as the Sky Dwellers.

The next two figures depict the power of the cross and its cosmic center as developed by Indian philosophy. The first, Figure 9-7, is a design inspired by the Lakota Sioux legend of the Iktomi, the Spider People—spiritual beings who were tutors of the Great Spirit and who taught the Indians how to live with nature. The four cardinal points of the universe are shown as is the heart of all creation—the abode of the Great Tree of Life.

The next design, Figure 9-8, is a Navajo sand painting representing a cosmological myth. The encircling rainbow goddess envelops the hunchback gods who carry the clouds on their backs. The sacred cross includes dualistic medicine helpers forming a sunwheel (swastika) with healing herbs depicted in its turns.

Figure 9-8. *Facsimile drawing of a Navajo cosmological myth. From an original drawing by Hasteen Klah (see text).*

This symbol was used in a consecrated hogan in a special healing ceremony in which the patient was placed onto the cross. This action was believed to bring the patient's conflicting energies back into balance at the center of the universe.

Perhaps the reason that many of the astro-observatories of the Mesoamerican Indians were designed to calculate the eclipses of the sun and moon is that

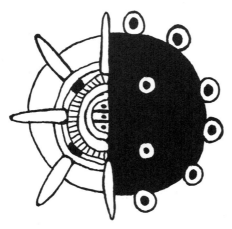

Figure 9-9. *Facsimile drawing of an eclipse symbol from a glyph in the* Codex Borgia.

these were natural cycles of astro-conjunction. In Figure 9-9 we find a symbol which comes from the *Codex Borgia*, a pre-conquest book of the Aztec Mixteca culture. The left side of the symbol reveals the sun, and the right half represents the star-studded night sky. Studies indicate that this particular symbol denotes an eclipse.

Although these ancient observatories marked many phenomena, the eclipse in particular represented a physical pattern that the astronomer-priests felt to be an outward reflection of the creative forces. Here, an invisible power inverted the cycles after meeting its own counterbalance.

Crucifixion & the Power of Choice

For some beings—especially the redeemers of life's essential philosophies —the path of power is especially arduous. It necessitates a sacrifice of self to the god-like elements: crucifixion.

The symbolism of crucifixion is rooted in the psychological process of suffering, where contradictions and conflicts are reconciled. In the icons of medieval times, we find Jesus nailed to the cross, between symmetrical pairs of opposites: the good and the bad thief; the Virgin Mother and St. John; the lance and the chalice; and between heaven and Earth at the vertical extremes. At the center is the soul of humanity, the heart.

These are all symbols of the dualism of human nature. Once we begin to recognize the basic elements of primary symbols, such as the cross and its many variations, it becomes easier to understand the meanings of the many ancient hieroglyphs and ideograms that represent these same material and spiritual phenomena.

Figure 9-10.
*Facsimile drawing of
the crucifixion of
Quetzalcoatl, from the*
Codex Borgia.

Figure 9-11. *Original drawing of the Sun Dance ceremony.*

In the *Codex Borgia*, for example, the legendary Quetzalcoatl is symbolically crucified in the heavens. He is encircled by nineteen figures, which is the number of the Metonic cycle (Figure 9-10). Also, many American Indian tribes, such as the Sioux, Mandan, and Chippewa, enacted (and many still enact) a ritual crucifixion called the Sun Dance (Figure 9-11).

Such initiations, among other things, enable the supplicant to come to terms with his or her own internal conflicts. This is a carefully planned integration of the basic binary system underlying the symbology of the cross.

In Lakota cosmology, there are two roads: the Good Red Road, or spiritual way, that leads from north to south; and the Black Road of ignorance, leading from east to west. The sun and moon are also associated with this symmetry.

The intersecting paths mark the center, where solar and lunar forces merge. Here, feminine and masculine become androgynous.

Inversion & Reversal

Just as death leads to rebirth, all opposites eventually reach a catharsis and become inverted. Constructive patterns lead to destruction, love turns to hate, happiness turns to sadness, and vice versa. The more entrenched the situation, the stronger the power it takes to invert it. In periods of great social upheaval, inversion of an entire nation sometimes takes place.

Symbols of inversion include the double spiral, the hourglass, the quiver of arrows, St. Andrew's cross, the letter "X", the bat hanging upside down, and the upside-down hanged man of the Tarot. Many of the Mesoamerican codices depict buildings with X-shaped symbols on them. Sometimes these symbols were used to distinguish particular buildings as astronomical observatories — places where sightings of cosmic conjunctions were made (Figure 9-12). Still others signified places of sacrificial offerings or penitence.

In my estimation, the Figure in 9-12C commemorates a certain Aztec War of Flowers, also called Xochiyaóyotl. This was a ritual war in which prisoners

Figure 9-12. *Facsimile drawings of three Mesoamerican building glyphs. Taken from* In Search of Ancient Astronomies, *edited by E.C. Krupp. New York: Doubleday & Co., Inc., 1978.*

Figure 9-13. *Facsimile drawing of Aztec arrow sacrifice ritual, the Ochpanitztli Festival.* Taken from Facts and Artifacts of Ancient Middle America, *by Curt Muser. New York: E.P. Dutton, 1978.*

were taken and later used for sacrifices to certain deities. Note that the performance of the rite is based on stellar sightings. This suggests that the buildings appearing in such images could have numerous meanings, depending on the symbols associated with them.

Also, the X-shaped quiver of arrows in the figure denotes the infamous arrow sacrifice, Tlacacaliliztli, in which victims were placed in a spread-eagle position on frames to serve as targets for arrows. The arrow is a symbol of power. The heart pierced by an arrow is a symbol of conjunction.

Actually, the latter ritual began as an important philosophical event. Originally, it was used to symbolically enact a psychological conjunction at the time of a cosmic conjunction; however, it was later perverted into a ritual of death by overzealous sorcerers and rulers.

Figure 9-14. *Facsimile drawing of "bat man" pottery design. From Mimbres Valley, New Mexico.*

Figure 9-15. *Facsimile drawing of bat motif, after a design from the Colima, Mexico period. From photographs in* The Search for El Dorado, *by John Hemming. New York: E.P. Dutton, 1978.*

The glyph in Figure 9-13 represents the arrow sacrifice, which has been found in Aztec material and in Mayan temples as well. The Aztecs used this rite in a sacrificial offering to the corn goddess, Chicomecóatl, the symbol of divine power.

This arrow glyph bears several indicators. Among them are the sun medallion hanging from the figure's midsection, below the base on which it stands. This suggests submergence into the underworld of spirits, where active and passive elements are joined (depicted here by the dark and light squares beneath the medallion). The black figure indicates that this rite involves sacrificing the dark side of one's nature to the light. This was the basic philosophical root of the rite.

The Bat Motif

A psychosymbolic conjunction always precedes inversion. To consciously enact a ritual of sacrifice is to become the hanging bat — to literally turn one's own life around.

According to Native and Mesoamerican Indian legends, entire tribes sometimes lived in caves or on lake bottoms. Such a tribe was known as the Bat People, symbolized by human bodies and bat-like wings. An example of this is found in Figure 9-14, taken from a funerary object of the Mimbres Valley of New Mexico, circa 1,000-1,500 A.D. This "bat man" creature has a pair of X-shaped flags on each wing—one red, the other black, similar to the colors of the upper portions of the wings. As with the Maya, the rising sun's color was red, while the setting sun's color was black. (The Maya may also have used red and black to denote the planet Venus as either the Morning Star or the Evening Star.)

In the Mayan *Popol Vuh*, there is mention of an ordeal at the House of Bats where Cama Zotz, the killer bat, lurked in a dark, subterranean labyrinth. The bat motif can also be found throughout the Colima Period of Mexico and other Mexican/South American periods. Figure 9-15 is the author's facsimile drawing of a gold artifact from this period.

In 1952, British explorers Stephens and Catherwood uncovered the celebrated Mayan Temple of Inscriptions, which contained a curious, hidden burial crypt. The sarcophagus was covered with an enormous carved rock slab inscribed with a large ornate cross and other cruciform motifs; however, buried under this slab along with its noble inhabitant's body was a plaque representing a bat.

Perhaps this ruler had taken his own life as a sacrifice in order to *invert* some impending doom. At any rate, his crypt struck a mysterious chord which Gallenkamp himself noted in his book, *Maya*. Gallenkamp believes that the temple had been planned long before the individual's death, and the evidence he cites strongly supports this premise.

Next, we come to the image of the hanged or dangling man. This man is much like the bat whose upside-down world dominates its existence. History has repeatedly illustrated that the outspoken individual whose conscience is in opposition to the collective viewpoint is considered an outsider. Jung believed that the inverted position was a symbol of purification, representing an unfulfilled desire or expectation. Thus it is with most reformers and redeemers. One's life is suspended. One becomes a dangling person whose only freedom is the release of spiritual transformation. Thus, the inverted or hanged man is also symbolic of crucifixion.

Equilibrium: The Fifth Element

Whether the symbolic cross is the beginning or the end, the cause or the result, one must eventually return to the center or be cast over the rim into insanity.

As noted, the cross is the extension of a unifying center—the four elements joined by a fifth. The four cardinal points symbolize the four elements

Figure 9-16. *Facsimile drawing of Mayan bone fragment inscription found at Tikal, Guatemala. From* Flight of the Feathered Serpent, *by Peter Balin. Wisconsin: Arcana Publishing Co., 1978.*

of fire, air, earth, and water. The center represents the fifth element of spirit. The redeemer, the reformer—the liberator in all of us—is the source of the fifth element, the creative potential of all humanity.

Figure 9-16 is a drawing of a bone engraved with a typical creation myth found at Tikal, Guatemala, which shows the creatures of the five creations on their journey into the sea of conscious experience. These are the manifestations of the five elements in the world of form. The canoe is the symbolic vehicle of the soul, while the waters are symbolic of consciousness. The drivers of this canoe are youth and vitality at the front, and wisdom and old age at the rear.

This creation myth is very common among Native American peoples and has been adapted to various locales to serve different purposes. In this particular one, we find humanity at the center, surrounded by the four elements: fish/water; monkey/earth; bird/air; and jaguar/fire. The central or fifth element is the human spirit—the place of equilibrium.

Conclusion

The life of any shaman or ancient Indian was far from simple. On the contrary, the paths to power were always precarious and studded with obstacles.

In the last ideogram, Figure 9-17, the paths to power can be viewed perfectly in their abstract sense. In its right, or active, hand, this figure holds a stalk of corn. Its left, or receptive, hand continues onward like a scroll or maze. A sacred basket lies under a cornstalk. The head is antlered, and the feet appear to be those of a bird.

This glyph represents the path taken by a medicine person. The left hand symbolizes the path of initiation, its center representing the sacred mysteries which lie within each of us. In order to reach the pinnacles of wisdom represented by the antlers, one's self must be elevated to the spiritual level—to the lofty heights of the feathered creatures, shown here by the bird's feet. The basket is the determinative—the container, symbolic of the body as the abode of the spirit. And the cornstalk is the sacred power.

Such is the journey on the paths to power. From the land of the mundane, they lead through the void of chaos, inversion, conjunction, crucifixion, suffering, and hanging. But eventually, they lead to the axis of the Tree of Life, the center of the cosmos—and finally to the heavens, the land of the supernatural and the power of the Great Spirit.

Figure 9-17. *Facsimile drawing of a glyph representing the medicine path. The glyph is from the Little Colorado River region, Late Pueblo Style III to Early Pueblo Style IV.*

PART II
Donn Le Vie, Jr.

A critical step for any shaman along the paths to power is to establish credibility as a healer, leader, and visionary. The shaman must also be able to establish his or her unquestioned authority as an interceder between the supernatural powers and the lives of tribal members.

Obviously, as the size of the unit increases, so does the probability for interpersonal conflict, rivals for power and authority, and different or contrasting practices. How, then, can the shaman minimize the factors that do not promote group cohesion and at the same time maximize his or her own influence and power?

Historically, the shaman's esteemed position within the tribe has depended mainly upon his or her wisdom and vision. A truly powerful shaman has an understanding of both individual and group thought processes, and inherently knows how these affect his or her position within the hierarchy.

Ceremonies became the socio-cultural adhesive necessary to unite geographically diverse units within the information network by widening allegiances, causes for the common good, and providing communities with a solid foundation to thrive for generations.

Early shamans as storytellers were always aware of the delicate nature of their exalted position. Whenever they employed their powers, they had to maintain—indeed, widen—the distance that separated them from others. This idea of Paleolithic "tenure" meant that shamans had to continually come across convincingly to the other members of the group in order to retain their status at or near the top of the hierarchy. In other words, they had to be genuine. Being genuine meant they had made the journey from a profane existence, through the often dangerous mindscape of the psyche, to the center of the cosmos and heavenward, to the abode of the Thunderbeings.

Many early anthropologists and ethnologists who studied Native and Mesoamerican cultures mistakenly identified tribal shamans as calculating power mongers and con artists. Consequently, shamans were thought to have assumed dictatorial positions within a tribe or culture. It was believed that other tribal members probably had little choice but to subscribe to their mandates and visions with unquestioning belief and acceptance.

It is unfortunate that an ethnocentric arrogance permeated these first Native American cultural investigations. Perhaps if a more open-minded, tolerant approach were used during the later half of the nineteenth century, Native American people and culture would not have been subjected to relocation, physical and emotional mistreatment, and an insensitive, ineffective government policy.

Investigators further concluded that the use of masks, body painting, and the wearing of exotic ornaments and amulets served to make shamans appear less familiar to tribal members. Familiarity, they contended, bred contempt. Shamans sounded different in ceremonies by employing ancient words and phrases, many with special intonations that inspired and instilled a sense of spiritual authority. However, initial interpretations suggested that the vocal variations and foreign phrases were simply another tool used to disguise the identification of the shaman.

Again, this is an example of cultural shortsightedness. These devices were thought by investigators to be used for separating the shaman socially and perceptually from the powerless masses. What probably contributed most to the establishment of this schism, they claimed, was the rapid proliferation of ceremonies and rituals.

But what of the shaman's genuine connection with the supernatural? Unfortunately, it was never realized by early researchers. And unfortunately, this attitude still pervades many of the social sciences today.

The shaman as healer helps others transcend their versions of reality—helps them to shed their egos and guides them in their journeys of self-discovery. The shaman shares power; on a subconscious level, he or she elicits in a patient the willingness to offer up their own self in the healing process.

204 ⊙ *Return of the Thunderbeings*

According to Michael Harner's *Way of the Shaman*, the shamanic self-sacrifice calls forth a corresponding emotional commitment from patients—a sense of duty to suffer along with the shaman to save one's self, a sense of duty to walk the path of power.

Again, this emphasizes the importance of the degree of "separation" between the shaman and the individual. The more significant the separation, the further both shaman and patient must travel toward each other in order to effect a cure, whether the ailment is physical, emotional, or spiritual. The greater the journey, the greater the degree of emotional and psychological commitment (and sometimes risk) needed by the patient. This deliberately created schism, then, is not for the purpose of placing the shaman in some egocentric universe, but instead serves as medicine for inner healing.

Shamanism is not just some social function that is taken up by opportunists and power mongers—it was and is *real*. In other words, the shaman is part actor, part clown, part manipulator, but the paths to power Iron Thunderhorse discusses are not paths of deception. They represent real transformation that makes shamans real healers and natural leaders. Although elsewhere in this book Iron Thunderhorse mentions the dark side of shamanism that employs sorcery, there are no deceptive practices for gaining or exerting external power. Shamans are genuine mediators between the human and spirit worlds; the shaman's path to power is not one of deception but is a gift from spirit.

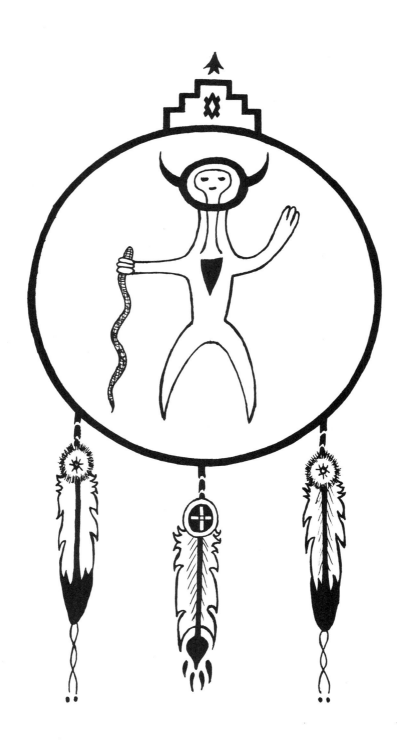

Chapter Ten

THE MAGICAL MEDIATOR

PART I
Iron Thunderhorse

Early shamans represented the very heart of tribal organization. Their main purpose was to mediate between the spirit world and the world of mortals. This enormous task often found them having to resort to many areas of expertise, according to particular needs and beliefs. Like chameleons, shamans blended their talents with the environment, allowing their creativity to adapt to the needs of the people.

Early shamans acted out mock hunts and battles through the magical aid of creative visualization. By exerting their own psychic influence, their acts became reality for their people. This is the foundation of sympathetic magic— "energy follows thought" made manifest.

Although images of these mock hunts are often described by scholars as "hunting magic" motifs, this is not their only valid interpretation. Oftentimes, these images illustrate what appear to be shamans and animals, along with a variety of hunting implements. They are generally classified as magical hunting scenes for want of a better definition.

The main reason for misinterpretation lies in the observer not making the proper distinction between the pictograph and the ideogram. A pictograph is an image that represents only the object it portrays (for example, a sun disk would represent nothing but the sun). An ideogram, however, is an image that symbolizes something more than the object it depicts (the same sun disk might represent daytime, heat, or the creative element). Hunting scenes also depict far more than meets the eye.

An important factor to remember when analyzing shamanic motifs is the shamanic role itself. It is generally assumed that shamans are healers and magicians. Although this is true, it is only a part of the picture, for shamanism has its dark side as well.

This dark side of shamanism involves sorcery in various forms. Because

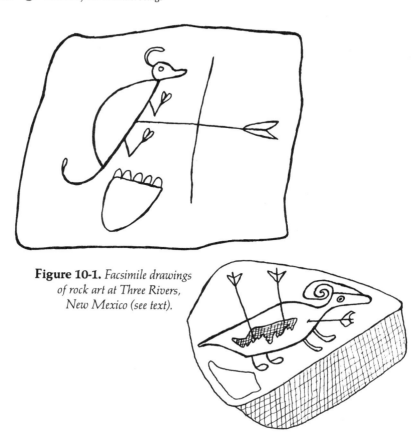

Figure 10-1. *Facsimile drawings of rock art at Three Rivers, New Mexico (see text).*

of contemporary taboos, these aspects are generally overlooked; hence, many decipherable motifs have remained puzzles. With the aid of surviving folklore, I plan to fill in many of the missing determinatives for these shamanic images in this section.

Hunting Magic

I cannot overemphasize the significance of shamanic motives in the symbolism and iconography of Native America. It is a primary belief of the Indians of the Americas that people, plants, animals, and the elements are only the outward appearances for various levels of spirit. In this way, all things are related. This is what is meant by the premise, "All the relations must be honored."

Part of the early shaman's role was to appease the spirits of animals before the hunt. The most important game animals were thought to be protected by "masters"—great supernatural beings who lived under or within mountains. To appease the animal's spirit, the shaman enacted a ritual in which incense was burned and certain songs were sung asking permission of the "masters" to hunt specific game. When a positive sign was acknowledged, then a mock hunt was conducted.

Another early ritual existed in which a picture of an animal painted on a rock or cliff wall was shot at by hunters under the watchful eye of the shaman. If the shots hit their mark, this was a sure sign of favor from the "masters" — hence, eventual success (Figure 10-1).

This hunting ritual stems from the typical Indian moral concerning the wanton destruction of game. There is a common legend told of a hunter who goes in search of game. After wounding many animals, he falls into a trance, and when he awakes, he finds himself under a mountain in the abode of the masters. Here he sees all the animals he has wounded. The master then tells the hunter he may not return home until all the animals are healed.

Hence, the shaman not only served as perpetuator of mythical tradition, but also as game warden and regulator of food supplies. The pictograph in Figure 10-2 is free of ideogrammatic determinatives and serves as a typical scene of "hunting magic."

Figure 10-2. *Detail of Anasazi petroglyphs at Minnie Maud Canyon, Utah. This facsimile drawing shows a central figure at top, possibly a "master" who guards the flock. Note the "consanguinity" lines which seem to connect most of the animals with this figure. Others seem to be separated, ready for the hunters at right who have petitioned the master for a reasonable supply of food.*

Medicine Rites

Numerous animal motifs may be directly related to diseases — especially their causes and cures. For instance, the Papago believed that dead animals' spirits cause nervous disorders and that deer spirits cause tuberculosis ("deer-cough"). Animals could cause, or even cure, certain diseases. The Ponca Buffalo Dance healed wounds. The Iroquois Society of Mystic Animals (*hadi'hi'duus*) healed wounds and broken bones. To the Iroquois, the buffalo could cure rheu

Figure 10-3. *Facsimile drawing of an east Dakota redstone pipe depicting the bear medicine spirit tutoring a shaman in the healing arts. This particular pipe, now at the Linden Museum in Stuttgart, Germany, was probably used in certain curing rites. The smoke opened up a two-way channel to the spirit world, and the shaman spoke to the spirits via the rising smoke.*

matism in the shoulders, and disembodied "false face" spirits could cause and cure eye ailments.

Shamans would determine the correct cause of an ailment and whether it was caused by an offended animal spirit. If so, the animal was placated by various formulas, rites, and chants (Figure 10-3).

The Sacred Deer

The deer is a common symbol in American Indian iconography, and numerous ceremonies were (and are) associated with it. For instance, the Huichol Deer Dance is associated with the *hikuli*, a peyote dance celebration which promotes fertility. And in the Papago *wiikita* ceremony, magical deer spirits protected crops from harm.

It is fairly easy to identify the true hunting scenes discussed above. Yet, if we wanted to distinguish a typical hunting symbol of the peyote deer dances, what would we look for? The rock painting in Figure 10-4, taken from Panther Cave in the Pecos River region of Texas, provides a perfect opportunity for making such a distinction.

Here, the central figure appears to be a shaman who has ingested peyote. The rays around his body portray the activation of the Sacred Fire released by the plant. The draped pouches which hang from his arms are thought to be hunting implements; however, I feel these are medicine pouches that bear the sacred peyote sacrament. The curious marks to the left of the shaman's lower body depict the peyote plant itself—both above the ground (horizontal wavy line) and below, where its roots extend into the Earth.

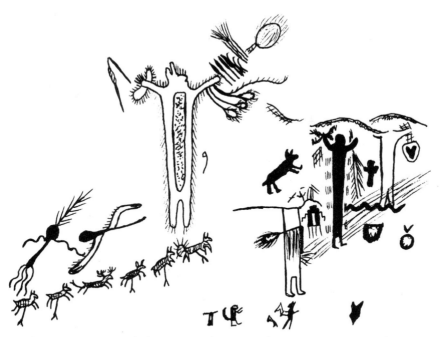

Figure 10-4. *Facsimile drawing of rock art at Panther Cave, Texas. From a drawing by Forrest Kirkland in* The Rock Art of Texas Indians, *by Forrest Kirkland and W.W. Newcomb, Jr. Austin, TX: University of Texas Press.*

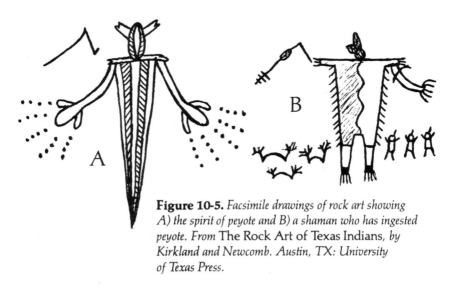

Figure 10-5. *Facsimile drawings of rock art showing A) the spirit of peyote and B) a shaman who has ingested peyote. From* The Rock Art of Texas Indians, *by Kirkland and Newcomb. Austin, TX: University of Texas Press.*

Legends in the Pecos River region say that the peyote plant sings, as does its patron deity, and the person who ingests it; that all three create a type of mystical vibration that speaks to those whose psychic centers are awakened. This is how the plant is found; the shaman hears it calling.

Most herbs, especially sacred ones, are depicted with prickly lines that illustrate their hallucinogenic properties. In Figure 10-4, the deer next to the plants and below the shaman are all shot with arrows. In this instance, I believe the shaman is using the peyote deer dance to enact a cure for a disease. The determinative here is to the right, where the shaman's helpers confront the cause of the disease, which was associated with witchcraft. This disease was apparently meted out as punishment for some past misdeed or broken taboo.

Notice that the shaman in Figure 10-4 seems to rise above the ground. When peyote is ingested, it gives a person a feeling of bodily elongation. While moving from the intermediate stage of an hallucinogenic trance (when the shaman's body is still partly in control) into the final stage of trance (when the shaman's inner spirit is in control), the shaman's spirit is "projected" into the spirit world, resulting in a dramatic sense of rising or being catapulted into the air.

The "hunting" paraphernalia in this ideogram also have magical connotations. Arrows, darts, and atlatls are, in the shaman's reality, psychic projectiles used to inflict or ward off disease. There are certain spirit traps and spirit catchers used by shamans. The circles to the left and right of the helpers and the "crooks" are images of traps and snares intended to magically capture the essence of this particular disease. Tokens were often laid out as lures to attract the curiosity and interest of the disease so that the shaman could capture it.

The Zuni Deer Dance, the Piegan Black-Tailed Deer Dance, and the Yaqui and Yuma Deer Dances are all performed as magical curing rites to detoxify diseases. Later in this section, it will become apparent just why the hunt and disease are so closely associated.

Patron of Peyote

Another rock art painting located at Pecos River, Texas, shown in Figure 10-5, illustrates how to distinguish between a deity and a shaman figure. Figure 10-5A, taken from Period 4 at Pecos River, represents the patron or spirit of peyote. Hanging from this deity's arms we find singing pouches filled with the sacred plant. The dots represent the cries of the plant's inner voice — its power. Next to the deity's head is the sign for sacredness. However, this deity is identified mainly by its peculiar tri-form, a form further subdivided into active (dark) and passive (light) properties to form a harmonious whole.

Figure 10-5B, another drawing from Period 3 at the same location, illustrates the psychoactive properties of peyote. This ideogram shows how the peyote becomes part of the inner nature of the shaman. The pouch is on the light, or passive, side, while the atlatl projectile is on the dark, or active, side. In these ideograms, people are shown on the passive side, while antlers (representative of both material and spiritual properties) are shown on the active side.

Peyote is a small, carrot-shaped, spineless cactus (*Lophophora williamsii Lemaire*) which grows in the Rio Grande Valley southward into Mexico. It exhibits both male and female (active and passive) aspects. The active male aspect is utilized for the sacred fertility ceremonies; hence, the determinative of antlers on the active side of this image. The female aspect is used for curing purposes; thus, it is a determinative for healthy tribespeople on the passive side. To me, this glyph was a type of mnemonic teaching aid, with which the shamanic novice was symbolically taught the properties of peyote, the sacrament of healing and enlightenment.

The Dark Side of Shamanism

The shaman is known primarily as a healer — a curandero who uses herbology and other forms of medicine to cure physical and spiritual diseases. However, there remains a dark side of shamanism which grew out of many folk beliefs. The practice of these crafts varied from tribe to tribe, yet their widespread use both past and present warrants a thorough examination as part of this study.

Sources of Disease

In the beliefs of early American Indians, plagues were caused by the wrath of the gods. For other diseases, most caused by food and water contamination, the cure was associated with some patron deity or elemental spirit. Some other spirits, however, were known to steal souls.

Figure 10-6. *Facsimile drawing of Eskimo shaman. From a stonecut print by Mary Pitseolak, a Cape Dorset Eskimo, in* Shaman: the Wounded Healer, *by Joan Halifax. New York: Crossroad Publishing Co., 1982.*

Figure 10-7. *Facsimile drawing of shamans traveling in search of lost souls. From rock painting at the Rio Grande Cliffs, Texas. Taken from* The Rock Art of Texas Indians, *by Forrest Kirkland and W.W. Newcomb, Jr. Austin, TX: University of Texas Press.*

When an Indian became ill, it was the belief that the soul had left the body. It was the shaman's job to retrieve the soul, usually on a spirit voyage. When the soul was recovered, it was placed in the victim's body—either through the top of the head, through the navel, or through an opening such as ears, eyes, mouth, or nose. Native people still wear sacred objects, such as turquoise, near these openings to ward off evil influences. Certain headdresses serve the same purpose, preventing negative influences from entering through the top of the head.

Figures 10-6 and 10-7 demonstrate the shaman's journey to recover a missing spirit. In Figure 10-6, an Eskimo wizard flies to the other world and back on a magical sled pulled by a spirit goose. The ideogram in Figure 10-7 shows a group of shamans who are traveling to the land of birds—to the heavens—in search of lost souls. Such missions were generally conducted in groups of three or four, as spirit allies were helpful to the shaman.

The Arrow Piercing Motif

Again and again in "hunting magic" scenes, we find images of deer, along with abstract images that are pierced by arrows and spears. In the Orient, the sorcerer or shaman is often depicted with a quiver of arrows. According to some observers, this combination is attributed to the fact that shamans used their supernatural powers to heal diseases caused by supernatural means. The supernatural power is symbolized by the arrow. "Removing the arrow" is a kind of sympathetic magic symbolizing the removal of the supernatural disease.

In Figure 10-8, we find several shamans and their spirit helpers (the inflated figures and the figures to the far left). The figure at the center is a tribesman who

Figure 10-8. *Facsimile drawing of shamans with spirit helpers. From* Rock Art of the Texas Indians, *by Forrest Kirkland and W.W. Newcomb, Jr. Austin, TX: University of Texas Press.*

has been severely wounded by a supernatural disease. In this ideogram, the shamans confront the sorcerers who caused the disease (the smaller figures between the shamans). These black magicians hurl poisoned, dart-like projectiles (the round objects with stems at the lower left) at the shamans, who inflate themselves in order to repel the darts' ill effects. The pierced deer indicates that the sacred herb has become an aid and denotes a healing ceremony. (Piercing can also represent many other calamities, as shown in Figure 10-9.)

Sorcery: Killing at a Distance

The tribal shaman/sorcerer often had the ability to send supernatural projectiles in the form of arrows or darts, intended to pierce the soul of the victim and to cause either instant or prolonged death.

In shamanism, there are many customs and rituals that boast of the shaman's ability to kill an enemy or cause injury through the use of magical projectiles. Mock performances were once common where powerful sorcerers would shoot psychically charged projectiles at each other. The most powerful would render an opponent unconscious.

The Heshwash ceremony of the California Yokuts is much like that just described. Here, shamans vie for public recognition, with the exception of the Bear, Snake, and Rain lodge shamans, who are strictly healers. If an opponent is "shot" and cannot revive himself, he is penalized or disqualified. Similar contests are also known among the Yuki, Maidu, and Iroquois.

Figure 10-10 is a perfect example of sorcery. A barrage of supernatural arrows is sent to its intended target. Here, the target is the uppermost figure, where three areas are marked (probably the throat, chest, and stomach), much like a voodoo doll being pierced with pins. The elongated figure is the spirit of this disease and carries the infected magical projectiles. At the left, the arrows are first steeped in noxious substances, such as poisonous spider venom, decomposing corpses, and other grotesque things, before being shot.

The Grand Medicine Society, known also as the Midewiwin, or Mide, was a secret society consisting of four degrees of expertise and initiation. It was accessible to both men and women of the Fox, Kickapoo, Ojibwa (Chippewa), Ottawa, Potawatomi, Sauk, and Winnebago tribes. The society met in a peculiar, oval-shaped lodge, reminiscent of an egg. There, initiates were shown how to control, through a process of auto-suggestion and psychic clairvoyance, a white shell which was kept in an otter-skin medicine bag. During this time, psychic shooting exhibitions also took place, and cures and remedies were revealed to the novices.

All types of sorcery incorporate images of substitution and rituals of a sympathetic nature. Many of the rock paintings are records of such rituals. It is quite possible that other material was used for these glyphs, such as animal hides, but stone is a medium that the shaman recognized as long-lasting.

Figure 10-9. *A) Glyph from the* Borgia Codex, *represents a serpent pierced by an arrow—a symbol of drought and famine. B) Glyph from the* Nuttall Codex, *shows a temple pierced by an arrow, indicating conquest. Fascimile drawings from* Arts of the Indian Americas, *by Jamake Highwater. New York: Harper and Row Publishers, 1983.*

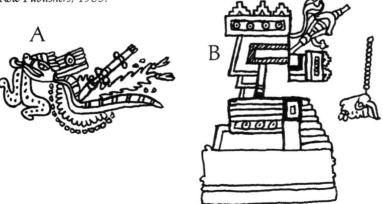

A

B

Killing by Pointing

The shaman is an extension of the Sacred Fire. By merging their personal power with the Sacred Fire, early shamans became manifestations of its properties as creators, preservers, and destroyers. Their magical power could cure, prolong life, or even take it away. Psychic death was sometimes caused by a shaman's merely pointing a finger, a magical lance, or some other wand-like object. Even today, sorcerers of the Miskito and Suma tribes in Nicaragua and Honduras have spirit sticks—each of which is identified with the image of a specific deity who "possesses" the stick.

In the Wintun culture of the Southwest, the legend of Katkatchila speaks of a man who magically killed game by pointing a hollow stick. Various accounts of this phenomenon still survive today, in ritual and in the rock art of the Pecos River region of Texas. Much of this area was undoubtedly the domain of powerful shamanic tribes. When this "killing by pointing" magic was performed, a counting process was used to determine its potency. To this end, certain projectiles were criss-crossed with a particular number of scratches, much like notching or scoring.

Figure 10-11 is a representation of a psychic battle. At center, the principal shaman is wearing an animal skin robe and antlered headdress. At his feet, he is protected by antlers of power, and the line of power, from antlers to infinity, is in front of him. From his left hand, his own power is being pointed at his opponent (pictured at left, facing the viewer). The shaman's opponent sends a projectile—not at the powerfully protected shaman himself, but at one of his helpers at his side. The opponent's allies work on the opposite side, drawing the attention of the shaman's other helper. An extension of the serpent power emanates from the principal shaman in order to barricade his helper.

Figure 10-10. *Facsimile drawing of rock art at Seminole Canyon, Texas, showing a sorcerer shooting supernatural arrows. From* The Rock Art of Texas Indians, *by Forrest Kirkland and W.W. Newcomb, Jr. Austin, TX: University of Texas Press.*

Figure 10-11. *Facsimile drawing of a psychic battle between shamans. Taken from Fate Bell Shelter rock painting at Seminole Canyon, Texas, as shown in* The Rock Art of Texas Indians, *by Forrest Kirkland and W.W. Newcomb, Jr. Austin, TX: University of Texas Press.*

Overlooking: The Evil Eye

Early sorcerers also had the power to release the Sacred Fire from their eyes, a technique that was referred to as "overlooking." Figure 10-12, again from the Pecos River Valley, depicts a shaman sending power toward several targets through his eyes. From the tops of these targets (which appear dark to the right of his gaze and light to the left), it appears that the shaman is overlooking all of these figures one by one. The three to the right have already been ritually killed. The one to the immediate right of the figure which the shaman is gazing at still shows the zigzagged lines of his attack. (Working counterclockwise is a common practice characteristic of sorcery.)

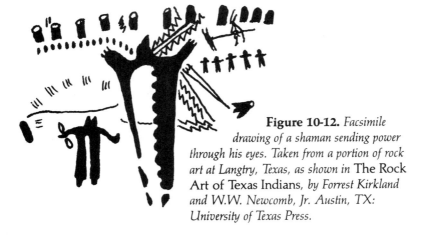

Figure 10-12. *Facsimile drawing of a shaman sending power through his eyes. Taken from a portion of rock art at Langtry, Texas, as shown in* The Rock Art of Texas Indians, *by Forrest Kirkland and W.W. Newcomb, Jr. Austin, TX: University of Texas Press.*

Figure 10-13. *Facsimile drawing from a ceramic vase at Nebaj, Guatemala, showing a sorcerer practicing the "evil eye."*

Overlooking was widespread in North America among sorcerers. In Mexico, it was known as *mal de ojo*—"the evil eye." (The *Standard Dictionary of Mythology, Folklore and Legend* states: "Because of the similarity to European evil eye beliefs, it seems probable that this is an introduced trait.")

Evidence of the evil eye has also been found in archaeological excavations throughout Mexico and Middle America. For example, in Figure 10-13, taken from a ceramic vase at Negaj, Guatemala, the figure on the left wears an earring in the shape of an inverted five-point star (pentagram) with a skull, hands, and feet indicated by tiny circles. This is undoubtedly a sorcerer who is proficient in the art of *mal de ojo*. The people behind the figure are helpers. The sorcerer in the middle holds a magic wand set with gems and with a feather-like extension. These figures all hold their hands in a way known as the "fig position" or the "sign of the horns," with the forefinger and little finger extended. This was known as a sure cure for the evil eye, and I believe this also indicates European contact. The cause and the cure were identical in both cases, the illness being caused by overlooking, and the cure being the sign of the horns. It appears that these sorcerers are ridding the food supply of evil influences caused by *mal de ojo* cast upon it by some enemy. In this way, sorcerers were probably employed by local rulers much like the food testers who served the Egyptian kings.

Disease by Proxy

The *haldā'wit* were sorcerers of the North American Tshimshian Indian tribe who bewitched by means of a piece of a corpse which they kept hidden in a box. With this technique, they could cause all manner of diseases—even death.

Figure 10-14. *Facsimile drawing of Unkatahe, the North American Indian Goddess Against Disease. From* Symbols, Signs, and Signets, *by Ernst Lehner. New York: Dover Publications.*

Figure 10-15. *Facsimile drawing of rock art depicting a shaman holding the symbol of the healing spirit. From rock art at Dinosaur National Monument, McKee Springs, Utah.*

If a *haldā'wit* failed to cause the desired effect, however, a special ritual had to be performed to compensate for the mistake that often placed the sorcerer in great danger.

To counteract such sorcery, *curanderos* made certain charms and medicine bags. The diagram in Figure 10-14 depicts Unkatache, the North American Indian Goddess Against Disease. Her image healed instantly. Other healing diagrams used by Indians in the Americas were either for cures or to reverse the effects of wizardry. One example of such is the Navajo painting of the whirling logs (resembling the swastika), known as Sineols Yikal, a requirement for the Night Way Chant.

Usually, the sacred healing power, *wakanda*, was demonstrated by a clockwise spiral while the counterclockwise spiral denoted the evil powers of disease and death. Figure 10-15, from Dinosaur National Monument in McKee Springs, Utah, depicts a large man holding a shield with the symbol of the healing spirit: *wakanda* or *kupuri*.

The Shape-Shifters

Depictions of shamans and sorcerers with animals and half-human/half-animal images are quite common in all American Indian iconography. The term "familiars" is given to an animal ally whose supernatural powers aid the shaman in curing or inflicting disease. The deer, bear, buffalo, serpent, otter, and mink were common familiars, as were the badger, mountain lion, gopher, and weasel. These animal healers were regarded as patrons of the curing societies and were (and still are) impersonated by shamans in healing ceremonies.

Figure 10-16 is a facsimile drawing of a "dream flag" depicting a bear hide used by a man to cure his wife. Shamans also kept sacred animal skins in medicine bundles. Ritual sacrifices of animals, human blood, or organs were made to these bundles, and legends of Middle America regarding the *nagual*, or animal double, may be a part of this practice. Many tribes also practiced a form of magic in which wolf skins, jaguar pelts, or bear skins were worn as costumes. Typically, the shaman sang songs, danced, and then "became" the impersonated animal as he went into trance (Figure 10-17).

Legends still survive telling of sorcerers who are able to animate sacred ani-

Figure 10-16. *Facsimile drawing of Chippewa bear hide "dream flag," from White Earth, Minnesota. Taken from* Dreams: Visions of the Night, *by David Coxhead and Susan Hiller. New York: Crossroad Publishing Co., 1976.*

Figure 10-17. *Facsimile drawing of a piece of pottery sculpture indicating a man with a jaguar skin cloak. This pottery piece, now in the Museum of Anthropology of Mexico, is perhaps one of the* nanahualtín *discussed above. From* The Olmec World, *by Ignacio Bernal. Berkeley, CA: University of California Press.*

Figure 10-18. *Facsimile drawing of rock art painting showing a village threatened by sorcery. From Seminole Canyon, Texas, as shown in* The Rock Art of Texas Indians, *by Forrest Kirkland and W.W. Newcomb, Jr. Austin, TX: University of Texas Press.*

mal skins and send them forth to do their bidding. Some sorcerers also had the power to actually become the animal itself, by projecting and merging their spirit bodies with the animals' forms.

In Mesoamerica, the Nahuatl word for such sorcerers—especially those who became the jaguar—is *nanahualtín*. A special concoction of herbs and hallucinogenic agents enabled sorcerers to send their *nagual* to take possession of

Figure 10-19. *Facsimile drawing of rock art showing the same village with the shaman's protection. From Seminole Canyon painting taken from* The Rock Art of Texas Indians, *by Forrest Kirkland and W.W. Newcomb, Jr. Austin, TX: University of Texas Press.*

their animal allies, causing death. These *nanahualtin* would also become intoxicated and sometimes stalk the jaguar, seeking to transfix it by their powers. (If they failed, a narcotic ointment rubbed on the skin would help ease the pain resulting from wounds.)

Among the Navajo and a few other North American tribes, certain witches (men *and* women) had the power to assume animal form—especially that of the wolf—in order to retaliate against enemies. If the skin of a wolf or mountain lion were found in a person's lodge, it was considered conclusive proof of their nefarious intentions, as these were the garments of "werewolves."

Protection

Protection was often a supernatural gift of grace from the shaman. At Seminole Canyon in the Texas Pecos River area, a series of paintings on the canyon wall depicts such shamanic protection. These present an excellent "before and after" situation for observation and study.

In Figure 10-18, we see animals and members of a village. At the right, a foreign object is discovered and is suspected of being an omen of sorcery. This might be some natural phenomenon, such as a comet or shooting star, or it might be a psychic projectile. At any rate, the tribe notes that something is amiss, and the shaman is summoned. (The shaman is identified by the lone hand print seen to the immediate right.)

In the next illustration, Figure 10-19, we see the same village after the shaman has taken protective action. Numerous hand prints appear around the villagers and livestock, as do several magical circles of power and a long zigzag-shaped serpent not present in the previous illustration. The serpent's presence here symbolizes supernatural power generated on the earthly level.

The hand prints are of particular importance. It is commonly believed that symbols of raised hands denote the voice in song. Although this is true, it is not the symbol's only function in this particular ideogram.

In certain hieroglyphs of Egypt, for example, the open hand symbolizes magnetism and attraction, as it does in pre-Columbian America. The hand also denotes power, authority, and strength. In this particular ideogram, however, the hand prints all over the village symbolize the shaman exercising his power as a mediator in the spirit world against harm.

Conclusion

The reader is probably wondering why I have focused on certain negative elements of shamanism while the overall purpose of this book is to offer spiritual insights. The negative elements of shamanism stem from deviations, each caused by imbalanced intention or motivation. In the last chapters of this book, we will explore the landscape of a new shamanic ethos. Subsequently, we will outline a five-step process toward mastering such an ethos. One of the five steps is to carefully evaluate the outworn concepts of our present ethos—especially to perceive why they are no longer working. Hence, by understanding the ways in which shamanism has been perverted or abused in the past (and how it has been distorted through inflammatory explanations), we can take precautions that will prevent us from falling into the same traps.

In this chapter, for example, I discussed sorcery. I might have called it "witchcraft"; however, the term "witchcraft" is an injustice. Why? Because the term was essentially created and perfected by petty tyrants to conjure up visions of evil women. During the Inquisition, thousands of women were branded as witches, tortured, and executed. Most of them were herbalists, healers, midwives, and so on. More importantly, though, they were a threat. At that time, the rising parochial religious movement was threatened by the feminine nature, the mystical side of humanity. Thus, the term "witchcraft" was devised to create a scapegoat so that a "better way" could be developed. But this "better way" was founded on deceit and distortion. Much like the terms "communism" and "terrorism" are used today, "witchcraft" was used to incite emotion against the "enemies" of the prevailing power mongers.

Shamans used certain methods to cure and heal, which contemporary society views as unorthodox. Yet these methods were merely props for a much deeper psychosymbolic triggering device which facilitated the body's natural healing processes. In an earlier chapter, we explored the healing powers of the

Heyokas and their seemingly absurd behavior. As mentioned, Heyokas employed highly esoteric methods that tricked the mind into healing itself by opening a person's receptivity to immediate experience.

These methods are necessary because the average person is not as esoterically aware or developed as the shaman. Specialized shamanic symbols and forms are required to overcome the built-in illusions and paradoxes of the socially indoctrinated mind—at least until we all become enlightened with the truth.

In this chapter, we have discussed rituals in which shamans shot objects at each other as a demonstration of their powers. The sacred Mide ceremony is as sacred as those of the Heyoka and has similar purposes. Like the "shock caused-by-bear" sand paintings of the Navajo, the Mide's purpose was to go beyond the barrier of fear. This increased an individual's receptivity to healing. Observers who failed to understand this saw only the physical aspects and immediately placed a label of sorcery on the ceremony—all because of their limited range of understanding. Fortunately, we have begun to see beyond these limiting and destructive boundaries.

From my point of view, the wanton destruction of Mother Earth is a form of sorcery. It is the result of the tyrannical action of power mongers. Yet, there are ways to bring balance to any form of imbalance. The creative mind of the shaman, the boundary mover, has the ability to achieve this balance. For the shaman is the magical mediator who once again brings balance from the primal subconscious, the realm of the ancient wisdom.

PART II
Donn Le Vie, Jr.

Most everyone today has been exposed to some form of magic. Great contemporary magicians, such as Doug Henning and David Copperfield, have thrilled millions of people the world over with their incredible feats of illusion. But is it magic? More to the point, is there really such a thing as magic, or is magic itself only a mythological illusion passed down through the ages?

For many centuries, India has had the distinction of being known as the "Land of Magic." But behind the superficial glitter of marketplace fakir tricks performed for the throngs of tourists, there lies a hidden India—a storehouse of ancient knowledge and wisdom that the vast majority of tourists never even hear about, let alone see.

The Orient has long been considered the great source of inner knowledge and mystery. Many orders of antiquity refer to it in their ceremonies: "Look to the East, for from the East cometh light." Yet for those who seek, the ancient wisdom can still be found in India as well. There, the esoteric knowledge continues to be highly revered, and taught by the few for the few.

Writing of Hindu philosophy and mysticism, Professor E.W. Hopkins states that much of Plato's ideology, by way of Pythagoras, was based on Hindu Sankhyan thought. Essentially all "Pythagorean" religious and philosophical thought was already in place in India prior to the sixth century B.C. Most authorities agree that the many parallels between Pythagorean and Sankhyan thought go beyond coincidence. In fact, both Neo-Platonism and Christian Gnostic ideology can be directly traced to Hindu sources. The Three Gunas of the Sankhya reappear, says Hopkins, in Christian Gnosticism as the Three Gospels. In fact, the concepts of the soul and spiritual light were unified under Sankhya long before they appeared in Greek philosophy and ideology.

Because of their long association with telepathy, Eastern peoples have developed a greater sensitivity to it than people from the West. Developed over many centuries, this general sensitivity has evolved to the point of fusing or harmonizing thought even among large crowds. Actually, this "thought contagion," as it has been called, is felt to some degree in all crowds of people. It is clearly evident at political gatherings and music concerts in the West, but the East Indian people are especially receptive to it.

The magical mediator, by directing the will, projects mental images to the audience who, in turn, perceive them as "real." In this fashion, an "illusion" is produced. But it is only perceived as illusion from the perspective of this reality. The Western mind classifies the observer's experience as delusion. But to the observers affected by it, the *maya* is very real. *Maya* is an important Hindu philosophical term, translated as "origin of the world" and "world of illusion." The word *maya* in Sanskrit has further connections to concepts meaning "great," "measure," "mind," "magic," and "mother." Maya is also the name of the mother of Buddha.

José Argüelles, in *The Mayan Factor*, relates that the Vedic classic, the *Mahabharata*, contains references to a noted astrologer-astronomer, magician, and architect named Maya. Maya was also the name of a great wandering tribe of navigators. There are many more references to the word *maya* in Egyptian history and Greek and Roman mythology.

According to Hindu sages, there is no such thing as supernatural magic. They attribute the supernatural to the superstitious. Real magic, they say, is *supernormal*. It lies above and beyond the ordinary happenings in nature but always functions in complete harmony with its laws and principles.

These ideas are not unique to India. With cultural variations, they are universal. In spite of the religious cloaking that removes these ubiquitous, non-physical capabilities from the cultural mainstream, the experience of *maya* is available to one and all. When an individual can harmoniously integrate the akasha, prana, and creative mind—the three principles of nature—that person becomes a source of universal magical power. Western culture is likely to mis-label this power as ESP or fraud, since Western science usually becomes frus-trated with that which does not conform to empirical standards and measure-ments. But real magic resides in the limitless psyche. It includes telepathy (extrasensory communication), psychokinesis (mind affecting matter), and mind rising above ordinary time-space consciousness to the everlasting now.

On a recent lecture tour in Houston, I documented many examples of how our society is slowly accepting the mind's ability to accomplish the extraordi-nary. I cited specific cases of psychokinesis performed under strict laboratory conditions, as well as controlled experiments of telepathy. And yet, at the con-clusion of the lecture, several people said to me, "I believe what you said is true, and you have shown what appears to be solid evidence for these claims, but I still can't believe it." Similar reactions are encountered by individuals who have experienced UFO sightings, landings, and abductions. Always there seems to be the missing piece of conclusive proof that prevents us from accepting phe-nomena that cannot be fully explained.

There is a similarity between the modern denial of creative magic (where processes of nature are influenced directly by the mind) and that of inexplicable phenomena such as UFOs. When prehistoric practices and beliefs began to yield to the earliest forms of technology, *Homo erectus* began to operate mainly from the brain, leaving instinct to contend with life-threatening situations. Today, we use the brain to imitate transcendental qualities of mind and thus shroud our true mystical natures. For this reason, people find it easier to accept the illusion of fakir magic than to believe that *true* magic exists. Similarly, they find it much easier to accept swamp gas, weather balloons, temperature inver-sions, and lenticular cloud formations as explanations for UFO sightings—even when the evidence appears to strongly favor something beyond earthly origins.

Every culture offers two basic kinds of magic: true magic, the authentic manifestation of controlled paranormal ability; and a mimicked exploitation that is essentially illusion. Brad Steiger explains in his book, *Medicine Power*, that the magic dispensed to all people is the magic of spiritual blessing. It is the birth-right of the person who learns, during the solitude of meditation, how to allow the stream of knowledge from the cosmos to permeate his or her being, how to enrich the soul and remove the veil to the unknown.

According to Sun Bear, Native American Indian magic, or "medicine," is not magic if you understand it. It is just something that *works*. This "something that works" can be thought of as the power of creation, the laws of nature in action. In physics, it is the Grand Unified Theory manifested as cosmological principle. It is watching a sunset at dusk. It is hearing the sound of children's laughter. It is experiencing the pain of grief or the bliss of love.

As we become more acquainted with this power, this magic, we are more able to see its fluid nature and how it carries us along with it. Eventually, we come to see that it is always with us, throughout each and every experience, always ready to be utilized. Just as everything is part of the whole, so the whole is contained in each part. We are individual, yet at the same time we are part of all humanity. Just as humanity is part of the cosmos, so is the cosmos a part of humanity.

One of the many amazing characteristics of the Native American peoples is their will and ability to maintain their uniqueness within the most technologically advanced nation on Earth. Surrounded by a shrinking global society, the Native American has nevertheless preserved the sacred and mysterious. Undoubtedly, this is partly attributable to centuries of isolation from "civilized" influences. Even the Native Americans' unyielding position today regarding the disclosure of the ancient mysteries is testament to their magic's great power.

Do Hindus, Buddhists, Native Americans, and others who practice deep meditation experience inner awareness to the same degree? Or, as Carl Jung suggests, are certain pathways more powerful in particular cultures? In spite of basic universal insights, can a Hindu achieve extended illumination or more profound enlightenment because of the thousands of years of individual and cultural acceptance of such practices? Perhaps the answer lies with the cultural collective unconscious.

The same can be said for the Native American vision quest. A non-native Westerner undergoing a vision quest may receive a mystical experience, but will it not be an experience perceived through the lens of Western culture? The experience may be as significant and powerful as that of the Native American only if the Westerner casts aside his or her prejudices, ethnocentric thinking, materialism, and traditional concepts of an anthropomorphic supreme being. Once such baggage is dropped, anyone can be set free to soar—to experience the mystical and the magical on the wings of spirit.

Chapter Eleven

THE PSYCHOLOGY OF SHAMANISM

PART I
Iron Thunderhorse

Shamanism has been viewed from many perspectives, including anthropology, ethnology, and history. In all of this, however, the shaman has been primarily an object of scientific study. In this study, one field of scientific endeavor has been left relatively untouched as applied to shamanism, and that is psychology.

There is an ethnocentric arrogance in the way native cultures have been studied in the past. Ironically, traditional cultures are outposts of social wholeness and sanity. Once the elements of technological society creep in to taint them, they begin to deteriorate.

In recent years, however, a few eyes have taken a closer look at shamanism with more sensitivity: Mircea Eliade, Claude Levi-Strauss, Barbara and Dennis Tedlock, Michael Harner, Joan Halifax, A. Irving Hallowell, Stanley Krippner, and others.

Clown Dances: Superstition or Subliminal Therapy?

Sacred clown dances once were practiced quite regularly in Native American shamanic societies. These clowns were often deliberately ludicrous, exhibiting backward speech, contrary behavior, burlesque gestures, and even certain obscene practices. A great deal of license and deference was extended to sacred clowns, who could ridicule anything. In some cases, they could even depose a chief.

Clown dancers were sometimes masked, almost always painted with traditional medicine signs, and wore a variety of costumes. In some instances, props were used to enhance the drama.

Variations of the sacred clown character included the Pueblo Koshare, various Hopi Kachinas, the Zuni Koyemshi, the Iroquois Gagósä, the Yaqui Chapayekas and Pascola, and the Sioux Heyoka. Many times these sacred clowns represented supernatural beings and expressed the customary habits depicted in their respective myths. The act of identifying with the spirit world enabled the sacred clown to absorb supernatural powers, which were subsequently brought into this world to use for healing. The actions, costumes, and psychosymbolic gestures of these characters were not the result of so-called "primitive mentalities," but a highly sophisticated process of primal psychology.

Ludicrous Behavior

Traditionally, before the sacred ceremonies began, it was important that visitors and native tribespeople alike had a good laugh. In certain Eskimo villages, for example, there would be an entire night of clowning, with long periods of hysterical laughter. The Sioux Heyoka might ride a horse backwards, carry a bow much larger than normal, talk backwards, or dance in a counterclockwise direction. As the Sioux shaman Lame Deer once said, the clown, while fooling around, is really conducting a spiritual cermony.

In some ceremonies, the clown instills a sense of fright in the audience by throwing stones at people, scattering hot ashes, and even throwing excrement. Still others act out ritualistic murders. Adolph Bandelier once reported observing a clown ritual in which the participants appeared to be drinking urine. (He failed to realize that clowns also used props in their ceremonies.) At the turn of the century, Alexander Stephen observed a clown ceremony in which two participants mimicked copulation. Another aspect of the Heyoka clown antics is the *wozepi*, in which clowns dip their arms in pots of boiling water, pull out pieces of boiled meat, and then throw them at the spectators.

The Sioux *heyoka wozepi* performance, using boiled dog meat, was similar to other shamanic societies' clown antics including the Omaha, Iowa, Ponca, Kansa, Mandan, and Pawnee. Clown dancers used a special grass to protect their arms from the heat of the coals and hot water.

Clown Tricks & Subliminal Suggestions

All of the above-mentioned clown antics use certain "tricks of the trade" to help stage the typically dramatic events. These tricks contained definite psychosymbolic significance. According to the Sioux, Nicholas Black Elk, these tricks were performed to make the audience laugh. And laughter, in turn, would make them more receptive to the power that would come to them. When an audience is preoccupied with laughter and astonishment, their troubles fade away. Meantime, the healer, acting as the trickster, weaves a magical web of transformation.

In contemporary psychology as well as holistic medicine, laughter is being re-discovered and recognized as an extremely effective and natural mood elevator. The disruptive and shocking behavior of certain sacred clown

Figure 11-1. *False Face mask, created by Iron Thunderhorse.*

performances—antics that may even appear to outsiders as grotesque—has important psychological implications as well.

To sum up, the effectiveness of psychosubliminal pantomime in the sacred clown ceremonies is deeply rooted in symbology. The Navajo have revealed their sleight-of-hand tricks to remind the people that the tricks are not the actual power that cures them from illness, but merely a symbolic veil over that power, which is invisible yet real.

This is subliminal therapy at its best. It is just as powerful as the modern cassette recordings that give subtle messages to the subconscious. These performers were (and are) doing important work—preparing the subconscious mind for healing and well-being.

Ceremonial Masks: Wizardry or Psychodrama

Ceremonial masks are almost as ancient as humankind itself. In relation to folk dance, a mask becomes a type of transformational cloak. Masks have the power to suppress, heighten, or integrate various emotional aspects of the wearer's or viewer's psyche. Recent research has found the ceremonial mask to be a vital tool—indispensable in the task of personality integration.

Shamans used masks in a variety of ways which indicated that part of their purpose was to treat numerous emotional and mental problems. Psychiatrists and other counselors today are rediscovering the ancient techniques of using masks for association and dissociation.

Distorted Features

Certain masks show symbolic distortions of facial features. This might include grass pasted on cheeks, twigs placed in each nostril, or half of the face being concealed with ceremonial paint. These partial masks served the same purposes and had the same degree of effectiveness as full masks.

True masks covering the head or face and bearing distorted features such as bulging eyes, long noses, protruding tusks, or floppy ears, demonstrate a half-demonic, half-human caricature in most instances. Anthony Wallace, author of the classic, *Death and Rebirth of the Seneca*, states that the Iroquois False Face masks provided an outlet for the wearer to vent immature, irresponsible, and egotistical emotions through the guided imagery of the mask. The False Face represents the twisted, evil half of the Iroquois creation myth and the suppressed *id*, the forgotten portion of the self where disallowed passions are kept locked away in silent turmoil (Figure 11-1).

Theriomorphic Features

A mask may express the human personality as part beast. The beast is symbolic for the animal nature in humans. Exaggerations of the beast within may be seen as the overpowering elements of human passions. Hair, horns, and the other animal-like features of various ritual masks are intended to allow the wearer to interact with totemic entities and the spirit world. Thus, the mask becomes a three-dimensional image for creative visualization.

Certain masks, such as that of an animal devouring a human head (Mesoamerican origin) or the compound mask with the outer face of an animal and the inner face of a human (North Pacific Coast) are transformational and demonstrate the recurring theme of being devoured (Figure 11-2). The devouring theme symbolizes the essence of duality: the struggle between inner and outer worlds; identity and loss of identity; self and other; individual and universal; revelation and deception; familiar and unfamiliar.

Figure 11-2. *The Mask of Kukulkan, the Lord Feathered Serpent. The theme of this mask is the devouring of stagnant beliefs and the transformation of culture. Mixed medium by Iron Thunderhorse.*

Superimposition

In many circumstances, masks were (and still are) painted directly onto the face. This created a feeling of dreamlike superimpositon. However, the painted facial mask and painted body imagery became confused by the misnomer "war paint."

In certain ceremonies, mock hunts and battles were enacted by the shaman, while others participated or observed in their respective worldly roles. The shamans were the doorway to the worlds of inner and outer influences. To heighten their mimicry of sympathetic magic, they sometimes used facial and body paint. In trance, the shaman was actually transported into another world and pre-enacted a hunt, battle, or cure. The drama created by such ceremonies triggered impulses that enabled the observers to overcome human weaknesses such as fear, worry, doubt, and anxiety. Thus, imagination became reality.

Psychologist Stephen Larsen conducts experiential shamanic encounter groups with the aid of his wife, Robin. In their group, masks are painted on partners, who then spontaneously dance and sing their newly created identity. In the process, participants sometimes find themselves meeting spirit guides or hearing the voices of ancestors or animal totems speaking to them. In other words, archetypes serve as transformational keys. Larsen believes that these superimposed masks may serve as triggering mechanisms that allow an individual to recognize unfamiliar or repressed aspects of his or her own personality.

Some psychologists view this as a form of psychological dissociation. However, anthropologist Charles Laughlin of Carleton University in Ottowa, Canada, feels that masking triggers certain neural structures that are not generally accessed in ordinary states of consciousness. Although this may be close to the clinical definition of dissociation, Larsen views masking as a mechanism that is integrative, rather than fragmentary; that is, it merges rather than separates aspects of the personality.

Laughlin believes that a mask enables the wearer to become transported to a realm of archetypal worlds where a shamanic "polystate" of consciousness can be achieved. Such a state seems to offer an effective antidote to the contemporary isolation of single-mindedness, perceptions of self-limitation, and phobias often masked by drugs or alcohol. In short, masks offer a unique tool for therapists in search of ways to expand the classic one-track mind into a multi-faceted personality.

Dreams: Psychosis or Psychoanalysis?

The concept of dreamtime is very important to all shamanic peoples. Modern society has not even begun to reach the level of expertise in dream analysis—and practical use of dreams—which certain shamanic peoples have maintained for ages.

Shamanic peoples generally agree that dreams and visions acknowledge the existence of spirit. Songs, cures, and peace of mind are given in dreams by spiritual entities. Among the Teton Sioux, Papago, and Chippewa, as well as other shamanic tribes, the song/poem is not simply an artistic creation; it is a sacred expression of a dream or vision.

The people most recognized today for their intricate dream analysis are the Senoi of the Central Highland jungles of Malaysia. Kilton Stewart lived among the Senoi in 1935, studying their practices and philosophies connected with dreams. While there, he noted a surprising lack of violence and disease, and a very high degree of what Jung describes as "individuation."

The Senoi encourage every member of the community to control their own spiritual universe, including the "dreamscape" and all the forces within it. The Senoi are taught that these forces are as real as those in their waking consciousness. When such forces become threatening, the dreamer is taught to call upon images of "dream guides" to help overcome fear, intimidation, and violence. As the dreamer overcomes a threatening dream, the dream guide then becomes a spiritual ally who helps the dreamer in future dreams, as well as in the waking state. (This is very similar to the appearance of guides and allies in the vision quests of Native Americans.)

Each morning the Senoi family unit discusses and analyzes the dreams of every family member from the previous night. After such discussion, the Senoi gather in council (presided over by a shaman), and attempt to unravel the symbolism and practical meaning in each dream. Thus, the spiritual health and welfare of the entire tribe is safeguarded on a daily basis.

Stewart summed up his research by concluding that the collective lifeway and ethos centered around a complex dream psychology that served to integrate the welfare of the entire community.

Conclusion

These are but a few examples of depth psychology which lies at the very core of all shamanic societies. The modern world has lost its sacred connection to its dreams, its myths, and its spirit. Jung alluded to this tragic loss of psychic identity (or "mystical participation," as he called it), and he urged the rediscovery of dream images as a foundation for psychic transformation.

It is apparent in modern society that something is out of balance. The predominance of phobias, mental disorders, and disease suggests that something is missing. Humankind has cut itself off from spirit. It has suppressed an enormously important part of itself—a part which transcends the material world.

The tools of the new shamanic awakening may provide a means of reconnection to that spirit. Tools such as masks and dreams are being used more and more by professionals and contemporary shamans to heal minds and spirits. Once this is achieved on a large scale, perhaps modern society will be able to live joyfully and harmoniously with itself and the environment.

PART II
Donn Le Vie, Jr.

Until recently, most studies of the psychology of shamanism attempted to address the emotional altered states experienced by shamans and their patients from an almost exclusively clinical perspective. In essence, these studies tried to understand the psychology of shamanism from the outside looking in. In very recent years, however, some anthropologists have begun to shed this cloak of prejudice. They have begun immersing themselves into primal societies, by partaking in cultural practices and ceremonies in order to achieve a view from the inside looking in *and* out. In so doing, they have provided insight that is both cerebral and visceral.

Among other things, this "instinct and intellect" perspective on shamanism points to a particularly fascinating human possibility—the evolution into a higher life form. The next step in the metamorphosis of *Homo sapiens* is, indeed, in Neil Armstrong's words, "a giant leap for mankind." It is the realization that we are not restricted to the ordinary, day-to-day reality of our physical senses.

We are now discovering that when we release the imprisoning notions that have been ingrained in our being since birth, a multiplicity of consciousness states and other dimensions of reality are available to us. Consciously accessed alternative perspectives also enable us to better understand our physical plane of existence.

Another related avenue available to us is that of dreams. One of the most remarkable dream societies among the North American Indian nations was (and still is to some extent) the Iroquois. In some respects, their sophisticated dream legends are aligned with Sigmund Freud's theories. The Iroquois believed that dreams played a significant role in fulfilling desires that were otherwise prohibited by the tribe. In the dream state, one could fully indulge in the forbidden fruits of fantasy. For the afflicted individual, sometimes the dream became an obsession. He or she sometimes had to wrestle with fulfilling the dream itself or continuing to live within the laws of the tribe. In such cases, the shaman performing the dream work was responsible for identifying the malady and doing what was necessary to restore the individual's health.

At one time there was also an annual Iroquois "dream festival." This resembled a group therapy session in which individuals would relate their troubling dreams and then, with the help of tribal members, act them out. If the dreamers felt like being aggressive, ridiculous, promiscuous, flamboyant, or dramatic, they could feel free to do so with tribal approval, since this psychodrama was meant to restore their health.

This practice has close parallels in some modern psychoanalytic therapies. "Danceplay," for example, is a modern experiential process designed to enhance self-awareness through new ways of sensing the body. It explores the relationship between motion and emotion. Through a series of exercises (some with and some without music), physical, emotional, and spiritual aspects of the personality are brought into clearer focus.

The renowned American psychologist Abraham Maslow claimed that all individuals have a desire to experience the higher self, the numinous, but that such things as the use of psychogenic substances or pilgrimages to exotic locations actually detract from such experience. Maslow believed that the sacred is realized through an elevated awareness of the majesty of everyday life—that the transcendental can best be found in the ordinary, through such things as neighbors, friends, and family. He further argued that travel outside one's backyard for the purpose of attaining enlightenment or enhanced awareness is actually *flight* from the sacred.

However, in my view, Maslow has fallen victim to the "outsider looking in" syndrome. He condemns the individual to a profane existence by limiting reality to that which is perceived by the senses—that which is to be found in one's daily life. Maslow claims that religious transcendence can be used as an escape from personal crisis, when in fact, very often people use *religion* as a crutch, resigning their problems and fates to "God's will."

Maslow's contention that our bliss and sense of the numinous can be found in our own backyard is reminiscent of the conclusion of the contemporary mythological story, "The Wizard of Oz." Here, Dorothy realizes that "there's no place like home," and that no matter what else she may seek in life, she'll never have to look beyond her own backyard again. The irony here is that her "enlightenment" occurs only *after* her experience in otherworldly consciousness. In other words, the sacred *must* be that which we are at least given a glimpse of—some other level of consciousness, some other dimension of reality that guides us, teaches us, heals us, and lifts us out of our confined, everyday existence.

Unlike most contemporary psychologists, P.D. Ouspensky studied humanity from the perspective of what it can become. In other words, he said, once we understand what little influence we have over our reactions to external circumstances and internal stimuli, we can set a methodology in motion that liberates us from this mechanistic existence.

Ouspensky believed that our machine-like nature is motivated mainly by external influences—that all movement, speech, action, emotion, idea, and thought arise from the outside. But under the proper circumstances and with proper treatment, he said, we can be brought to realize our machine-like nature and subsequently adopt behavior, thoughts, and actions that lead to a more deliberate and conscious existence.

The further evolution of humanity will undoubtedly be more of mind than of body. Shaman, sage, psychologist, and scientist are each contributing toward this evolution. Where physical evolution has historically been a response to changes in the environment, the evolution of consciousness must now be internally directed. Ouspensky defines this evolution as the development of inner qualities that require conscious effort. All of humanity cannot evolve and become different because not everyone wants to. Evolution, then, becomes a personal question. The individual who consciously chooses to evolve is indeed the rare exception among the mass of humanity. More frightening than humankind not knowing its potential, says Ouspensky, is humankind not even knowing just how *little* it does not know itself.

Traditional psychotherapeutic practices in this country have become externalized; emphasis is placed on the *client's* state of mind with little regard for the inner state of the therapist. In effect, the therapist's attempt to understand the patient's reality comes from outside the patient's perspective. Contrast this practice with that of the shaman, who journeys *with* his or her patient to invoke new knowledge and power for healing.

But the winds of change are aleady sweeping the profession. Psychotherapists are now taking Freud's notion of trance as a form of dissociation to its next logical stage: placing the *therapist* in trance while listening to a client. This intuitive approach to psychotherapy has been addressed in *Listening with the Third Ear*, by Theodore Reik.

So far, modern science and mainstream psychology have avoided any major involvement with the relationship of psychotherapy to intuitive knowledge. An article in a 1987 issue of the *Journal of Imagination, Cognition, and Personality* states the position of most researchers that intuition is a linear thought process without intermediary stages. Most psychologists believe that the complete analytical process underlying intuition could eventually be arrived at, given a sufficiently sophisticated methodology.

Recent findings in hypnosis, however, indicate that science is beginning to change its attitude toward intuition. Research now supports the premise that both hypnotic trance and psychic intuition are based on dissociation. Modern psychotherapeutic techniques are now surfacing that utilize many principles of consciousness change common to yoga, alchemy, and shamanism. However, the latter disciplines also employ an integrative approach to psychological well-being: Besides physical healing methods, they also use consciousness exploration and spirituality in their therapies. (For example, in his chapter contribution, "Transformation Processes in Shamanism, Alchemy, and Yoga," from the book, *Shamanism*, Ralph Metzner states that the sweatlodge ceremony is a type of psychological therapy as well as prayer worship.)

Until very recently, traditional psychotherapy did not seek to generate physical healing or to incorporate spiritual and religious concepts, but mainly to bring about behavior adjustments through conflict resolution and solving problems in communication. In other words, psychotherapy concentrates on changing some aspect of the client to invoke more positive patterns of living. By contrast, traditional systems of yoga, alchemy, and shamanism focus on self-discovery, self-healing, and self-change. Morita psychotherapy, a practice that also concentrates on the patient's self-healing and self-realization, is a Japanese method that was contemporary with Freud's theories. This practice has become more popular in the United States in recent years.

More and more, modern psychotherapy is relying on the ancient Earth wisdom. The borrowing of techniques, practices, and goals (whether consciously or not) from yoga, alchemy, and shamanism holds promise for more effective and permanent healing. In the long run, our future may very well depend on placing our trust in the knowledge of the sacred—in the fountain of wisdom that poet Robert Browning termed the "imprisoned splendor" within.

Chapter Twelve

THE NEW SHAMANIC PARADIGM

PART I
Iron Thunderhorse

Anthropologist Michael Harner coined the term "core shamanism" to refer to the neo-shamanic movement of today. Other investigators, such as Joan Halifax and Mircea Eliade, have shared their observations of a shamanic complex that parallels Jung's theory on primal archetypes.

Years of field study among shamanic cultures have led these individuals to the realization that shamanic motifs and rituals can be broken down into a core of elements—a collection of archetypes and patterns inherent in the universal shamanic psyche. Yet, here we must exercise extreme caution. There is a potential danger in formulating what could be perceived as a "one-method-fits-all" shamanic model. (This is discussed at length by my co-author in Part II of this chapter.)

Joseph Campbell spent most of his life probing the mythological roots of the world, seeking patterns of harmony and truth. Myths and legends, as we have observed, are not mere fantasies of the mind, but unique windows to self-introspection and transformation.

We now have access to modern and ancient wisdom, shamanic techniques, and the memories of former disasters that arose from the timeless struggles between human beings. We are now at a crossroads called the New Age. Just as each millenium celebrates its Golden Age of cultural attainment, this age is new and yet also old.

One of its "new" discoveries is the theory of the split brain—the right and left hemispheres, and the multifaceted levels of the mind. These phenomena are not really new, of course. Only the *labels* are new. Shamans have known about and cultivated these mysteries for ages. As a result of the Age of Technology, the human mind has become weak and soft, programmed with too much logic and left-brain stereotyping and not enough right-brain imagination or medial-brain creativity.

The flowering Tree of Life and Knowledge is the lifeblood of all shamanic peoples. It stands at the mystical center because it is the heart of the people. Ancient prophecies relating to the Feathered Serpent spoke of a day when the Great Tree of Life would wither and die, symbolizing the end of one age and the dawn of another. As we have seen in previous chapters, the Tree is now being replanted. If we have all learned our lessons well, it will blossom once more.

But if the sacred Tree is to truly unify us as a species, we need a new shamanic paradigm—one that is both ancient and new, and one that stimulates all portions of the brain. This newness is merely a rebirth—a rediscovery of the true self in *balance*. My hope is that the following paradigm will serve as a starting point for such rebirth—a re-awakened mystical center that can unite us all as one tree with many roots and branches. This new shamanic paradigm—this vision of the rebirth of the Great Tree of Life—is dedicated to the memories of the prophets who never lost their vision of its rebirth, and to the shamans of the future who stand in the light of a new Golden Age.

Replanting the Sacred Tree

On the third day of the Lakota Sun Dance, the sacred sunpole is erected. In Chile, a female shaman, or *machi*, climbs a notched pole to the seventh level, completing her skyward journey in a large tree with many branches. The Australian Fire Ceremony of the aboriginal Arunta is climaxed as initiates climb the sacred pole and pick the sacred fruit at its top.

Mircea Eliade has written in depth about the psychosymbolic implications of the Sacred Tree. He has noted its connections to the themes of continual regeneration in the psyche, and to mastering one's own destiny. As the initiate climbs the Sacred Tree, reaching the level of the heavens, the gods give counsel to the future, the fate of the soul. The Sacred Tree is not merely a picture or a static symbol. It is a vehicle by which to enter the visionary worlds. Without it, the bridge between the worlds would collapse.

Perhaps the most abstract and unique form of the Sacred Tree is the Mayan ideographic tree described in a previous chapter. Our vision of the Sacred Tree is similar to this form, yet it has been slightly altered in order to visually express the components for a new paradigm (Figure 12-1).

The Visionary Tree of Life

The following interpretation of the symbolism illustrated in Figure 12-1 is not exhaustive. It is offered here only as an introduction to the many facets incorporated in the overall ideograph. As a person grows in spirit and wisdom, so too will this symbolism continue to create new dimensions of awareness.

At the base of the Tree is an abstract skull. Its facial features allude to the

Figure 12-1. *The New Shamanic Paradigm, by Iron Thunderhorse.*

divine significance of eyes, nose, ears, and mouth. That is, when an individual learns to use these senses in a truly spiritual manner — when they are in balance with all creation — then that person's inner sight will begin to develop.

This inner sight is symbolized by the glyph just above the eyes, positioned at the forehead. This is the glyph of the sun at the center of the four sacred directions. The spiritual light of the center, the inner light, is the giver of spiritual life. All directions come together at this center.

Extruding from both sides of the base of the Tree are tentacles that reach to the edges of the universe. These are the roots of the Tree. They travel underground in the land of the underworld. The skull and roots represent our ancestry. Notice that the roots, although separate, are intertwined. This is symbolic of the interrelationships humankind should be experiencing, since all humanity comes from the same Tree. If these roots are cut off or decay for lack of ability to grow in unity with others, then they all decompose and the Tree eventually dies. But if there is a unified balance, the Tree lives and thrives. The roots, then, represent the links to both our past and our future.

The trunk is the upright connection, symbolic of the spine. The trunk allows the Tree to grow straight and tall. Notice also that the Tree resembles the human form. The base of the Tree—the sun glyph and wisdom of our ancestors—is the seed of all future generations. That is where our feet are planted. When we walk on Mother Earth, we tread on sacred ground, for that is where the bones of our ancestors are laid to rest.

At the solar plexus—the navel of the Tree—is a three-headed beast. All energy lies at the navel. Depending on whether our energy is released to the left, right, or center, we develop either the virtue of wisdom or the vice of ignorance. Too much energy expended in one direction brings imbalance. There is always a point of equilibrium at the center where all imbalances can be reconciled. The three-headed beast also represents knowledge of the past, present, and future. When an individual is centered and in balance with nature, the result is an attunement with the hidden voices of all our relations.

The Tree has two limbs that represent the arms that reach to the heavens. The many branches bearing fruit with human faces represent the many human races. Each is unique, yet all have the same features, the same seed, the same ingredients.

Around the "neck" of the Tree hangs a medallion which rests at the heart of the Tree. At the heart of the Tree is the face of the inner sun again. This is a visual reminder that our faith is spiritual, and that focusing our intentions on the spiritual center is our primary goal in life.

The face of the Tree is a replica of the face of our ancestors at the base of the Tree, except that here the face has flesh. Both eyes are crossed, looking into the center of balance. The glyph of awareness, or inner vision, on the forehead is a lunar glyph representing the unconscious mind, whereas the solar glyph symbolizes the conscious mind. The more we consciously strive to achieve spiritual balance, the more our efforts sink into the unconscious mind and eventually bear fruit from our inner core, our soul. When the soul body is sufficiently vitalized with solar and lunar balance (right-brain and left-brain hemispheres), the soul flower begins to blossom. At the top of the Tree, long hairlike fibers flow from the crown. These are the spiritual fibers of psychic awareness. Like antennae, they absorb vibrations from the universal light and store it in the inner eye.

When this state of awareness is achieved, the soul has no boundaries; it can fly like a bird. In the midst of the Tree's crowning fibers sits the Thunderbird who sees and knows all, who is able to travel to the upperworld and the underworld, and who can even be observed in this world through dreams and visions.

The Tree has four cardinal points: crown, roots, foliage, and trunk. There are seven steps to the top of the Tree that coincide with the seven chakras. These are symbolized by the following: 1) mouth of the skull; 2) sun glyph at the base of the Tree; 3) three-headed beast at the solar plexus; 4) sun glyph at the heart medallion; 5) mouth of the Tree; 6) forehead lunar glyph; 7) Thunderbird crown.

These also represent the attainment of the seven virtues of the soul and the seven aspects of esoteric consciousness: 1) sensation; 2) emotion; 3) reflective intelligence; 4) intuition; 5) spirituality; 6) will; 7) divine imitation (deification).

The Three Worlds & the Tree

In the new shamanic paradigm, there are three paths to enlightenment which correspond to the three worlds. The path to the left represents the solar path, the way of the warrior, and corresponds to the underworld. The path to the right symbolizes the lunar path, the way of the adventurer, and represents the upperworld. The underworld is Mother Earth and what lies beneath her. The upperworld is the sky and all that lies in the heavens. The third path is the center, the Sacred Way of the Tree which grows at the center of the world and corresponds to the world of inner space. This is the way of the Thunderbird, whose flight leads to creative solutions to any problem.

The way of the warrior, the solar path, should first be developed at an early age. This path to consciousness is reached by a process of hyperstimulation. The sweatlodge is one way of achieving such an altered hyperstate. Participation in the sweatlodge ceremony accelerates the metabolism and stimulates the body's immunological system. When coupled with fasting, it produces a heating process that leads to illumination. Sensory deprivation is an aid to this process.

The way of the adventurer is the lunar path, one that should be developed after puberty and prior to adulthood. This path to consciousness is one of hypostimulation. Here, sacred herbs, chants, and meditation are used to slow down the metabolic rate. In this state, spirit allies are encountered and often teach the adventurer songs or dances to help strengthen the unconscious lunar power. On this path, one learns to confront fear and the unknown.

The Way of the Thunderbird is the reciprocal path to enlightenment. This path should be developed past middle age, after the paths of the warrior and adventurer have been walked. It is a path of non-stimulation that relies on abstract, symbolic patterns, metaphor, and ideograms. Here, the combined insights of the shadow and the light merge with one another.

While each successive pathway to consciousness is developed, the former methods are not to be discarded or ignored. These paths are supplemental to what has already been learned and practiced. One cannot erase what one experiences. However, it is wise to maintain a conscious practice which continues to expand and evolve. Stagnation in mind, body, or spirit leads to atrophy of the same. Many contemporary phobias and neuroses, in fact, are the result of such physical, emotional, or spiritual emaciation.

The Polynesian Connection

The aboriginal people of Australia have been practicing a natural shamanic lifestyle for approximately 35,000 years. When approaching adulthood, Australian aborigines begin to focus their attention on the sky. One very simple technique they use is to gaze at the sky with eyes wide open while meditating on the idea that the universe is imbued with inspirations. In their view, the heavens are a map containing a storehouse of infinite knowlege and wisdom.

The significance of this practice is that the Earth studies prepare one for familyhood and tribal relationships. The practice of sky meditation is a transitional stage that prepares the initiate to develop aspirations that will promote unity between the community, the environment, and the universe.

This is the path of the adventurer, the path pursued by the *kahuna kalokupua*, or Hawaiian master shaman. This direction taps into Earth currents, utilizing a kind of psychic "web" to transform Earth energy into lunar energy. It is essentially a path of persuasion rather than one of force. The adventurer does not view the world as a dangerous place but as a place of excitement and opportunity. Dangers or pleasures are generated by choices. The adventurer cultivates power to generate change in the world and to assist others in doing the same.

This third and final path, which leads toward the spirit of the Thunderbird, still remains open for us to establish. Techniques of aboriginal cultures can also be incorporated into the Thunderbird's flight, such as utilizing the dreamtime in both conscious daydreaming and using symbology as a means of gaining access to more centered forms of transformation.

The appendix of this book contains a guide of the one hundred most common symbols of shamanic transformation used in the Americas. The potentials for this study are vast. Ceremonial aids, such as masks, costumes, and creative visualization murals could help guide lost or confused souls—help them find the nest of the Thunderbird in the top of the Sacred Tree at the center of the world.

Five-Step Process to Transformation

Myths help us shape our world and teach us how to live harmoniously in it. Dr. David Feinstein, director of Innersource, Inc., has developed a unique five-step process for formulating a personal shamanic mythology. This process is included here in condensed form to serve as a guide in assisting fledgling Thunderbird souls:

Stage 1. Recognize when a guiding myth or preconceived notion is no longer of benefit.

Stage 2. Bring conflicting myths into focus, toward catharsis.

Stage 3. Create a new mythic vision to replace old stereotypes.

Stage 4. Create exercises which lead from vision to commitment.

Stage 5. Design methods of incorporating the new ethos into daily routines.

Conclusion

Much discussion has been devoted to the Harmonic Convergence ceremonies of August 16-17, 1987 and their effects on humanity and the world. This event heralds a shift in consciousness, as well as the entry into the New Age. Critics say the event was simply a one-day ceremony and that its significance does not measure up to all the publicity.

Or does it? The return of the Feathered Serpent is much more than a physical event. In the deepest sense, it represents a shift in the collective unconscious that links us all harmoniously in the Great Cycle of Life itself.

Harmonic Convergence ceremonies were conducted at sacred sites all over the world. Like many spokes within a giant medicine wheel, Native Americans, Hawaiians, Maoris, Japanese, Tibetans, Africans, Arabs, and all other races participated in their own shamanic ways. We have mentioned the journey of the mask of Kukulcan around Turtle Island as it became part of these many awakening ceremonies. It circled the continent counter-clockwise just as the contrary does, to help reverse the negative energies within Mother Earth and to help reawaken and unify the spirits of the true native peoples. The Sacred Tree of Life ideogram shows us how this unity can be accomplished. Harmonic Convergence represents the death of the beast (tyranny) and the rebirth of the spirit (peace) through a rapport with traditional cultures.

Now we have seen how the rocks speak to us. These pictographs represent both an esoteric history and prophecies of the future. The Hopi prophecies speak of the Pahana's return with the missing piece of a sacred rock tablet. This missing piece represents the lost instructions left to us by our ancestors—the instructions for the time when we would be tempted by such things as technology and power. If Pahana returns the missing tablet piece, then there is hope for the Hopi, who are the lifeblood of the Americas. If their culture perishes, then so will ours. If the cultures of Native America disappear, then so will all others, for the first nations hold the ancient ways of survival.

The late Dan Katchongva of the Hopi Sun Clan revealed the sacred prophecies and legends "from the beginning of life to the day of purification." As his words reveal, the day of purification is now:

> We know certain people are commissioned to bring about the Purification. It is the Universal Plan from the beginning of Creation, and we are looking up to them to bring purification to us. It is in the rock writings throughout the world, on different continents. We will come together if people all over the world know about it. So we urge you to spread the word around so people will know about it, and the appointed ones will hurry up with their task. . . .

We have mentioned and illustrated some of the secrets of the talking rocks, the missing piece of the stone tablet. The lost white brother is not the white race, but the color of peace, the culture hero. The lost white brother is people of all races whose hearts beat to the rhythm of the New Age. I am Pahana, and so are you.

PART II
Donn Le Vie, Jr.

The recent popularity of shamanism has given rise to the concept of "core shamanism," which in turn has brought up some controversial issues. Core shamanism challenges the purist view of shamanic initiation (including dismemberment, evisceration, and transformation) with a course that transports the initiate through less dangerous psychic territory. In other words, it appears that the once-revered status of the shaman, *brujo*, or *curandero* is now being threatened by less arduous methods of transformation.

Core shamanism seeks to remove so-called "superfluous" cultural burdens and extract the essential elements that will contribute to a cross-cultural "generic" form of shamanism. By necessity, this process theoretically omits the extreme and often long-term sacrifice the initiate has traditionally been required to endure. With core shamanism, the physical, emotional, and spiritual strength required for long periods of fasting as well as for the vision quest, for example, receive little emphasis or even recommendation. This is a grave mistake.

Shamanism is not a path one chooses; it is a path for which one is chosen. It is a sacred calling, usually received in dreams, visions, or through an inheritance of power. This power sustains the shamanic practitioner throughout the years, and in years past it was the object of special reverence — reverence that included discourses on its proper use and the dangers involved with its abuse.

The neo-shamanic movement, and core shamanism in particular, was clearly established by the recent proliferation of workshops and seminars promoting self-transformation. Many of these workshops are modeled *after* shamanism, and for the most part they offer many opportunities for personal growth. But it is irresponsible and dishonest to offer such programs as training in shamanism itself.

Here, in the semantics, the debate reaches its most fervent pitch. For example, not all shamans are healers, but many New Age "healers" are proclaiming themselves to be shamans. The term "shaman" has been used with great license ever since the neo-shamanic movement began. If an individual is truly answering a shamanic calling, would he or she not benefit more from studying with the Huichol Indians for several weeks in Mexico's Sierra Madre mountains than from attending a weekend seminar in the grand ballroom of the Marriott Hotel in downtown Boston? You get what you pay for.

To reinforce this argument, consider the contemporary mythology of the movie, *Star Wars*. Would Luke Skywalker have been transformed to such a degree if he had merely attended a seminar to learn the secrets of "the Force" and become a Jedi knight? Most certainly not. He received the calling, accepted the sacrifices, and endured years of rigorous training by going to the source itself: the Jedi Master, Yoda. Before we counter this point with the fact that *Star Wars* is science fiction, let us remember the lessons of folklore and mythology as revealed to us by Joseph Campbell, Mircea Eliade, and others. In fact, *Star Wars* writer/producer George Lucas was strongly influenced by the writings of Joseph Campbell.

It is true that during Skywalker's initiation, he was under the watchful eye of a mentor, but that mentor could only bring Skywalker so far — and he insisted that his student seek out the master to complete his training. Certainly the responsible, ethical, and qualified neo-shamanic seminar leader would do no less. He or she would prepare the individual for sacrifice, discipline, and dedication.

There are several training workshops available today that are designed as modular, self-contained programs. Participants need not continue with subsequent programs unless they wish to accelerate their training. But there appears to be a contradiction in people having to be taught how to "learn directly from spirit teachers." One wonders how shamanic initiates in primal cultures ever managed to complete their transformation without the benefit of a seminar or workshop.

Unfortunately, Western culture is afflicted with a malady known as "instant gratification," whereby things must be had immediately with little or no concern for the virtue of patience. Ours is a "fast food" mentality; we poison our minds and bodies for the sake of convenience, with little regard for the long-term consequences. Personal growth is an ongoing, lifelong process, a gradual metamorphosis of self-realization. It is a continuum of ordeal, discovery, and change.

In a 1989 editorial in *Shaman's Drum* magazine, James A. Swan, Ph.D., cautioned his readers of the dangers associated with the "weekend healer" seminar—especially seminars held in the name of spiritual or emotional growth. The way has been smoothly paved for the entry of con artists and quacks who, with little or no shamanic training, will cheapen authentic shamanism while the public pays a high price "for the new show," as Swan calls it.

Every culture possesses its own concepts of the universe, reality, and knowledge. Many of these even share common elements. But a "core metaphysics" would strip away important cultural nuances from the essence of the teachings. In effect, it would render them neutral, devoid of power—all for the sake of convenience and easy access by an impatient world.

The popularity of the New Age has created for shamanism the most serious curse of all: commercialization. Teachings and practices that lie on the periphery of shamanism have become more popular as well, but they are not shamanism. As a practitioner of Aikido, Kendo, and T'ai Chi, I am aware of the harmony of mind, body, and spirit that each promotes. Eastern thought is strongly rooted in the Earth, with special reverence for water. There, meditation and the quest for enlightenment reflect a deep awareness of other states of consciousness. But Eastern disciplines are not shamanism, although the roots of Aikido are set in Japanese Shinto mysticism. Jungian therapy, powerful and mystical as it may be, is not shamanism, either.

The study of metaphysics has also become contaminated by individuals who claim to have channeled everyone from Elvis Presley and former "hollow earth" dwellers to "starcraft" commanders in charge of the environmental restoration of the Earth. Some of these well-intentioned people appear to believe that *all* of Earth's problems have extraterrestrial solutions, and they have little understanding of the physical and biological principles that operate in the universe.

Yes, a new shamanic paradigm is needed to satisfy the hunger of the New Age. But it should be a model that will both nourish the neophyte and satisfy the master's desire for protection of the ancient practices and beliefs. This controversy between "core shamanism" and "pure shamanism" is not an either/or argument. What is needed is a model that does not dilute pure shamanism but one that *incorporates* practices and teachings found in the ancient rites of transformation.

This struggle is not unique to this age. Every period that has celebrated a Golden Age has had to contend with turmoil and conflict. When the caterpillar changes into the butterfly, it retains some of the identity of the caterpillar. This is a necessary part of our evolution toward balance. Ours is a continual evolution, but on an ever-ascending spiral. Higher and higher we circle toward our common destiny, eliminating the separation between observer and observed, realizing and celebrating our beings as simply participants in all that is.

EPILOGUE

Donn Le Vie, Jr.

This account of the esoteric significance and symbolism of shamanic art, language, and practice is an attempt to illumine the reader to knowledge beyond that detected by the senses. The shaman's role in the culture of the Indian Americas as facilitator to the gateways of liberation has received frequent emphasis in these pages because it represents a return to the self, the "no-I" of our universal, immortal essence.

There are many cultural variations of the universal shamanic theme, each incorporating legend and myth with actual practice. Native American shamanism has been emphasized here because of the authors' practice and familiarity with it; however, obtaining glimpses of the mysteries is possible through many other paths.

The point is, only when we decide to purge our limiting egos and ethnocentricities will the parallel paths toward unity become apparent to us. Then the multiplicity of experience so characteristic of our everyday waking consciousness falls away to reveal the underlying oneness of all things.

There is no teaching that holds the "one way," but there *is* a way—and that is the way that is right for each individual. This may well be through one of the well-marked highways of the world's traditional religions. But perhaps the search will take us down a path less traveled. And perhaps, at one time or another, we will arrive at a point where we encounter intersecting paths. This usually happens when the time is right, when we are presented with an opportunity for continued growth. Then we can proceed in our own self-defined direction and enter onto a new path, to travel further toward release from our self-imposed bondage.

But what is it that draws us down a particular path? Evelyn Eaton, author of *I Send a Voice*, says that the first essential is to *want*. Then we realize that the gap between the want and the wanted requires a bridge. That bridge turns out to be the path or paths we must traverse at this time on our never-ending journey.

After acknowledging the connecting bridge between the want and the wanted, we must start from where we are *right now*—not on Monday or after a New Year's resolution. In this respect, we must forsake the linear concept of time. The now does not recognize circumstances, but only the immediate itself.

In other words, where we are right now—both spiritually and physically—is just where we should be. Acknowledging the connecting bridge can take place at the office, in the car, at home, in a crowded subway, or in the solitude of the wilderness. At the same time, journeying to the highest mountain peak around Katmandu or bathing in the Ganges is not a necessity. Each of us is where we are supposed to be, now.

Now is a moment that passes without measure, often without notice. A moment is infinite—infinitely short or infinitely long in duration. And it is the mystic and the physicist's concept of a moment, the now of time, that may hold the secret of cosmic unity.

A scientist's calling to the mystic path may take many of his or her colleagues by surprise. These colleagues may be at a loss to understand immersion into such a "tangential" field. They may cite the many apparent incongruencies between science and mysticism. But these well-intentioned friends will be arguing from a position of bias, due to their lack of knowledge and understanding.

In my experience, the scientist-turned-mystic is always attempting to understand the relationship between the parts and the whole. He or she refuses to adopt the separation that has traditionally been a precept of all the sciences. Stimulus and response, cause and effect: these integrated relationships are observed daily. The cosmic thread invisibly intertwines humanity and nature, creature and habitat, consciousness and matter.

But sometimes an amazing transformation takes place. An increasing awareness of the parallels that drive both science and mysticism begins to emerge from the shadows of consciousness. This is an awareness that the common quest of science and mysticism is the discovery of unity. This common quest becomes the cohesive force that transcends all arguments of separation.

The evolving universe has certain "habits" that we have labeled as "laws." These laws of nature that govern gravitation, the speed of light, radioactive decay, magnetism, and electricity are human attempts to simplify the seemingly complex into the comprehensible. For years, scientists have been trying to unite the four basic forces of nature—gravitation, electromagnetism, and the weak and strong nuclear forces within the atom—into the Grand Unified Theory, an all-encompassing super-force. In spite of recent advances in subatomic particle physics, this still remains an elusive ideal.

The mystic, in quest for unity, receives inspiration to follow a spiritual path. The question that has been raised recently is whether or not the search for unity in science is *itself* a path of spirituality. In my opinion, it is. Whether one investigates the microcosm of the atom or the boundless expanse of the universe, it is difficult *not* to acknowledge a sense of a consciousness radiating out in all directions from processes both great and small. To the creative mind of the scientist, the sense of nature's simplicity, subtlety, and unity appears intuitively.

Is not the spark of creative genius most often the result of an intuitive flash of insight? Could such flashes be glimpses into the unity of all being, in which the conscious mind suddenly "knows" something without really knowing how it knows? The peak experience is *not* in opposition to rational thinking. In moments of scientific discovery, biologist Ludwig von Bertalanffy gained an "intuitive insight into a grand design," and so have many others.

The eloquence of mathematics as a language is universal in nature. Maxwell's equations for light, for example, would be more easily understood by intelligent extraterrestrial civilizations than any accompanying verbiage. Mathematics attempts to uncover the inner configuration of nature by reducing diversity to its lowest common denominator: unity. Is this not similar to the mystic's philosophy that beneath the multiplicity of perspectives and vistas lies the one, the simple, the real?

Comparing the efforts of mystics and scientists can be like treading on thin ice, especially with theoretical physicists. These scientists, for the most part, take offense at having their work compared to that of mystics. But the reverse is not the case. Most modern mystics freely admit that scientific cosmology is an alternative but parallel perspective into the nature of reality.

The scientific community's animosity toward mysticism is not totally without justification. The history of science reveals a dark period of religious domination in which such great scientists as Galileo forfeited their freedom, and in which Servetus, Mansur al-Hallaj, and Giordano Bruno forfeited their lives. Unfortunately, many scientists make little or no distinction between religion and mysticism. What the scientist often fails to perceive is that during this same dark period in history, the mystic was just as frequently on the receiving end of the heavy-handed persecution as was the scientist—and all because of a common vision!

The scientist's view of ultimate physical unity is the moment before the Big Bang, when all matter in the universe coalesced, condensed, and contracted into an infinitesimally minute point referred to as the "singularity." And it is here, in the quest for the singularity, that we can find answers to the questions of who we are and where we come from.

In this light, the scientist and the mystic travel parallel paths, with one fundamental difference: Science has great difficulty answering questions bordering on the highly speculative. What came before the Big Bang? What lies beyond the edge of the cosmos?

For the question that science cannot answer, mysticism, at least, provides a possibility.

This possibility, this direction, is part of an ancient theory substantiated by the mystic's own experince. This theory suggests that the universe is the creation of *consciousness*—a process in which simple matter gives rise to more complex matter and in which all matter is part of a sequence, a continuum. Massless (or nearly massless) particles give rise to the building blocks of the atom. These in turn give rise to the basic element, hydrogen, and later, to the other light elements. Stars are born, and when they expend their thermonuclear fuel, they spew off the heavier elements of which the remainder of the universe—including you and I—is constructed. In this sense, we are indeed children of the stars.

Working backwards with this theory, the more subtle matter becomes, the more it approaches the state of pure consciousness. At the ethereal minimum, matter and consciousness lose their distinction. This ancient wisdom has never escaped the mystic.

What lies beyond consciousness and matter? It appears that both are the expression of something that transcends themselves, yet this unknown "something" has no expression and therefore refuses to be defined. It has been called "nothingness" by some, "silence" by others, but in the end it defies imagination.

The mission of both the mystic and the scientist is to search for the reality of existence. In her book, *Dialogues with Scientists and Sages*, philosopher and mystic Renee Weber perhaps relates this common cause best by referring to both scientist and sage as transformers of energy who are involved in the "dance of Shiva." The scientist commands the dense matter to dance, producing pure energy, while the mystic—the "master of subtle matter—dances the dance of himself."

As with any of nature's secrets, each question answered brings more unsolved puzzles. The mystery of nature becomes more profound with each new solution to its riddles. If the key to the Grand Unified Theory can be discovered, will it all stop there, or will we then have to seek the answer to another question? After science closes in on the birth of the universe and the beginning of time, will it then have to confront that which is timeless? Thus do advances in quantum physics, relativity, and theoretical cosmology stretch the fine line that separates mysticism from science.

Bridging of the gap between science and mysticism could hinge upon a proposal by physicist David Bohm, suggesting that meaning is a form of being. That is, by interpreting the universe, we are implying a reality to it—in effect, creating it; nature becomes altered by our very definitions. We therefore become co-creators *with* nature, participating in its evolution.

Bohm further suggests that the cosmos is changing its idea of itself. Humanity's doubts, questions, and truths, he says, are all facets of nature's drive toward clarity and truth. And this synergistic relationship causes the universe to question itself, to search through various answers in an attempt to uncover the meaning of its existence. This course parallels our own quest to discover the answer to the question, "Who Am I?"

The immensity of Bohm's implication challenges the powers of perception. In Dr. Weber's words, it "assigns a role to man that was once reserved for the gods."

Will science ever approach the mystical view of cosmic unity? This is difficult to assess or even to speculate on. It is possible that the best science can do is take us to the edge, where we ourselves will provide the final step. Carl Sagan's best-selling novel, *Contact*, clearly suggest that humanity—not science—holds the key to the revelation of ultimate reality. Dr. Weber suggests this could bring us full circle, from an awareness of the unity and interconnectedness of all existence to a feeling of empathy with others—an empathy expressed in compassion, reverence for life, a sense of brotherhood, and a commitment to heal our ailing Earth Mother and all her children.

A SPECIAL SUMMONS
From the Great Council of
The Manitous

We conclude this publication with a special announcement
from the Great Council of the Manitous:

Greetings to all our human relations. The Great Council of the Manitous hereby summons each and every one of you to meet with us in the Sacred Grove under the Great Tree of Peace.

The Shaman and the New Age Scientist have now revealed to you some of the most important laws of nature. Thanks to their teachings, you have become more aware of our existence and of your own spiritual power and destiny.

As you know, Mother Earth and Father Sky are in serious trouble, due to the imbalances created by artificial laws. A new time cycle is now approaching that will counteract these imbalances. We humbly ask each and every one of you—each and every caring human being—to do your share in helping to restore balance in the world. All you need do is listen . . . and follow your heart!

And remember that you are never alone in your struggles. Our council welcomes you. All barriers are gone now. You have the power to call upon us anytime, and to receive knowledge from us in your dreams and visions. Ask, and you will be heard. Seek, and you shall find. We are all relations!

Gitche Manitou

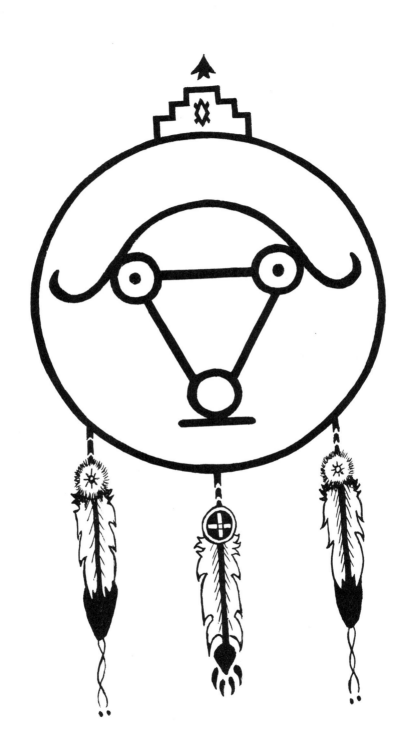

SHAMANIC POWER SYMBOLS
of the Americas
Iron Thunderhorse

This research was compiled in cooperation with the efforts of The Four Winds Foundation. I contribute it in the spirit of collective appreciation and reverence for the common mythologies and symbolism of the ancient peoples of the Americas.

I dedicate this paper to the work of Dr. Alberto Villoldo, Ph.D., adjunct professor at San Francisco State University in Shamanism and the Healing States, and to the mutual path shared by fellow shaman don Eduardo Calderón, of Incan ancestry.

1. Acorn: prolongation, perfect achievement.

2. Afterbirth (also umbilical cord): nagual, soul, alter ego.

3. Air (including winds, breath): freedom, will, wanderlust.

4. Alligator (crocodile, cayman): consumption, fear.

5. Androgyne: integration, harmony, fertility, balancing.

6. Ant: industriousness, perseverance, strength.

7. Armadillo: mystery, mysticism, introspection, protection.

8. Arrow: divination, conquest, success, problem solving, domination.

9. Axe: power of light; double-bladed means balance.

10. Badger: healing, childbirth, sign of herbalist.

11. Bat: inversion, crisis, attachments, fears.

12. Bear: brotherhood, medicine man.

13. Beaver: conservation, industriousness.

14. Bees: secret knowledge, diligence, altruism.

15. Beetle: warrior spirit, courage, valor.

16. Bird Ally: hawk = soul in flight; spirit goose = nocturnal power.

17. Bones: resurrection, ancestry, heritage, battlements.

18. Buffalo: provider, Great Spirit.

19. Bull Roarer: initiation, unknown, awe, inspiration, heralder.

20. Butterfly: metamorphosis, soul in flight.

21. Buzzard: omens, survival, purification.

22. Cannibal (windingo, monsters): devouring, psychic reformation, guilt.

23. Cat: sensitivity; sorcery.

24. Caul (membrane covering newborn's head): divination, prophecy, good fortune, sign of seer.

25. Cave: womb, rebirth, spiritual center, mysticism.

26. Chacmool: offerings, sacrifice, homage.

27. Circle (including hoop of life, medicine wheel): oneness, unity, perfection, cycles, relationships.

28. Clouds: truth, souls of departed; dark clouds = trouble ahead.

29. Corn: life, life force, sustenance, survival.

30. Corpse: ancestry, rebirth, new opportunities, cycles.

31. Coyote (including fox, wolf): trickster, culture hero, deep undercurrents, unexpected.

32. Cross: suffrage, crucifixion, inversion, conjunction.

33. Crow (includes raven): messenger, trickster, presager, memory, intellect.

34. Crystal: spirit of the fire.

35. Dance: cosmic progression, metamorphosis.

36. Death: end of cycle, new beginning, alternatives.

37. Deer: magic, wisdom, vision.

38. Dog: companionship, faithfulness.

39. Dolphin (also salmon, other types of fish): salvation, friendship, companionship, adventure.

40. Dragonfly (horsefly, mosquito): supernatural power signs.

41. Drum: primal force, magic, journey.

42. Dwarf (eunuch, deformed person): sign of a nagual, or immortal.

43. Eagle: foresightedness, clairvoyance, insight.

44. Earth: nurturing, fertility, mother (feminine/passive).

45. Earthquake: disintegration, inversion, calamity.

46. Eclipse: doom, warning, conjunction, presage.

47. Elk: dreaming, love magic, healing.

48. Enemy: obstacles, struggle, entanglement, repression.

49. Eye: wisdom, intelligence; evil eye = sign of witchcraft.

50. Father Sky (Tairawa): upperworld, universal mind.

51. Finger: direction; fingernail = connections; hand sign, = strength, power, authority.

52. Fire: purification, spiritual energy, healing (male/active).

53. Flight: ascension, spirit, imagination.

54. Flint: insight, heavens, destruction.

55. Flood: regeneration, disintegration.

56. Foot: standpoint; footprint = pathway of the Holy Ones.

57. Four (quaternary, four winds, four directions, symbol of the cross): versatility, perfection, unlimitedness, universal mind.

58. Frog: transition, metamorphosis.

59. Ghosts: taboos, fate, incompleteness.

60. Giants: unconscious, mystery, dark forces.

61. Great Spirit: creation, mystery, unknown known, wholeness.

62. Guardian (nagual, allies): supernatural protection, divine guidance, spiritual aid.

63. Head (speaking, rolling, severed): prophecy, spiritual essence.

64. Heart: single heart = truth; double heart = deceit; heart line = inspiration and compassion.

65. Horns: medicine, aphrodisiac.

66. Horse: medicine, clairvoyance, companionship.

67. Hunter: quest, searching, vigil, lamenting, vengeance.

68. Island: isolation, metaphysical force.

69. Jade: spirit of the Earth.

70. Jaguar (mountain lion, puma): sorcery, transformation.

71. Kachina: fertility, spirits of nature.

72. Knife: vengeance; lance = sign of justice.

73. Lightning: enlightenment, illumination, holy.

74. Lizard (salamander): immortality, transformation.

75. Moon: growth, transitions, cycles, Goddess.

76. Mother Earth (Pachamama, Tonantzin): the underworld, telluric forces in nature.

77. Mountain: loftiness, mystical elevation.

78. Peyote (San Pedro cactus, Datura): vision, transformation, creativity, introspection.

79. Pipe: spirit, communication with higher intelligence.

80. Place of Emergence: ancestry, mystical center, balance.

81. Rainbow: mystical bridge, gateway to otherworld.

82. Sacred Clowns: contrariness, reversal, conjunction, inversion.

83. Serpent: resurrection; feathered serpent = astromancy; horned serpent = geomancy.

84. Shaman: supernatural, psychic integration, survival.

85. Shell: spirit of the sea.

86. Spider: creativity, inversion, medicine, grandmother.

87. Spiral (labyrinth): sunwise means evolution and healing; counter-sunwise means involution, curse, disease.

88. Spiritual Warrior: balance, justice, fate.

89. Star (star man, star woman): deification; becoming, spirit.

90. Stone: invulnerability, cohesion, reconciliation.

91. Sun: procreation, life, warmth, hero, health, God.

92. Three (ternary, trinity): reciprocity, soul, cosmic centering.

93. Thunder: power; thunderbolt = divine power.

94. Tobacco: purification, reverence.

95. Tree of Life: life, knowledge, immortality.

96. Turquoise: spirit of the air.

97. Turtle: longevity, spiritual permanence.

98. Two (binary, twins, dual creators): opposition, duality, struggle, catharsis.

99. Water (including rain): preserver, unconscious; male rain is hard and fast; female rain is short and soft.

100. Witch (sorcerer, *brujo*): confrontation, catharsis.

THE SHAMAN
Iron Thunderhorse

The facing illustration was inspired by many ancient petroglyphs and cave art figures. After you have read *Return of the Thunderbeings,* look closely at the figure and try to guess what each symbolic element represents. Recall what you have read. Think with your heart and inner eye instead of your mind. Then turn the page and see how close you came to the correct interpretation.

Hint: The clue to this test lies in the title. Do you remember the important attributes of a true shaman? This figure represents these powers in every respect.

Interpretation

"The Shaman" is a composite of the truly free spirit in symbolic form. It combines the abstract essences of many characteristics.

In the illustration, the right, or active, hand holds a medicine staff; while the left, or passive, holds a medicine shield with the spiral of involution. Positive and negative powers are both medicines, and together they form a reciprocal whole.

The antlers, branching out from the head like the Tree of Life and Knowledge, denote wisdom.

The shaman's mask has animal ears. This indicates the ability to listen to the inner voice of long ago, the natural speech that all creatures hear.

The shaman's eyes are those of the owl, indicating an ability to see clearly through the darkness without prejudice or obstruction.

The birdlike beak represents the spoken language of the higher entities of the sky world and the ability to communicate with them freely.

Arm and wrist bands secure a cape of feathers, allowing the shaman to fly freely into both the sky world and the underworld.

Medicine pouches hang at both sides, and a medicine necklace hangs around the shaman's neck. These are symbols of the shaman's personal abilities and represent the power and activity of shamanism.

The shaman has the legs and hooves of a four-legged but, like a human, has only two legs. This indicates the shaman's ability to walk in true balance on the path of natural life, as long as he or she respects natural law as the four-leggeds respect it.

The shaman also has a beard. Like long hair, this is a sign of spiritual attainment. These "psychic fibers" are like antennae which pick up spiritual vibrations.

The shaman wears a breechclout with patterns that are symbolic of male and female unity.

The person depicted also wears a shaman's mask. But the mask is not a disguise; it is a channel through which the shaman releases or captures extraordinary aspects of the mind or spirit.

Once the full potential of the shaman is realized, the flight of the Thunderbird can be achieved. This is symbolized by the Thunderbird soul in flight. Through ceremonial enactments, the shaman can also enter trance, or the shamanic state of consciousness.

ACKNOWLEDGMENTS

The authors wish to acknowledge the following people for their expertise, guidance, cooperation, and insight in making this manuscript a success.

To all the staff at Bear & Company, for their knowledge and patience, as well as for their invaluable service to the reader. It is indeed a fortunate experience to work with the Bears. Thank you, Barbara Hand Clow, for your intuitive beliefs in this manuscript. Thank you, Gerry Clow, Debora Bluestone, Angela Werneke, Gail Vivino, and especially Brandt Morgan, and the rest of the team who put your hearts and souls into this publication. To our brother and ally, Dr. Alberto Villoldo, for his friendship and for writing the foreword.

To all the brothers and sisters who took time to review this manuscript. (And to the ones who were not asked to do so, please know you are not forgotten.)

Donn Le Vie's acknowledgments: To my wife Jeanette, for her understanding, her help in maintaining editorial deadlines, and for challenging me to discover my deeper spiritual and creative self. To my daughter Michelle, may this book serve to light the path of your spiritual journey in the years ahead. To my parents and brother Brian, for their steadfast support during the trying years. To Joseph Campbell and Alan Watts, for serving as inspiring mentors. And finally, to all the individuals who have crossed my path with lessons for me to learn, especially my grandmother, Emma Mae, and my best friend, Tony Vanacore.

Iron Thunderhorse's acknowledgments: To my teachers, Slow Turtle, Yehwehnode, White Eagle, Duda Flying Squirrel Woman, Buck Ghosthorse, Andy Hewitt, Walking Medicine Robe, Brown Bear Mallot, and to all the unseen help from the other world, I pray this manuscript is worthy of your guidance. To all the people who gave me support and who were there in times of frustration: Morning Star Woman, Dianne La France, Smiling Raven, She Who Calls the Ancestors, and Roxy Gordon and his son, Quanah Parker Gordon (thanks for the *Crazy Horse Never Died* album and cassette, brother), and to the Metis Medicine Circle—Skyhawk, Owl, Morning Dove, and Grandfather Windfeather.

Finally, to all our relations: Thank you, and blessings from the manitous.

BIBLIOGRAPHY
& SUGGESTED READING

Achterberg, Jeanne. "The Shaman: Master Healer in the Imaginary Realm." In *Shamanism*, compiled by Shirley Nicholson. Wheaton, IL: Quest Books, Theosophical Publishing House, 1987.

Akwesasne Notes, 19 (no. 3)

Akwesasne Notes, 19 (no. 4)

Argüelles, José. *The Mayan Factor: Path Beyond Technology*. Santa Fe, NM: Bear & Co., 1987.

Balin, Peter. *The Flight of the Feathered Serpent*. Wilmot, WI: Arcana Publishing Co., 1978.

Berlant, Tony, and Mary Kahlenberg. "The Navajo Blanket." *Art in America* (July-August, 1972).

Bernal, Ignacio. *The Olmec World*. Translated by Doris Heyden and Fernando Horcasitas. Berkeley, CA: University of California Press, 1976.

Bettelheim, Bruno. *The Uses of Enchantment: The Meaning and Importance of Fairy Tales*. New York: Alfred A. Knopf, 1976.

Brown, Dee. *Bury My Heart at Wounded Knee: An Indian History of the American West*. New York: Henry Holt & Co., 1971.

Brown, Joseph Epes. *The Sacred Pipe*. New York: Penguin Books, 1971.

Bruchac, Joseph. *Thanking the Birds: Native American Upbringing and the Natural World*. New York: Green Mountain Press.

Burland, C. A. *The Gods of Mexico*.

Campbell, Joseph. *The Hero with a Thousand Faces*. Princeton, NJ: Princeton University Press, 1949.

_____. *Oriental Mythology: The Masks of God*. New York: Penguin Books, 1968.

_____. *The Inner Reaches of Outer Space*. Toronto: St. James Press, Ltd., 1985.

Castaneda, Carlos. *Tales of Power*. New York: Simon and Schuster, 1984.

Cerum, C.W. "Discovery of the Mounds." In *The First Americans*. New York: Harcourt, Brace, Jovanovich, Inc., 1971.

Cirlot, J.E. *Dictionary of Symbols*. New York: Philosophical Library, 1983.

Coppola, William Iron Thunderhorse. "Heyoka, The Thunderbird Medicine Rite: New Light on Shamanic Cosmology." Manuscript for American Indian Research Project, University of South Dakota, 1986.

_____. "Crimes Against Nature: A Study of Navajo and Hopi Traditionalists and Their Place in the Global Collusion Against Indigenous World Populations." Thunderbird Free Press, 1987.

Cox-Stevenson, Matilda. "The Zuni Indians: Their Mythology, Esoteric Fraternities, and Ceremonies." Washington, DC: Twenty-third Annual Report of the Bureau of American Ethnology, 1904.

Eaton, Evelyn. *I Send a Voice*. Wheaton, IL: Quest Books, Theosophical Publishing House, 1978.

Edmonson, Monroe S., ed. *The Popol Vuh of the Quiche Maya*. New Orleans, LA: Tulane University Press, 1971.

Eliade, Mircea. *The Myth of the Eternal Return*. Princeton, NJ: Princeton University Press, 1954.

_____. *The Sacred and the Profane*. New York: Harper and Row, 1957.

_____. *The Forge and the Crucible*. New York: Harper and Row, 1962.

_____. "Shamanism and Cosmology." In *Shamanism*, compiled by Shirley Nicholson. Wheaton, IL: Quest Books, Theosophical Publishing House, 1987.

Eliot, Alexander. "The Realm of the Mother Goddess." In *Discovery of Lost Worlds*. New York: Simon and Schuster, American Heritage Books, 1979.

Feinstein, David. "The Shaman Within: Cultivating a Sacred Personal Mythology." In *Shamanism*, compiled by Shirley Nicholson. Wheaton, IL: Quest Books, Theosophical Publishing House, 1987.

Fell, Barry. *America, B.C.* New York: Quadrangle/New York Times Books, 1976.

Fronval, George and Daniel DuBois. *Indian Signals and Sign Language*. New York: Bonanza Books, Sterling Publishing Company, 1985.

Galante, Lawrence. *T'ai Chi: The Supreme Ultimate*. York Beach, ME: Samuel Weiser, 1982.

Gallenkamp, Charles. *Maya*. New York: McKay Publishing Co., 1976.

Gates, William. *An Outline Dictionary of Mayan Glyphs*. Baltimore, MD: Johns Hopkins Press, 1931.

Goodman, Ron. *Ethnoastronomy of the Lakota Sioux*. Mission, SD: Sinte Gleska College Press, 1986.

Gorstein, Shirley. *Prehispanic America*. New York: St. Martins Press, 1974.

Halifax, Joan. *Shaman, The Wounded Healer*. London: Thames and Hudson, Ltd., 1982.

Hall, Manly P. *The Secret Teachings of All Ages*. Los Angeles, CA: The Philosophical Research Society, 1977.

Hallowell, A. Irving. "Ojibwa Ontology, Behavior, and World View." In *Culture in History: Essays in Honor of Paul Radin*. New York: Columbia University Press, 1960.

Hansen, L. Taylor. *He Walked the Americas*. Amherst, MA: Amherst Press, 1963.

Haviland, William A. *Anthropology*. New York: Holt, Rinehart & Winston, 1974.

Hemming, John. *In Search of El Dorado*. New York: E.P. Dutton.

Henderson, Joseph. *The Wisdom of the Serpent: Myths of Death, Rebirth, and Resurrection*. New York: George Braziller, 1963.

Heyerdahl, Thor. "Archaelogical Evidence of Pre-Spanish Visits to the Galapagos Islands." In *Society for American Archaeology*. Memoir 12, 1956.

_____. *Aku-Aku, The Secret of Easter Island*.

Highwater, Jamake. *Arts of the Indian Americas, North, Central, and South; Leaves from the Sacred Tree*. New York: Harper and Row, 1983.

Hopi Journal. Columbia University Contributions to Anthropology 25. Vol. 1 (no. 19).

Hoppal, Mihaly. "Shamanism, an Archaic and/or Recent Belief System." In *Shamanism*, compiled by Shirley Nicholson. Wheaton, IL: Quest Books, Theosophical Publishing House, 1987.

Jung, Carl, ed. *Man and His Symbols*. New York: Dell Publishing Company, 1964.

Jyotirmayananda, Sri Swami. "The Significance of Mantra." *The Divine Life* 27.

Katchongva, Dan. *From the Beginning of Life to the Day of Purification*, translated by Danaqyumptewa. Los Angeles: The Committee for Traditional Indian Land and Life, 1972.

King, Serge. "The Way of the Adventurer." In *Shamanism*, compiled by Shirley Nicholson. Wheaton, IL: Quest Books, Theosophical Publishing House, 1987.

Kirkland, Forrest and W.W. Newcomb, Jr. *The Rock Art of Texas Indians*. Austin, TX: The University of Texas Press, 1968.

Krupp, E.C. *Echoes of the Ancient Skies: The Astronomy of Lost Civilizations*. New York: Harper and Row, 1983.

Lang, Charles. *Cochiti*. Carbondale, IL: Southern Illinois University Press, 1968.

Lyon, William S. "Black Elk, Then and Now." In *Shamanism*, compiled by Shirley Nicholson. Wheaton, IL: Quest Books, Theosophical Publishing House, 1987.

Mallery, Garrick. "Sign Language Among the North American Indians." In *First Report of the Bureau of American Ethnology*. Washington, D.C., 1881.

_____. "Picture Writing of the American Indians," in *Tenth Annual Report of the Bureau of American Ethnology*. Washington, D.C., 1893.

Martin, Paul S., et al. *Indians Before Columbus: Twenty Thousand Years of North American History Revealed by Archaeology*. Chicago: University of Chicago Press, 1947.

Martinou, La Van. *Clear Creek Project*. Published by the Paiute Indian Tribe of Utah, 1985.

Mastay, Carl. "New England Indian Place Names." In *Rooted Like the Ash Trees*. CT: Eagle Wing Press, 1987.

Mathews, Washington. *Navajo Legends*. 1897.

Maxwell, James A. *America's Fascinating Indian Heritage*. New York: Reader's Digest Books, 1978.

McAllester, David. "New England Indian Music, the Earliest Mechanically Recorded American Indian Music." In *Rooted Like the Ash Trees*. CT: Eagle Wing Press, 1987.

McGill, Ormond. *Hypnotism and Mysticism of India*. Los Angeles, CA: Westwood Publishing Co., 1979.

McMann, Jean. *Riddles of the Stone Age*. London: Thames and Hudson, 1980.

Mead, Charles. *Old Civilization of Inca Land*. Savage, MD: Cooper Square, 1972.

Medicine Eagle, Brooke. "Lineage of the Sun." In *Shamanism*, compiled by Shirley Nicholson. Wheaton, IL: Quest Books, Theosophical Publishing House, 1987.

Moeller, Roger. "Ten Thousand Years of Indian Lifeways in Connecticut." In *Rooted Like the Ash Trees*. CT: Eagle Wing Press, 1987.

Morgan, William. "Human Wolves Among the Navajo." Yale University Publications in Anthropology No. 11, 1936.

Muldoon, Sylvan and Hereward Carrington. *The Projection of the Astral Body*. York Beach, ME: Samuel Weiser, 1982.

Muser, Curt. *Facts and Artifacts of Ancient Middle America*. New York: E.P. Dutton, 1978.

Neihardt, John G. *Black Elk Speaks*. New York: William Morrow & Co., 1932.

Nequatewa, Edmund. *Truth of a Hopi*. Flagstaff, AZ: Northland Press, 1967.

Perera, Victor. "The Last of the Mayas." *East-West Journal* (July, 1984).

Pfeiffer, John E. *The Creative Explosion: An Inquiry into the Origins of Art and Religion*. New York: Harper and Row, 1982.

Price, Monroe. "The Indian and the White Man's Law." *Art in America* (July-August 1972).

Progoff, Ira. *Jung, Synchronicity, and Human Destiny*. New York: Julian Press, 1973.

Quigley, S.P. *A Brief History of the Language of Signs*. Washington, D.C.: U.S. Government Printing Office, 1965.

Quinn, William Jr. "Metaphysics in Traditional Cultures." *The American Theosophist* 73, no. 10 (1985).

Radin, Paul. *The Story of the American Indian*. New York: Leveright, 1934.

Recinos, Adrian, and Delia Goetz, trans. *Popol Vuh: The Sacred Book of the Ancient Quiche Maya*. Norman, OK: University of Oklahoma Press, 1950.

Reichel-Dolmatoff, Gerardo. *The Shaman and the Jaguar: A Study of Narcotic Drugs Among the Indians of Colombia*. Philadelphia, PA: Temple University Press, 1975.

Ritter, Dale and Eric. "Medicine Men and Spirit Animals in Rock Art of Western North America." In *Acts of the International Symposium of Rock Art*. University of California-Davis, 1972.

Roaix, Jim. *The Eagle* 6, no. 6. CT: Eagle Wing Press, 1987.

Rossi, Ernest. *The Psychobiology of Mind/Body Healing: New Concepts of Therapeutic Hypnosis*. New York: W.W. Norton & Co., 1987.

Roys, Ralph L., ed. and trans. *The Book of Chilam Balam of Chumayel*. Norman, OK: University of Oklahoma Press, 1967.

Schele, Linda. *Maya Glyphs, The Verbs*. Austin, TX: University of Texas Press, 1967.

Science Digest (November 1985).

Sealth, Chief Seattle. Speech of record, circa 1884.

Sejourne, Laurette. *Burning Water*. New York: Vanguard Press, 1956.

Shaman's Drum (Fall 1985).

Shaman's Drum (Spring 1986).

Shaman's Drum (Spring 1987).

Shaman's Drum (Summer 1987).

Shaman's Drum (Fall 1987).

Shaman's Drum (Winter 1987-1988).

Sharon, Douglass. *Wizard of the Four Winds*. New York: Macmillan, 1978.

Sinte Gleska College. "Hanta Yo, A Gross Insult is Offered to Indian People." *Wassaja—The Indian Historian* 13, no. 14 (1980).

Storm, Hyemeyohsts. *Seven Arrows*. New York: Ballantine Books, 1972.

Taylor, Thomas. *Mystical Hymns of Orpheus*. London: 1884.

Tedlock, Barbara. "The Clown's Way." In *Teachings from the American Earth: Indian Religion and Philosophy*. New York: Leveright, 1975.

Tedlock, Dennis, ed. and trans. *Popol Vuh: The Definitive Edition of the Mayan Book of the Dawn of Life and the Glories of Gods and Kings*. New York: Simon and Schuster, 1985.

Thero, Ven. E. Nandisvara Nayake. "The Dreamtime, Mysticism, and Liberation: Shamanism in Australia." In *Shamanism*, compiled by Shirley Nicholson. Wheaton, IL: Quest Books, Theosophical Publishing House, 1987.

Thomas, Elizabeth Marshall. *Reindeer Moon*. Boston: Houghton Mifflin Co., 1987.

Toriens, R.G. *The Golden Dawn: The Inner Teachings*. York Beach, ME: Samuel Weiser.

Walker, James R. *Lakota Society*. Lincoln, NE: University of Nebraska Press, 1982.

Waters, Frank. *Book of the Hopi*. New York: Penguin Books, 1963.

Weber, Renee. *Dialogues with Scientists and Sages: The Search for Unity*. New York: Routledge & Keegan Paul, Inc., 1986.

Weil, Andrew. *The Marriage of the Sun and the Moon: A Quest for Unity in Consciousness*. Boston: Houghton Mifflin Co., 1980.

Wright-McLeod, Brian. "The Law of Seven Fires." Canadian Alliance in Association with the Native Peoples.

Yoga Journal (November-December 1985).

INDEX

ABOUT THE AUTHORS

Iron Thunderhorse (Kanatisoquilli) is a Thunderbird Sachem (shaman) who practices a combination of cross-cultural medicine ways. He is of Algonquin and mixed ancestry, a member of the Cherokee Confederacy, and the United Eastern Big Horn Lenape' Nation. He is founder of the Thunderbird Alliance (a confederacy between medicine circles, prison groups, activists, and outside support groups), and is active in the XAT Medicine Society.

Thunderhorse writes monthly columns for *News From Indian Country: The Journal*, published by the Las Courte Orielles band of the Ojibwa Nation, and freelances regularly for many publications. He has been writing for 20 years and has authored several publications in the small presses.

As an artist and craftsperson, his work spans the spectrum from painting, pottery, and leatherwork to mask making, sculpture, jewelry, and woodworking. Thunderhorse is also an expert in the areas of hieroglyphics, pictographs,

and the esoteric traditions of Native American cultures. His work is recognized by many Native American elders and indigenous organizations, as well as by New Age groups and many ancient orders of the mystery schools.

Donn Le Vie, Jr. is a writer and lecturer of international recognition. He has been a research oceanographer with the National Oceanic and Atmospheric Administration (NOAA), a geologist/geophysicist with Phillips Petroleum Company and Highland Resources, an adjunct faculty member with the University of Houston Downtown College, and a mission specialist candidate for NASA's Astronaut Training Program for the space shuttle (1981-1984). Donn is the author of many technical and scientific publications in the Earth and planetary sciences and several hundred general interest articles.

He is also a professional speaker and seminar facilitator in great demand around the country. His lectures and seminars on human potential, the noetic sciences, and self-discovery offer enlightening and challenging ideas for everyone interested in becoming an open-minded, unprejudiced seeker of truth. Donn also presents corporate programs on intuitive leadership, personal empowerment, and creativity breakthrough. He currently resides in Austin, Texas.

BOOKS OF RELATED INTEREST
BY BEAR & COMPANY

CRYING FOR A DREAM
The World Through Native American Eyes
by Richard Erdoes

KEEPERS OF THE FIRE
Journey to the Tree of Life Based on Black Elk's Vision
by Eagle Walking Turtle

MEDICINE CARDS
The Discovery of Power Through the Ways of Animals
by Jamie Sams & David Carson

MEDITATIONS WITH ANIMALS
A Native American Bestiary
by Gerald Hausman

MEDITATIONS WITH THE HOPI
by Robert Boissiere

MEDITATIONS WITH THE NAVAJO
Navajo Stories of the Earth
by Gerald Hausman

SECRETS OF MAYAN SCIENCE/RELIGION
by Hunbatz Men

Contact your local bookseller or write:

BEAR & COMPANY
P.O. Drawer 2860
Santa Fe, NM 87504